W. G. SEBALD – A CRITICAL COMPANION

W. G. SEBALD – A CRITICAL COMPANION

Edited by
J. J. Long and Anne Whitehead

EDINBURGH UNIVERSITY PRESS

© editorial matter and organisation
J. J. Long and Anne Whitehead, 2004, 2006
© the chapters their several authors, 2004, 2006

First published in hardback by Edinburgh
University Press in 2004
Edinburgh University Press Ltd
22 George Square, Edinburgh

Typeset in Sabon and Gill Sans
by Servis Filmsetting Ltd, Manchester, and
printed and bound in Great Britain by
The Cromwell Press, Trowbridge, Wilts

A CIP record for this book is available from
the British Library

ISBN-10 0 7486 2469 4 (Paperback)
ISBN-13 978 0 7486 2469 0

The right of the contributors
to be identified as authors of this work
has been asserted in accordance with
the Copyright, Designs and Patents Act 1988.

CONTENTS

ACKNOWLEDGEMENTS

George Szirtes's 'Meeting Austerlitz' was first published in *The Rialto*, and grateful acknowledgement is made to the editor of that periodical for permission to reprint the poem here. Permission to reprint a still from *Der Führer schenkt den Juden eine Stadt* was granted by Beit Terezin. Anne Whitehead gratefully acknowledges the funding support offered by an AHRB Research Leave award and a University of Newcastle upon Tyne Internal Research Fellowship. The School of Modern Languages at the University of Durham generously funded some of the photographic and textual permissions. The editors thank Jackie Jones and Carol Macdonald at Edinburgh University Press for their commitment to and enthusiasm for this volume, and for their invaluable help and advice, particularly at the project's inception. Special thanks are due to all of our contributors for adapting so readily to a tight production schedule. Finally, thanks to Marita le Vaul-Grimwood and Mark Gillingwater (they know what for!).

Grateful acknowledgement is made to Maggie Evans for her help in securing permission to reproduce copyright material, and to the following sources for permission to reproduce material previously published elsewhere:

Quotations from *The Emigrants*
The Emigrants, by W. G. Sebald, translated by Michael Hulse, published by Harvill. Reprinted by permission of The Random House Group Ltd.

Quotations from *Vertigo*
© Eichborn AG, Frankfurt/Main, 1990
First published in Germany under the original title *Schwindel. Gefühle*
English translation © Michael Hulse 1999

Quotations from *The Rings of Saturn*
© Eichborn AG, Frankfurt/Main, 1995
First published in Germany under the original title *Die Ringe des Saturn, Eine englische Wallfahrt*.
The Rings of Saturn, by W. G. Sebald, translated by Michael Hulse, published by Harvill. Reprinted by permission of The Random House Group Ltd.

Quotations from *Austerlitz*
Austerlitz, by W. G. Sebald, translated by Anthea Bell (Hamish Hamilton, 2001), © the estate of W. G. Sebald, translation © Anthea Bell, 2001. Reproduced by permission of Penguin Books Ltd.

Quotations from *On the Natural History of Destruction*
On the Natural History of Destruction, by W. G. Sebald, translated by Anthea Bell (Penguin Books, 2003, 2004) © The estate of W. G. Sebald, translation © Anthea Bell, 2001. Reproduced by permission of Penguin Books Ltd.

Photographs taken from *The Emigrants*
© Eichborn AG, from *The Emigrants*, first published in Germany under the original title *Die Ausgewanderten* by Eichborn AG, Frankfurt/Main 1993

Photographs taken from *The Rings of Saturn*
© Eichborn AG, from *The Rings of Saturn*, first published in Germany under the original title *Die Ringe des Saturn, Eine englische Wallfahrt* by Eichborn AG, Frankfurt/Main 1995

Photographs taken from *Vertigo*
© Eichborn AG, from *Vertigo*, first published in Germany under the original title *Schwindel. Gefühle* by Eichborn AG, Frankfurt/Main 1990

Photographs taken from *Austerlitz*
Austerlitz, by W. G. Sebald, translated by Anthea Bell (Hamish Hamilton, 2001), © the estate of W. G. Sebald, translation © Anthea Bell, 2001, pp. 257, 258, 351. Reproduced by permission of Penguin Books Ltd.

A NOTE ON REFERENCES AND TRANSLATIONS

Wherever possible, contributors have quoted from the English translations of Sebald's works, but page references to the German editions have been provided for those wishing to consult the originals. The table below lists the abbreviations used. Full publication details are given in the bibliography at the end of the volume.

Abbreviation	English Title	German Title
A	*Austerlitz*	*Austerlitz*
BU		*Die Beschreibung des Unglücks*
E	*The Emigrants*	*Die Ausgewanderten*
LL		*Logis in einem Landhaus*
NHD	*On the Natural History of Destruction*	*Luftkrieg und Literatur*
NN	*After Nature*	*Nach der Natur*
RS	*The Rings of Saturn*	*Die Ringe des Saturn*
UH		*Unheimliche Heimat*
V	*Vertigo*	*Schwindel. Gefühle*

Page references will be given first to the English translation, then to the German edition. So, for example, the reference 'E: 15/24' means that the quotation can be found on page 15 of *The Emigrants* and on page 24 of *Die Ausgewanderten*.

For all other works, published translations have been used wherever possible. All other translations are by individual contributors.

W. G. SEBALD: CHRONOLOGY

1944	Born in Wertach im Allgäu, Bavaria, on 18 May
1963–6	Studied German and comparative literature at universities in Freiburg and French-speaking Switzerland
1966–8	Worked as *Lektor* (German language assistant) at the University of Manchester
1968	Completed MA thesis on Carl Sternheim
1968–9	Worked as schoolteacher in St Gallen, Switzerland
1969	Publication of MA thesis as *Carl Sternheim: Kritiker und Opfer der Wilhelminischen Ära*
1969–70	Returned to his post as *Lektor* in Manchester
1970–5	Appointed as Lecturer in German at the University of East Anglia in Norwich
1975	Worked at the Goethe Institute in Munich
1976	Returned to lecturing post in Norwich
1980	Publication of Ph.D. thesis as *Der Mythus der Zerstörung im Werk Döblins*
1985	Publication of *Die Beschreibung des Unglücks*, a collection of essays on Austrian literature
1988	Awarded personal chair in European Literature at the University of East Anglia
	Publication of *Nach der Natur* (translated as *After Nature*, 2002)
1989	Founded British Centre for Literary Translation
1990	Publication of *Schwindel. Gefühle* (translated as *Vertigo*, 1999)
1991	Awarded Fedor Malchow Prize for *Nach der Natur*
	Publication of *Unheimliche Heimat*, a second collection of essays on Austrian literature
1992	Publication of *Die Ausgewanderten* (translated as *The Emigrants*, 1996)
1994	Awarded *Berliner Literaturpreis* and the Bobrowski Medal, and the *Preis der Literatour Nord*
1995	Publication of *Die Ringe des Saturn* (translated as *The Rings of Saturn*, 1998)

1997	Awarded Mörike Prize, the Heinrich Böll Prize, and the Wingate Prize for Fiction
1999	Publication of *Luftkrieg und Literatur* (translated as *On the Natural History of Destruction*, 2003)
2001	Publication of *Austerlitz*
	Award of the Heinrich Heine Prize
	W. G. Sebald dies on 14 December
2003	Publication of *Unerzählt* and *Campo Santo*

PART I
CONTEXTS

Wertach Im Allgäu

↓

Manchester

↓

Norwich

I

INTRODUCTION

J. J. Long and Anne Whitehead

1

W. G. Sebald's untimely death in December 2001 robbed European literature of one of its most distinctive and important voices. The same year had seen the publication of *Austerlitz*, which had rapidly become an international bestseller. He had been awarded the Heinrich Heine Prize of the City of Düsseldorf, and was widely tipped as the next recipient of the Georg Büchner Prize, Germany's most prestigious literary award.

Sebald had turned to literature relatively late in life. Born in Wertach im Allgäu, a hamlet in the Bavarian Alps, in 1944, he took up a teaching post at the University of Manchester in 1966, and eventually settled in Norwich, where he enjoyed a successful academic career at the University of East Anglia. He published extensively on nineteenth- and twentieth-century literature, and was appointed to a Personal Chair in European Literature in 1988. In the same year, he also published his first major literary work, *Nach der Natur* [*After Nature*], after which his reputation grew slowly but steadily in Germany. His first two books attracted positive reviews, but he remained something of cult figure, known only to a small number of aficionados, until the publication of *Die Ausgewanderten* [*The Emigrants*] in 1992. *The Emigrants* was a runaway success, went to a second hardback printing, and was the first of Sebald's works to appear in paperback. It was also the first to be translated, and established Sebald's reputation beyond the borders of his native land. In Great Britain and the United States in particular, Sebald's work was greeted with arguably greater critical acclaim and public enthusiasm than had been the case in the German-speaking world. As a result of the success of *The Emigrants*, translations of his earlier and subsequent texts followed: *The Rings of Saturn* and *Vertigo*. The publication of *Austerlitz* in 2001 was widely greeted as the summa of his work to date. It will now stand, of course, as his last major prose work; his oeuvre must be regarded as closed. This *Critical Companion* represents an attempt to provide an assessment of his multifaceted and impressive contribution to contemporary fiction.

In the course of his literary career, Sebald made distinguished contributions to several genres. His first major publication was the long quasi-narrative poem *Nach der Natur* [*After Nature*], and he returned to poetry in his collaborative work with two artists. *For Years Now* (2001) is a slim volume of pithy, elliptical verses written in English and accompanied by the geometric graphics of Tess Jaray, while *Unerzählt* [*Untold*, 2003] is a posthumous volume of thirty-three similarly brief lyrics, each printed opposite the image of a different pair of eyes, drawn with exquisite precision by Jan Peter Tripp. Sebald also produced a number of occasional poems and short stories, and several books of literary criticism, including *On the Natural History of Destruction*, a controversial polemical essay about literary representations of the Allied bombing of German cities. But the texts on which his critical reputation and public success largely rest are his four volumes of narrative prose: *Vertigo*, *The Emigrants*, *The Rings of Saturn* and *Austerlitz*. None of these works is easy to categorise in terms of genre; each mixes biography and autobiography, history and fiction, travelogue and documentary. This generic hybridity, however, is far removed from the kind of ludic textual experimentation associated with certain strands of postmodernism. On the contrary, Sebald's works are informed by a profound ethical and political seriousness. They evince an almost encyclopaedic knowledge of European cultural, social and political history – particularly the history of colonialism – and an enduring concern with what is arguably the defining historical event of recent times: the Holocaust.

Sebald's work can be seen as a response to these multiple pasts. Taken together, *Vertigo*, *The Emigrants*, *The Rings of Saturn* and *Austerlitz* constitute a project of ambitious if not audacious scope. In them, Sebald seeks to explore man's historical relationship to his environment, the effects of economic and political history on nature and on the lives of individuals, and the nature of memory, be it collective, familial or individual. But he is also intensely concerned with questions of representation, with the forms in and through which individual and collective memory, historical knowledge and the cultural heritage can be communicated from one person to another or passed down though the generations.

These concerns determine not only the thematic content but also the formal features of Sebald's texts. They are highly self-reflexive, containing meditations on the ethical and epistemological pitfalls of writing in particular and representation in general. These meditations are in turn linked to the problem of perspective, in both the literal and figurative sense: a recurrent topos of Sebald's writing is the desire for a stable perspective or vantage point from which the object, be it a landscape or a historical event, can be reliably represented, even if the possibility of such a vantage point is ultimately recognised as an illusion. The thematisation of vision is rendered more concrete and more complex by the inclusion of heterogeneous photographic material, which raises questions about the relationship between visual image and verbal narrative. Sebald's stories of loss and destruction, exile and return, forgetting and remembrance are mediated through complex forms of narrative embedding, as the story of the narrator's journey, investigation, or quest functions as a framing narrative within which other stories can be integrated. By thus drawing attention – by explicit or implicit means – to his own representational strategies, Sebald thematises the question of transmission of historical knowledge and personal and collective memory. Furthermore, his narrators are also engaged in the transmission of cultural values, writing extensively about the art and literature of the past. Indeed, this literature permeates the very texture of Sebald's prose. The abundance of quotations, allusions and intertextual references testifies to Sebald's indebtedness to his literary forebears, while the hypotaxis of his style – simultaneously extravagant and leisurely – bears obvious traces of the Austrian writers (notably Adalbert Stifter and Thomas Bernhard) on whom Sebald wrote so eloquently.

As this brief and inevitably partial sketch of the thematic and formal aspects of Sebald's prose suggests, his works deal with many issues that are of central concern not just to scholars in the humanities, but to Western culture more generally. The chapters in this *Critical Companion* have been organised around four key thematic headings that address what we perceive to be the salient features of Sebald's work: Landscape and Nature; Travel and Walking; Intertextuality and Intermediality; and Haunting, Trauma and Memory. These categories are not, however, watertight; productive points of agreement and debate can be found both within and across the four central sections. In the remainder of this introduction, we set out some of the intellectual contexts that are central to Sebald's work and to the essays in this volume, and outline the approaches of the various contributors, in the hope of stimulating further debate about one of the most representative writers of recent decades.

2

Sebald's work is situated at the confluence of numerous discourses, contexts and debates. His integration of photographic images into verbal narratives raises questions of the role of the visual in memory and the construction of narrative, questions that are central to the discipline of visual culture studies. His essay on the aerial bombing of German cities was published at a time when the ethics of articulating the very real suffering of Germans during the Second

World War was emerging as an urgent and heated historiographical debate in Germany and beyond. Sebald's self-conscious and pervasive quotation of and allusions to past writers invite engagement with theories of intertextuality. But perhaps the two most important contexts, both for an understanding of Sebald's work and for the essays in this volume, are first questions of nature and second Freudian and post-Freudian discourse on memory and trauma.

As Simon Schama argues in his work *Landscape and Memory*, the role of landscape in the imaginary of different national cultures varies hugely from one national community to the next. The forests of Poland, for example, functioned as a powerful symbol of, and often surrogate for, national independence. The English greenwood stood for the ancient rights and liberties of an indigenous sylvan folk that were constantly imperilled by aristocrats of Norman descent, while for settlers in North America the vast trees in the western regions bore witness to man's transcendental connection to his creator. In these cases, landscape clearly serves to bolster and legitimise national ideologies, and the same is true of the German forest. The foundational account of the Teutonic woods and the Germanic tribes that dwelt therein was provided by the first-century Roman historian Cornelius Tacitus. For Tacitus himself, stressing the difference between the civilisation of Rome and the barbarism of the Germanic tribes served its own legitimating function, even if it was tinged with subtle criticism of Rome (Schama 1995: 83–6). Yet his descriptions of the warlike, non-agrarian, self-sufficient and self-abnegating Germanic people proved to be a powerful myth of origins for those who, from the early sixteenth century on, sought to establish the grounds of a German national identity in opposition to the Latin south. It was an extraordinarily persistent myth, resurfacing at various points in Germany's discontinuous history as a marker of German identity.

Throughout the nineteenth and twentieth centuries, conceptions of landscape and nature continued to play a prominent role in debates about German identity. Germany's transition, in 1871, from a particularist patchwork of states to a unified nation state dominated by Prussia was, as Elizabeth Boa and Rachel Palfreyman have observed, 'marked by tensions between regional and national identity which were intensified by the extreme rapidity of industrialization and urbanization' (2000: 1). One response to the process of modernisation was the so-called *Heimatbewegung* (*Heimat* movement). *Heimat* is a term that denotes 'home' in the sense of a (predominantly rural and agrarian) place, but its semantic range is vastly extensible, and the notion of *Heimat* has indeed been enlisted in the service of a broad spectrum of ideological positions. The *Heimatbewegung* itself, for example, included a variety of activities such as environmental planning and countryside protection, the promotion of local history and museums, rambling, folk festivals and tourist guidebooks. The discourse of *Heimat* as it developed during the late nineteenth and early twentieth centuries was organised around a series of oppositions that 'set country against city, province against metropolis, tradition against modernity, nature against artificiality, organic culture against civilization, fixed, familiar, rooted identity against cosmopolitanism, hybridity, alien otherness, or the faceless mass' (Boa and Palfreyman 2000: 2).

Sebald's interest in questions of *Heimat* can be gauged from the title of his collection of essays on Austrian literature, *Unheimliche Heimat*, 'unheimlich' here meaning unhomely as well as uncanny, and signalling that for nineteenth- and twentieth-century Austrian writers *Heimat* was never an untroubled notion. Wherever Sebald's work evokes landscapes and other aspects of the natural world that have been irrevocably spoilt by the industrial expansion of modern societies, he is clearly drawing on the oppositions that, as we have seen, inform *Heimat* discourse. Yet he also appears to take a longer historical view of landscape; his literary engagement with the natural world is not restricted to the problem of *Heimat* and modernity, but extends into medieval and early modern conceptions of nature too, as Greg Bond and Colin Riordan show. Furthermore, landscape functions as a vehicle for articulating wider issues of representation, and these are addressed by Simon Ward and John Beck as well as Riordan and Bond.

As we have mentioned, memory plays a central role in Sebald's work, and many of the key questions he addresses also arise in contemporary memory discourse. Since the early 1990s, the problem of memory has become a central preoccupation for those working in the disciplines of literature, history and cultural studies. Scholars are increasingly concerned not only with what is remembered of the past but also with how and why it is remembered, and the attendant issues of aesthetics, politics and ethics remain matters of heated controversy and debate.

As a founding figure in the conceptualisation of trauma and a tireless theorist of memory, Sigmund Freud continues to occupy a central position in the current discourse of memory. The traumatic neuroses of the First World War precipitated Freud's most influential work on trauma, in particular the two closely related essays 'The Uncanny' (1919) and *Beyond the Pleasure Principle* (1920). 'The Uncanny' is ostensibly a study of a literary genre and aesthetic response, but the essay was written as Freud revised *Beyond the Pleasure Principle* and it extends into the darker territory of the death drive. Freud investigates our sense of 'unhomeliness', the propensity of the familiar to suddenly become defamiliarised and dreamlike, provoking in us feelings of anxiety and dread. Through the sensation of déjà vu, the conviction that an event or experience has already happened before, the uncanny is linked to the traumatic compulsion to repeat. For Freud, the uncanny represents something which has long been familiar to us but which has been repressed from consciousness, something which ought to have remained hidden but has come to light. The uncanny is indissociable in Freud's thinking from traumatic repression and repetition, and it has gained resonance as the condition of contemporary haunting. The notion of the uncanny provided Freud with a way of thinking through the First World War, but it has proved an equally useful concept for thinking about the post-1945 period.

In *Beyond the Pleasure Principle*, Freud grappled with the problem of repetition. He was particularly concerned with the tendency of traumatised people to repeat painful experiences in their dreams, which could not be satisfactorily explained as an attempt to achieve libidinal satisfaction. Freud acknowledged a 'beyond' of the pleasure principle, which he termed the death drive, and which acts independently of, and at times in opposition to, the pleasure principle. In the book, Freud significantly expanded his definition and account of trauma. He argued that a defensive shield or barrier is designed to defend the organism against large quantities of stimuli from the external world that threaten the stability and organisation of the psyche. Trauma represents a breach in the ego's protective shield, which sets in motion a defensive reaction or response. The psyche seeks to master the stimulus that has broken through the defences by a process of binding. Repetition works towards binding and acts to gain a retrospective mastery over the stimulus. In Freud's conception, then, psychic trauma is caused by the ego's lack of 'Angstbereitschaft', the preparedness to experience fear or anxiety. Fright produces a disorganisation of the ego and repetition represents the defensive response of the organism.

Sebald's work is steeped in psychoanalytical thought and he consciously integrates Freudian terms into his writing. Sebald is a highly selective reader of Freud, however, and he focuses overwhelmingly on 'The Uncanny' and *Beyond the Pleasure Principle*. For Sebald, trauma is inescapably bound up with repetition, and his narratives both retrace the past and explore the inescapability of the past in the present. He draws on 'The Uncanny' to reconfigure the German *Heimat* or homeland as an unhomely territory, which is characterised by disorienting coincidences, repetitions and doublings. More broadly, he demonstrates that contemporary Europe is unhomely, haunted by the spectres of the past, and especially by the traumatic history of the Holocaust. His insistent use of repetition consciously draws on *Beyond the Pleasure Principle*, and Freud's book leads us to question whether Sebald's repetition is solely a backward movement or propulsion which signals the inexorable hold of the past. Is repetition also, as in Freud, a form of binding or mastery, which positions Sebald's writing as a mode of working through the past? Is repetition for Sebald, as for Freud, ambiguously suspended between a backward and a forward momentum?

Trauma theory is central to the current discourse of memory. Cathy Caruth is a particularly influential proponent of trauma theory, whose work comprises a distinctive combination of deconstructionist literary theory and psychoanalysis. Caruth proposes a model of trauma which is defined by belatedness and missed experience. The traumatic event is necessarily subject to deferral and registers only belatedly after a period of latency or delay. Trauma brings about a rupture in memory, it breaks continuity with the past, and it places identity in question.

The memory lapses of trauma are conjoined with a compulsive reliving or re-experiencing of the traumatic event, which takes the form of uncontrolled experiences of hallucination, nightmare or flashback. Trauma does not disappear, but returns in all too literal a manner. The notion of belatedness in Caruth is not confined to the trauma or pathology of the individual but encompasses subsequent generations, so that groups or individuals who have not themselves experienced trauma can 'inherit' the memories of those who have died.

Sebald is clearly conversant with the discourse of trauma theory, both in his novels and in his critical essays, and this is especially evident in *The Emigrants* and *Austerlitz*. As a member of the post-war generation, Sebald insists that the shadow of the war falls over him and that he cannot escape from it. His novels address the relation of the generation after to the trauma of the war, and assess the impact of the Holocaust on German collective identity. Sebald's writing raises crucial questions concerning intergenerational trauma. Is the transgenerational transmission of trauma an appropriate model for describing the impact of the war on those who come after? How does the trauma of the individual relate to collective trauma? What role or responsibility does the second generation have in representing a trauma that is not their own? Although Sebald is often described as a melancholic writer who is locked in a frozen relation to the past, there is a complex dialectic between memory and forgetting at play in his writing, which gestures towards the fundamental ambiguity and complexity of trauma. He is profoundly imbricated in the ongoing dilemmas and debates of trauma theory and he occupies a central position in contemporary memory discourse. Freudian and post-Freudian psychoanalysis occupies a central position in several chapters in this volume, most notably those by John Zilcosky, Maya Barzilai and Carolin Duttlinger. They also, however, engage in dialogue with Freud, using Sebald's texts recursively and pointing up the limitations of the psychoanalytical framework. Other contributors, such as Jan Ceuppens, Wilfried Wilms and Russell Kilbourn also engage in dialogue with Freud, even where they seek alternative models of memory.

3

This volume begins, rather unconventionally, with a poem: George Szirtes's 'Meeting Austerlitz: In memoriam W. G. Sebald'. In the light of Sebald's untimely and shocking death, it offers a meditation on friendship, loss and memory. But it is also a lyrical engagement with Sebald's work: Szirtes takes up and develops the themes of walking and travel, employing similar techniques of allusion and quotation, and, like Sebald, embedding his philosophical speculations within a precisely delineated object-world.

The fact that Sebald's books have found a large popular readership across Europe and North America has perhaps obscured the fact that they are simultaneously responses to specifically German concerns. Martin Swales adopts such a 'double optic', pointing out in his 'Theoretical Reflections on the Work of W. G. Sebald' that a full appreciation of Sebald's status as a writer entails an understanding of a distinctly German inflection of the wider European novel-writing tradition. Sebald's prose writings are deeply indebted, both aesthetically and philosophically, to a peculiarly German kind of novelistic discourse. Whereas the novels of the great French and English realists treated the minutiae of social and economic life in basically secular and materialistic terms, Swales points out that German writers of the nineteenth century tended to read the phenomenal world as a cipher through which intimations of the metaphysical reveal themselves to the attentive observer. Drawing on Hegel's *Aesthetics*, he shows that Sebald writes in precisely this tradition, the myriad documentary details being inseparable from the signification of spiritual entities.

Greg Bond's essay 'On the Misery of Nature and the Nature of Misery' introduces the section on 'Landscape and Nature'. As if to illustrate Swales's contention that Sebald's work is concerned to hint at a spiritual dimension beyond phenomena, Bond shows that Sebald's depiction of the natural world reveals a 'baroque metaphysics of landscape, wherein there is nothing behind the scenes but the empty grin of death'. Sebald was especially keen to refute what he terms the 'ideological concept of nature', according to which nature is viewed as a compensatory sphere that evinces none of the shortcomings of the social world. Bond argues that nature and man do not form two terms of a binary opposition, but that human and natural history are in some sense continuous, nature merely using man to further its own destructive work. Bond expresses scepticism about the ability of Sebald's landscapes to carry the metaphysical weight with which he burdens them, but he also argues that Sebald's melancholy is occasionally relieved by glimpses of hope, be they the utopian landscapes of *Austerlitz* or the recurrent sightings of the butterfly man.

Colin Riordan's reading of *After Nature* shares some common ground with Bond, but he adopts a very different critical approach. Riordan demonstrates that, even at a theoretical level, a notion of nature that is in some sense pristine and untouched by human beings is utterly untenable, not only because everything we regard as nature has been transformed by human action but also because the very concept of nature is a social, mental and linguistic construct that is ultimately indissociable from human signifying practices. It is precisely this inseparability of the natural and the social that facilitates Riordan's eco-centric reading of Sebald's poem. Riordan uses the term 'ecology' to denote not a target of political activism but a value system in which the environmental context of human life is viewed as intrinsically valuable and becomes the central object of textual inquiry. *After Nature*, Riordan argues, rightly accords nature a central place in its portrayal of human history, presenting nature in two forms: as a malleable entity subject to transformation by human agency, and as an eternal, elemental power that is indifferent to human endeavour.

In the final essay in the section 'Landscape and Nature', Simon Ward adopts a rather different perspective, discussing the thematic and formal status of the ruin in Sebald's prose work. Ward points out that the representation of ruins in Sebald's texts goes hand in hand with reflection on the position and perspective of the observer. So while ruins appear as the result of a natural-historical process of destruction, they also function as sites of projection or hallucination, realms in which the imagination engages with and transforms the material environment. This reading of the ruin allows Ward to take issue with Andreas Huyssen's accusation that *On the Natural History of Destruction* merely reinscribes the trauma of the Allied air raids on German cities in the Second World War through quotation and repetition, and performs a politically dubious reduction of recent German history to natural history (Huyssen 2001). Ward shows that while Sebald's texts aesthetically appropriate the traces of the past, they also reflect on and call into question this process of appropriation. By highlighting the mediated nature of transmitted experience and stressing the necessary unreliability of any perspective, Sebald's art is itself a ruin, caught up in processes of self-erasure even as it constructs its textual worlds. Artistic production is simultaneously a natural eruption of material and a self-conscious process of destruction, and this represents a dialectical response to the metaphysics of the natural history of destruction that ostensibly informs Sebald's texts.

The section 'Travel and Walking' opens with John Beck's chapter, 'Reading Room: Erosion and Sedimentation in Sebald's Suffolk'. While landscape is of interest to Beck, the structuring metaphor of his analysis is walking as a kind of reading, and vice versa. Beck's meditation on walking, reading and the environment in *The Rings of Saturn* becomes a means of exploring the question of representation. Sebald ironises the futility of man's rage for order by showing how nature continually reclaims and destroys the products of human work. But he also reflects in melancholy fashion on the fact that system-building of all kinds – from imperial rule and capitalist expansion to the labyrinthine literature of Borges – paradoxically rely on the destruction of the world they seek to dominate. Sebald cannot, however, escape the seductions and consolations of systems: *The Rings of Saturn* itself offers a self-legitimising order that substitutes the world of the scholar's preoccupations for the debased culture of consumption and historical amnesia that the narrator inhabits. While threatening to reproduce the very same 'tyranny of representation' that it criticises, though, *The Rings of Saturn*, Beck argues, offers a metacommentary that destabilises the system from the inside: the accumulation of interconnected information leads not to an ever tauter system of control, but rather to increasing indeterminacy, instability and disappointment.

Massimo Leone's 'Textual Wanderings: A Vertiginous Reading of W. G. Sebald' likewise addresses the question of walking, seeing the Sebaldian narrator as a *flâneur*, that emblematic figure of modernity who strolls aimlessly through the city streets, and whose gaze both appropriates and projects meaning onto the urban landscape. Leone analyses the specific techniques by means of which Sebald's narrators set out to find meaning within, or create meaning out of, the ordinariness of everyday language and the built environment. In contrast to Swales, Leone sees this as a mystical rather than a philosophical enterprise. By destabilising the familiar structures of space (through *flânerie*) and language (through association and repetition), Leone argues, Sebald's narrators open up a perspective on the hidden meaning of things which is both a result and a cause of a consciously sought vertigo.

As we have seen, the Freudian uncanny exerts a particularly strong influence in Sebald's writing and is a key element in his response to and figuring of the Holocaust. In the closing essay of Part III, John Zilcosky draws out the ways in which Sebald overturns the formal expectations of the travel-writing genre through his evocation of the uncanny. Sebald undermines the conventional travel narrative, in which the traveller gets lost in order to find his way home, by revealing that in today's uncanny world it is impossible to really lose one's way. Sebald's travellers trace the trajectory of the uncanny: unable to lose their way, they are also unable to return home and so wander through an unsettling and disorienting terrain. Zilcosky is also alert to Sebald's continual reconfiguring of the uncanny. In *Vertigo*, Sebald explores Freud's theory that male heterosexuality is a site of the uncanny, for the man finds in the woman's genitals the familiar, and his experience is one of return or of not getting lost. Sebald questions whether homosexuality offers an escape from the system of eternal heterosexual return, but although sexual straying or drifting is figured in the novel as a desired goal, it is one which is not pursued by the narrator. In *The Rings of Saturn*, the uncanny extends towards the death drive, so that the inevitable return, or the inability to get lost, leads to a state of lifelessness and paralysis. *The Emigrants* connects the figure of uncanny return to the Holocaust, for all four of the stories enact a compulsive homecoming to the ruins of German-Jewish history. Although Zilcosky does not extend his reading to *Austerlitz*, Sebald consolidates in this novel his treatment of the uncanny in *The Emigrants*, and underlines the significance of Freud's concept as a figure for contemporary haunting.

Martin Klebes's discussion of Sebald's *Vertigo* and Kafka's story-fragment 'The Hunter Gracchus' introduces the section on 'Intertextuality and Intermediality'. Klebes is also concerned with travel to a certain degree: Manfred Frank's attempt to integrate 'The Hunter Gracchus' into a history of the motif of the neverending journey forms the starting point of his analysis. But Klebes's real concern is the indeterminacy of textual meaning, which subverts Frank's assertion that the history of a motif can function as a privileged interpretative framework for the interpretation of Kafka's story. Klebes shows that Kafka's Gracchus is a profoundly ambiguous figure, a character who is both native earthling and eternity-bound stranger, both guest and host, both at home everywhere and at home nowhere, and who simultaneously remembers perfectly and remembers nothing at all. 'The Hunter Gracchus', then, would appear to problematise the very semantic stability on which Frank's analysis depends. Klebes goes on to explore Sebald's use of Kafka in *Vertigo*, a link that is mediated through photography in the story 'Al'estero' and through citations from 'The Hunter Gracchus' and Kafka's letters and journals in 'Dr K. Takes the Waters at Riva'. Rather than offering a key to the meaning of *Vertigo* or providing some sort of referential anchor, however, intertextuality and photography in Sebald's text thwart the possibility of authenticity; we are denied any reliable access to the narrator's psychology or experience, and any reliable insight into Kafka's emotional life. Like 'The Hunter Gracchus', *Vertigo* is characterised by a semiotic drift which ultimately implies scepticism of any historical schema that seeks, like Frank's, to arrest the play of textual meaning.

The second and third essays in Part IV deal with memory and the visual from two different perspectives. Russell Kilbourn analyses the role of architecture and cinema in the memory discourse of *Austerlitz*, arguing that such an approach is not incompatible with psychoanalysis, but rather demonstrates the irreducibly metaphorical nature of Freud's spatial model of the psyche. Drawing on the work of both pre-modern and poststructuralist thinkers, Kilbourn links Austerlitz's experience in the Ladies' Waiting Room of Liverpool Street Station to the mnemonic structures of classical rhetoric, Augustine's *Confessions* and apophatic theology, a strand in theological thought that seeks to define God negatively (that is, by saying what God is not). As in classical rhetoric, memory in *Austerlitz* is figured as an exteriorised, purely imaginary space that reproduces the structure of the protagonist's displaced long-term memory of his parents and the *Kindertransport*. This, argues Kilbourn, is the first of the novel's ironic *katabases* or trips to the underworld, the others being the return to Marienbad with Marie de Verneuil and Austerlitz's immersion in the Nazi propaganda film about the Theresienstadt ghetto and H. G. Adler's historical study thereof. In all cases, Austerlitz seeks to 'bring back' the other in order to gain knowledge of the self. But in what is perhaps the novel's most pessimistic turn, Austerlitz's very discovery of who he is, was, or might have been, deconstitutes rather than produces his subjectivity, leaving the reader uncertain as to which version – if either – of Austerlitz's biographies is the 'authentic' one.

Carolin Duttlinger's reading of *Austerlitz* shows that Sebald's preoccupations overlap with two key concerns in trauma theory, namely, how trauma is registered or experienced, and the relationship between acting out and working through. Duttlinger argues that in *Austerlitz* Sebald draws on the current discourse of photography, loss and trauma, in order to figure photography as a symptom of Austerlitz's traumatised condition. As Ulrich Baer has pointed out in *Spectral Evidence: The Photography of Trauma* (2002), photography parallels the traumatic experience, for it records that which is not necessarily registered by consciousness. Sebald extends this analogy, however, gesturing towards the dilemma of the second generation by suggesting that photography can also substitute for traumatic experience, facilitating the viewer's engagement with incidents that were not experienced in the first instance. In his description of Austerlitz's scrutiny of his photographs, Sebald deliberately evokes the concept of working through, suggesting that the photograph preserves an event to which the subject can only later attach a meaning. However, he quickly undermines the possibility of working through by emphasising the precariousness and the transience of both photograph and memory. For Duttlinger, Sebald repeatedly emphasises the aporia of traumatic experience. Although photographs can aid a moment of recollection, this memory will inevitably turn out to be fleeting and will rapidly fade into the surrounding darkness.

The question of trauma also forms the basis of the first essay in the section 'Haunting, Trauma, Memory'. Sebald's critical essay *On the Natural History of Destruction* implicitly draws on the discourse of trauma theory to suggest that the bombing raids over Germany were overwhelming historical events. He echoes Caruth's notion of trauma in his claim that the German victims of the bombing could not have access to their experiences and that they could not be integrated into narrative memory, because a collapse of witnessing had taken place. As Wilfried Wilms points out, however, Sebald contradicts the very model of trauma he invokes by suggesting that the Germans suffered from an unwillingness rather than an inability to mourn the bombing war. Sebald's shift of agency implies that the Germans actively forgot or repressed their experiences, extending his argument into the moral realm. The post-war Germans impose their own silence and fail to transmit the history of their suffering to the next generation. The question of how traumatic experience is registered marks a crucial slippage in Sebald's argument, so that the Germans who experienced the bombing raids are precariously positioned between the roles of victim (traumatised and rendered inarticulate by their experiences) and perpetrator (actively silencing and failing to pass on the story of their experiences). Wilms rightly questions whether we can view Sebald's study – and especially its blind spots – in relation to the second generation. Is his analysis distorted by the second-generation taboo on representing Germans as victims rather than as perpetrators? Certainly, Sebald feels the need to lay the blame and failure on the side of the German, who renders the massive destruction of his home and life a taboo subject. Wilms compellingly suggests that Sebald himself is caught within the very dilemmas that he seeks to analyse. The silence and trauma at the heart of *On the Natural History of Destruction* is experienced by the second generation as well as by those who experienced the bombing raids, and it powerfully affects how the war is remembered or constructed in the present.

Jan Ceuppens's account of Sebald's spectrology also deals with questions of history, memory and repetition. But for Ceuppens, psychoanalysis no longer forms the central theoretical framework. Rather, he draws on Jacques Derrida's reading of Marx in order to explore the dialectic of repetition and uniqueness in *The Emigrants*. The key problem for Ceuppens is whether a singular, authentic or, to use Derrida's term, 'pure' representation of historical trauma is possible, or whether one is always of necessity bound to repeat the discourses and narratives of the past. Instead of seeing these as irreconcilable opposites, though, Ceuppens devotes much of his attention to the ways in which Sebald enlists the logic of haunting and repetition in order to remain faithful to the singularity of a person or event. If singularity can never be attained in its pure form, it can nevertheless be hinted at, and continues to exist in the form of a promise.

The volume closes with Maya Barzilai's essay 'Facing the Past and the Female Spectre in *The Emigrants*'. Barzilai builds on the scepticism of contemporary feminist critics, who have noted a fundamental problem in Freud's theory of the uncanny: it privileges a male response to the trauma of woman's perceived lack. For Barzilai, Sebald replicates the problems in Freud by privileging male bonding and aligning female figures with the traumatic aporia of the Holocaust. In *The Emigrants* women either act as conduits of memory, who relate what they have been told of the past, or they represent the simultaneously threatening and captivating encounter with death. Through a close historical-cultural reading of 'The Uncanny', Barzilai demonstrates that, in a period of intensifying anti-Semitism, Freud repositioned the uncanny as a sexual rather than a racial category. Sebald reassociates the uncanny with the figure of the Jew, and in the post-1945 context this connection evokes the highly ambivalent and troubled nature of post-war German-Jewish relations. As Barzilai points out, Sebald's is a risky strategy, for it is difficult to determine whether he foregrounds misogynistic and anti-Semitic figures in order to heighten our awareness of contemporary sexism and racism, or whether he inadvertently reinforces their disturbingly persistent heritage.

2

MEETING AUSTERLITZ

George Szirtes

i.m. W. G. Sebald
December 2001

1

The cold sat down with frozen fingers. Cars
were iced up, the pavements were treacherous.
Boys in t-shirts drifted through doors of bars
in quiet market towns. The shops were a chorus
of seasonal favourites, every one the same.
We were jollying ourselves up for Christmas
without much money and no sense of shame
because this was a time for giving and for joy.
We were all good intentions. So the postman came
and went, lorries delivered supplies, the boy
with the papers zipped about on his bike,
parents were packing the latest must-have toy
(each one expensive, every one alike),
the butcher's whole family were busy serving
and no one had fallen ill or gone on strike.
On ungritted roads motorists were swerving
to avoid each other. Nothing had come to bits
in the houses of the whole and the wholly deserving,

nothing was incomprehensible or beyond our wits
and I myself was taking a quiet stroll
in the nearby fields when I met Austerlitz.
It was some way off the road and he was the sole
patch of dark in the bright mid-afternoon.
Hello Max, I said. And he looked up with that droll
melancholy expression. There was the faintest moon
visible in the sky. Both day and night,
he grinned. It'll be dusk pretty soon.
In *Lalla Rookh*, if I remember right,
I've not read Thomas Moore for several years,
there's a veiled prophet, Hakim, who radiates light
and draws the moon from a well. When it appears
it eclipses the real moon. Perhaps we have invented
the sad pale thing there with its terrible shears.
The air was frosty, oddly tobacco-scented,
thick grey clouds rose from his mouth as he spoke.
I could not be certain whether the wisps that entered
my mouth were frozen breath or cigarette smoke:
everything had a double or existed
in some version of itself wrapped in a winter cloak.
It was as if an enormous window had misted.
Austerlitz was looking across the field.
Beyond the window, there were buildings twisted
into macabre shapes. Some creature squealed
in the distance. A car growled briefly past.
Then silence, complete and vacuum-sealed.

2

I could not believe that Austerlitz was dead.
Though others had died that year his death was strange.
His voice had internalised itself in my head
and I kept listening to see how it would arrange
the furniture it found there. Certainly
it would improve things. Almost any change
would do that. A puff of dust from the library,
swirling like ashes, had settled across his prose,
its flavour tart, magical and scholarly,
as tired as the world. Each cadence had to close
on what remained of it. A collection of postcards,
a guidebook, a streetmap. The attempt to impose

order was a perilous task, all but beyond words
while the alternative universe of flux
offered no sympathy and kept no records.
His were meticulous, a kind of *fiat lux*
compounded of atoms. My mind being a mess
I wanted his vision blowing through the ducts.
Though Austerlitz had died the tenderness
of his precision was consoling. No-one
could start at quite that angle to the homeless
intellect. It was the winter sun.
His voice moved in the frozen field and I
would follow it and beg him to carry on.

3

I was writing about wrestlers. There were books
and videos and interviews. I thought
long about the body, the way it looks
and functions, the way the body fought
its enemies – other bodies, disease,
the weather, the impossible onslaught
of information, and the curious sleaze
it took to – but also its courage, miraculous
cogency and ability to please.
My half-century had passed. I was feckless
and wanted to listen to what Austerlitz
might say on the subject, however ridiculous.
I knew a good man once, of regular habits,
he began, a doctor, who lived just there
beyond the field. In reasonable spirits
you'd have thought. It was a bad affair,
a long way from his birthplace. He was ill
of course, but others sicken without despair
quite breaking through like that. We can distill
our terrors and make them hang like a grey mist
beyond the garden, somehow peripheral,
and I considered him an optimist
compared to me, though that's a matter of style.
Body and mind, the way they co-exist,
is by breeding madness which festers a while
but sooner or later starts jabbering, and then
at last it is as if an imbecile

had always possessed you. Your wrestling men
are like the demons that Jesus exorcised,
playing at swine herded into a pen
or ring, and we pretend to be surprised
when they break free and tumble from a height.
Demons are inevitably oversized
by our usual standards. We remain polite,
value nobility, and the poor doctor was the most
courteous of people until that night.
Things just add up, especially the lost
things. He breathed out and the air stood still
before it vanished slowly like a ghost.

4

But I was not prepared to let him go
so easily. I knew that in his mind
there was a tendency to counterflow
and double exposure. He would unwind
the world of memory and wind it up again
a little off-centre as though it were a blind
or hedge against bad luck. You can't explain
history to itself, he said. It has
neither ears nor eyes. Humankind must train
itself to refocus or employ mirrors.
That morning I had leaned forward to shave
and thought to see myself in my true colours,
but the face was broader and I seemed to have
no focal point at all. The nose was there,
and eyes, ears, mouth, chin, cheeks, but nothing gave
the parts coherence. The face was just too bare,
I could not glimpse it as another could
in another dimension, less self-aware.
I remembered my mother's face in childhood,
my father's worried look, my children's deep
otherness, my wife's eyes, and saw the blood
that ran through all of us like dreams in sleep
in faint streams of reality, a secret plumbing
telling us who we were, what we could keep
and what we'd have to lose in whatever was coming.
But we were standing still in the stiff grass.
It was almost dusk and the cold was numbing.

Perhaps we were statues and time would pass
leaving us unaltered, or him at least.
His words were turning to silver behind glass
like any mirror, although the mouth had ceased
moving and his breath was only in my head
stirred by a wind directly north-north-east.

5

We're born in joy, we live joy and we die
into joy, say the masses crowding on the shore
of the Ganges. You listen to the cry
of the holy men, said Austerlitz. The more
they cry, the greater the joy. You speak the name
of the god and it appears in shadows on the floor
or in the seeds of a plant, everywhere the same.
But names are like dreams we disappear into
where all things seem to fit into the frame
of their narrative. It is names we journey through:
they're landscapes of whatever happens and goes
on happening as we progress, neither old nor new.
Take photographs, the way a flashbulb blows
your swollen shadow up against the wall
behind you. A momentary perception grows
into an image of itself. It is an oddly comical
sensation. Frozen motion. Blind field. I stared
at the panoramic photograph of my old school
seeking my younger face, darker and thicker haired
lost cousin among all the faces trapped
in the moment. It was, I think, time that shared
us, not us that did the sharing, however rapt
the attention the camera gave us. We were stopped
in our tracks by it as if time itself had snapped
shut. We were part of something that was cropped
and stern but opened out again into time
that carried on either side of the camera propped
on its tripod. Look how our mouths mime
to the words we are speaking now. It is late,
said Austerlitz, watching the stars climb
to their stations. The gods of joy can wait
forever, and so can we. It was cold. I stood
trembling beside him, trying to concentrate

as the fields disappeared into the wood,
till my own image hung for a second then went
absent, not for a moment but for good.
He too watched it go, then slowly bent
his head and leaned it on my shoulder, as he had
the last time we had met, like a penitent,
and I was touched. It was terribly sad
to think of it. A car was drifting by
as in an old film. I took the nearby road
back into town just as snow began to fly.
Christmas lights dripped from windows winking
their enormous eyes at the dark sky.

6

We'd met at the station once, in the café.
It was cold then too, both of us shivering
and we said hello to each other then moved away.
I saw the crippled bushes weathering
with dead traveller's joy. At Manningtree
quicksilver mudflats and channels feathering
water with light, a water tower, the Marconi
factory at Chelmsford. The whole train-
ride was a kind of speculative journey
into melancholy in a steady rain
of terraced houses, the imperium
of the great city spreading like a stain
across suburbs, from village to reclaimed slum
in three generations. The great hotels
at the terminus, spire and dome and drum,
were ghost planets of marble and precious metals,
metaphors for a solar system whose core
had disintegrated in a peal of bells
echoing forever along one shore
or another. Water ate away each edifice,
both centre and periphery. The roar
of crumbling brickwork and the shriek of ice
in the North Sea. Gulls swirling in a high
circle over pigeons, terrace on terrace
like slow waves. I saw you pulling your wry
face again. The place was grim. I sat down
nursing my coffee and a piece of dry

Danish pastry. You'd vanished into town,
and I waited for my train and played with the sugar,
holding a lump in my spoon, letting it drown.

7

My bookmark is a little headed note:
the Esperia Hotel in Athens. The room
looked out on a side street which seemed to float
in an almost permanent state of gloom
and only when the sun rose to noon height
did it penetrate there beyond the boom
of traffic at the front where all the light
available had gathered. The TV showed
a micro-second of hard porn as bait:
a tongue, a vulva, a thrusting groin, glowed
then disappeared. Something silky froze
into permanence, in an elsewhere you could decode
with a machine. So a piece of silk could close
the gap between worlds, Austerlitz observed,
quoting somebody. The picture that shows
the young girl in the garden, her lips faintly curved
into a smile, is touching because she is lovely
and gone. Going is what we have deserved
and welcomed. The puzzled small dog on her knee,
the doll at her feet, the bentwood chair, the flowers
behind her are silky cellulose. Photography
has made them into dwarfish ghosts, sleek showers
of light beating down an endless slope.
My feet are sliding even now. There are a few hours
left, if that. The bookmark remains. The soap
by the basin. The towels. The curtains. The name
of the hotel, which, as you know, means hope.

3

THEORETICAL REFLECTIONS ON THE WORK OF W. G. SEBALD

Martin Swales

W. G. Sebald's work is suspended between two sharply contrasting narrative possibilities. On the one hand, there is a high degree of literariness in evidence: echoes of earlier literary forms and periods and of specific writers from Classical Greece to key figures of High Modernism (Rilke, Kafka, Proust, Nabokov) abound. On the other there is a register that unmistakably bespeaks and expresses documentary solidity and authenticity. Passages of factual observation and description are legion, photographs are constantly incorporated into the main text. What this strange coexistence of, on the face of it, incompatible rhetorical strategies achieves is a set of questions directed at us, the readers. We find ourselves wondering at, and wondering about, Sebald's particular narrative achievement.

Our uncertainty is compounded by the fact that, at one level, the voice that speaks in that prose (and there is often a 'spoken' quality to it) feels personal; it is manifestly and recognisably Sebald. Yet at the same time that prose feels not only impersonal but meta-personal – almost a summation of the condition of European prose at the end of the twentieth century; and that condition is intertextually rich, speaking of and through the modes and moods of modern narrative from the eighteenth century on. In this paper I want to provide a sense, in both theoretical and historical terms, of the kinds of context that are pertinent to the task of understanding Sebald.

Let me begin with the simple proposition that Sebald, however much he was a European writer, was deeply embedded in the tradition of German prose writing in both its theoretical and its practical forms. I venture to suggest that we need to have a sense of this German inflection of the European tradition if we are to get Sebald's work in focus. Two propositions in respect of the rise and development of the European novel can, I think, help us at the outset. One is that the novel is born of the urgent emergence, in the eighteenth century, of subjectivity as the governing value in human affairs. The other is that the European novel explores that subjectivity under two contrasting but related aspects. One has to do with the specificity of human experience, as expressed, say, in the epistolary novels of Richardson, Rousseau or Goethe. The other has to do with social experience, which forms the central thematic concern of the realistic novel from Defoe and Fielding, via Stendhal, Jane Austen, Balzac and Dickens to George Eliot, Flaubert, Turgenev and Hardy. In both strands of novel-writing the individual subject is at issue; and that central concern can take on a greater or lesser degree of on the one hand psychological and on the other socio-historical definition. The constant interplay of inward and outward matters, of personal and corporate issues, of private and public imperatives is the lifeblood of the European novel from the early eighteenth century to our times.

In the context of this broad corpus of narrative possibilities, German prose, it has to be said, plays at best a modest role. It is only really in the twentieth century that German-language novels become part of the canon of European 'classics' – with Kafka, Thomas Mann, Musil and others. But it was that long German tradition that Sebald was steeped in, and it is a tradition that provides a particular configuration of the repertoire of European narrativity. Two aspects need to be stressed at this juncture. One is that German culture, from the mid-eighteenth century on, is characterised by an intense inwardness of theme and mode. This has often been linked to what is perceived as the 'belatedness' of the German-speaking lands before 1871: the lack of national unity produces a particularism of self-definition, a provincialism of theme and attitude. There is, for example, no capital city that can equal the vibrant worldliness of London or Paris in English or French culture from the eighteenth century on. The lack of outward vividness is, however, offset by a vivid commitment to human interiority. Arguably, it is that inwardness of theme that produces the second aspect of the German narrative tradition that I want to stress: its theoretical sophistication. Broadly speaking, it is true to say that, prior to the appearance of the New York edition of Henry James's works, where the remarkable prefaces to each novel offer a developed and sophisticated theory of the novel, European novel-writing of the eighteenth and nineteenth centuries generates little by way of serious novel theory. Remarks on the nature of the novel are often confined to brief, unsystematic comments in forewords, casual notes and jottings by the writers themselves, whereas, from the early nineteenth century on, German prose is sustained by a significant theoretical component, one shared by both practitioners and critics alike.

The key witness here is Hegel. In his lectures on aesthetics he offers a set of brilliant reflections on the emerging modern bourgeois novel:

> The novelistic (*das Romanhafte*) is chivalry become serious again, with a real subject-matter. The contingency of external existence has been transformed into a secure order of civil society and the state, so that police, law-courts, the army, political government replace the chimerical ends which the knights errant set before themselves. Thereby the knight-errantry of the heroes as they act in more modern novelistic fictions is also altered. As individuals with their subjective ends of love, humour, and ambition, or with their ideals of world-reform, they stand opposed to this substantial order and the prose of actuality which puts difficulties in their way on all sides. (Hegel 1975: 592, translation modified)

> The novel (*der Roman*) in the modern sense of the word presupposes a world already prosaically ordered; then, on this ground and within its own sphere whether in connection with the liveliness of events or with individuals and their fate, it regains for poetry the right it had lost, so far as this is possible in view of that presupposition. Consequently, one of the commonest, and, for the novel, most appropriate collisions is the conflict between the poetry of the heart and the opposing prose of circumstances and the accidents of external situations. (Hegel 1975: 1092, translation modified)

Hegel works with the dialectical interplay of two categories, which he understands both thematically and stylistically: prose and poetry. For Hegel, the novel is the form that has the time and energy available to chronicle the prosaic condition of social life (institutions, practicalities and so on). In this sense the novel is as prosaic as the world which it chronicles. Yet the protagonists of the modern novel, Hegel argues, are inspired by a need for poetry in their lives, for finer experiences than those represented by mere worldly success. And, in consequence, the novel, as literary mode, acquires a reflective, spiritually questing, poetic register; it has room both for the characters' own thoughts and for narrative self-reflection, for symbolic intimations that make the prosaic a transparent medium through which one can perceive the possibilities of higher, finer signification.

Hegel's commentary is truly remarkable, and his dialectic of poetry and prose provided the conceptual framework for, and sets the seal on, much significant discussion of narrative modes in Germany. The terms and character of the ensuing theoretical debate may be recognisably German; but the issues raised are part of the European mainstream.[1] Above all else, what that whole German tradition articulates is a sense of and feel for the complex and ceaseless interplay of materiality and mentality. In my view, precisely that interplay, in shifting configurations, is at the heart of Sebald's creative achievement. His writing constantly has a descriptive force to it, a need to acknowledge materiality. Yet that materiality is the precipitate of a specific 'geistige Lebensform', a specific mode of mental and spiritual existence: sometimes in the sense that certain historical, political and social ideologies are recognisably at work in the characters' lives (hence the entrapment about which Sebald writes so well); but sometimes in the sense of spirituality as a need, a quest for some kind of signification beyond common perception.

Such arguments may sound somewhat rarefied and abstract. Perhaps it is helpful, then, at this juncture of the argument, to remind ourselves of the literary criticism that Sebald produced. His essays are, of course, works of analysis in their own right – and often very fine analysis. But they also provide hints and pointers that illuminate the condition of his own creative endeavour. Many commentators on his work have drawn to attention to his (slightly old-fashioned) fondness for 'fine writing', for a certain spaciousness and stateliness of expression. There is an element of truth in this. But it seems to me important to understand Sebald's literary indebtedness less as a kind of surrender to the dead hand of well wrought prose than as an engagement with a corpus of theoretical issues which quickened both his critical and his creative work.

Virtually all his critical writing is concerned with German – particularly Austrian – prose writing. Common to all his essays is the need to define the world portrayed in any particular fiction and to extrapolate from this some sense of the universe of discourse and signification which the writer in question inhabits and to which he gives expression. At one level, then, there is a clearly descriptive thrust to Sebald's critical project: he charts for us the world as described in the literary works under discussion. But that world, detailed though it is (and Sebald, like the writers he cherishes, loves detail) is not there simply in and for its materiality. Rather, it is informed by and expressive of a particular mentality. Sometimes (as in *Die Beschreibung des Unglücks* [The Description of Misery/Misfortune]) Sebald defines that mentality in primarily psychological terms. But the psychological picture that emerges is not primarily there to generate mood or emotional atmosphere. Rather, the particular instance of human temperament is invested with a cognitive force. The misery or misfortune ('Unglück') highlighted in that collection of essays is the bearer of a kind of epistemological authority; that unhappiness, that melancholy becomes a profound form of knowing. The same interpretative strategy is at work in the later volume of essays, *Unheimliche Heimat* [Uncanny/Unhomely Homeland]. Once again, Sebald lovingly charts the fictive world created by his chosen writers, constantly reading it as the expression of an omnipresent mental landscape. And then he goes on to explore that landscape for its socio-political and cultural implications (as emblematic of the fraught quest, on the part of Austrian writers, for a sense of *Heimat* or belonging). In Sebald's criticism, then, physical description becomes a mental world which is understood as an instance of both psychological and socio-political cognition.

Perhaps it will be helpful if I here give three examples of Sebald's criticism at textual close quarters. I shall refer to his last collection of essays, *Logis in einem Landhaus*, first published in 1998. The volume is prefaced by a brief introduction, at the end of which Sebald observes that 'one has to reckon with numerous difficulties when enumerating things' (*LL*: 7). It is an intriguing remark, which could well have come from Stifter or Kafka or Handke, one feels. Why should it be difficult to produce an inventory of things? One answer, as we shall see, has to do with the notion that things enact, in their disclosure to human perception, a mysterious drama of being and non-being. In consequence, description becomes an act not just of stenography but of philosophically strenuous constatation. At two points in the essays Sebald gives us a clear intimation of what he has in mind. In the piece on the Swiss novelist Gottfried Keller, he draws attention to a mutilated drawing by Keller, which is now housed in the Zürcher Zentralbibliothek and is reproduced in Sebald's text. It is a watercolour of a landscape with trees. It came into the possession of a Heidelberg actress Johanna Kapp, to whom Keller was very attracted. Towards the end of her life she was threatened by madness. She cut out about a quarter of the picture; and it is that partly dismembered picture that was returned to Keller after her death. Sebald comments:

> We do not know what led her to such a drastic step, nor do we know how Keller felt when he held the mutilated painting, that had been returned to him from Johanna's estate, in his hands once again. But perhaps he, too, felt that the snow-white void that opens up right there beneath the nigh-on transparent landscape is more beautiful than all the miraculous colours of art. (*LL*: 123)

A similar comment occurs in the final essay of the volume, which concerns the painter Jan Peter Tripp. His work is amazingly, overwhelmingly realistic. It is, Sebald suggests, almost too realistic to be real. He argues that, behind the illusionism there is 'a terrifying depth'. And he continues: 'This is, so to speak, the metaphysical lining of reality' (*LL*: 181). The link with Keller's watercolour is, I think, inescapable, as is the link with Sebald's creative prose.

The fact that we have now on two occasions been considering pictures may serve to remind us of the role of the photographs in Sebald's narrative texts. This is a large and complex issue which I cannot go into at any length here.[2] Suffice it to say that the photographs affect us in two different ways, and their dual effect recalls the point about duality of register with which I began this paper. They seem to be documentary material akin to a set of corroborative illustrations, and yet they also partake of and create a whole symbolic texture of evocative images. Hegel would have fully understood the co-presence of prosaic and poetic modes.

Sebald's prose is, then, both true to, and a debate with, the complex legacy of German and European narrative fiction. At one level, art, for Sebald, can be prosaic to the point of documentary. He attends circumstantially to physical things, to places, to settings. Yet those places are supremely sites of human signification: the material entities bespeak spiritual entities. The physical is expressive by virtue of the 'lining' (to use Sebald's own term) that is made of metaphysical presences. That perceived mentality can, of course, take many forms: it can be a melancholy, or punch-drunk, or entrapped, or wounded condition; it can be a kind of renegade, desperate spirituality, an outraged quest for other, better, things. But whatever form the mental universe takes, it is implicitly invoked rather than explicitly evoked. What Sebald depicts is the materiality rather than the mentality, materiality made eloquent by the implied 'metaphysical lining'. In this strangely quickening interplay of substantiality and insubstantiality, Sebald's art provides a summation of some two hundred years of European prose.

If I have endeavoured to contextualise Sebald within his artistic lineage or *Herkunft* (understood both historically, theoretically, and generically), it is because I believe that such a framework can help us more justly to perceive the extent and nature of what he has to offer us. The matter of *Herkunft* embraces not only the style and mode of his writing but also its theme. For him, *Herkunft* is all-pervasive. It is the sedimentation of past living that produces present forms of being; it is a community of landscape cultivated, buildings inhabited, lives lived and stories told. Sebald acknowledges that past with no sense of secure exorcism. The past cannot be laid to rest – neither psychologically nor socially nor politically nor aesthetically nor ethically; the legacy of European civilisation, to paraphrase Walter Benjamin, is also the legacy of European barbarism. The narrative act, then, serves neither to soothe nor to assuage; it does not make things better. But it does make these (material and mental) things knowable. And somehow, in Sebald's hands, that seems achievement enough.

NOTES

1. I have tried to argue this case more fully in my study *Epochenbuch Realismus* (Swales 1997).
2. On photography in Sebald, see Boehncke 2003, Harris 2001, Long 2003 and Carolin Duttlinger's chapter in this volume.

PART II
LANDSCAPE AND NATURE

4

ON THE MISERY OF NATURE AND THE NATURE OF MISERY: W. G. SEBALD'S LANDSCAPES

Greg Bond

THE GREAT STORM – IDEAL LANDSCAPES

> Finally, in the autumn of 1987, a hurricane such as no one had ever experienced before passed over the land. According to official estimates over fourteen million mature hard-leaf trees fell victim to it, not to mention the damage to conifer plantations and bushes. That was on the night of the 16th of October. (*RS*: 265/315)

In *The Rings of Saturn* W. G. Sebald describes the great storm of October 1987, which he experienced at his home in East Anglia, as an opening of the gates of hell, and the wind that is released ravaging the trees in the park that he can see from the windows of his own house. In the months that follow, the wood from fallen trees is removed, and the erstwhile woodlands come to resemble dry steppes, because the vegetation is smothered by a covering of clay. This chapter of *The Rings of Saturn* ends with the stillness of death – the birdsong that was once so lively has given way to chilling silence.

Sebald's apocalyptic English landscape in chapter 9 of *The Rings of Saturn* begins with the end – the word that introduces the events of the night of 16 and 17 October 1987 and the following months is 'finally'. What precedes this final destruction is a series of destructive acts perpetrated on – or by – the landscape of East Anglia and Suffolk. Dutch elm disease has virtually eradicated elms, and killed within fourteen days one of the most perfect trees Sebald had ever seen. It is not only the elms, for the poplars, ash, beech and oak trees have lost their splendour too. Early in the nineteenth century, parks, such as the one in Ditchingham, where Sebald is (allegedly) pictured in a photograph leaning against an enormous Lebanese cedar, and presumably the one adjacent to Sebald's own house, were established throughout the south of England, and a large number of trees was planted. Most of these have now gone, and have not been replaced. Here Sebald gives his readers no clues as to who is responsible for these changes to the landscape, concentrating instead on the frozen image of the end of a process that set in during the nineteenth century with the large-scale colonisation of the landscape of Europe. There is also no invitation to question Sebald's evaluation of the state of southeast English woodlands – his statements in *The Rings of Saturn* are presented as the final word.

In *Logis in einem Landhaus*, in his essay on Gottfried Keller, Sebald includes a two-page fold-out reproduction of a watercolour by Keller, entitled *Ideale Baumlandschaft* [Ideal Sylvan Landscape]. This is also featured on the book's dust jacket. The painting shows a wooded landscape, with a lake in the foreground and mountains in the distance. There is no sign whatsoever of human intervention; no buildings and no people are featured. Human intervention in nature figures large in Sebald's discussion of Keller's work. Using the natural image of a virus, he writes of the 'effects of virulent capitalism on the natural environment' (*LL*: 103), and cites a passage from Keller's *Martin Salander* in which trees are cut down to make way for building projects. The landscape has become barren and dry. Sebald concludes: 'It is not Keller's meanest achievement, that he recognised so early the often irreparable damage that the proliferation of capital inexorably triggers in nature, in society, and in the emotional life of man' (*LL*: 104).

Here there is cause and effect: the cause is capital, economic expansion, and the effect is a wasted landscape, quite the opposite of the seemingly untouched landscape of Keller's watercolour. But the untouched landscape in the work of art is not innocent, for the work of art itself is damaged. Around a quarter of this image is missing, so that it looks like an unfinished work. In fact, a portion was neatly cut out by the actress Johanna Kapp, according to Sebald one of a number of ill-fortuned loves in Keller's life, who died 'ill in the head' (*LL*: 123). Here the disfigured landscape in a work of art mirrors Keller's failure to gain the enduring love of a woman, and humankind's misguided or ill-fated affairs of the heart. If there is a reason here for the intervention in a landscape, then it is the suffering that comes with the human longing for love.

These two images – the trees of England in October 1987 and Gottfried Keller's ideal landscape – could be complemented by countless more episodes from Sebald that explore the interaction between humankind and landscape, or man and nature. Sebald's technique of narration leads him to dwell on a subject or image in contemplation, until it reveals what is intended to come over as a final overwhelming insight: the silence of an English countryside where no birds sing, or the ideal white emptiness where Keller's picture has been cut away, which transcends what remains of the ideal landscape itself. Sebald's books are all based on series of such premeditated flashes of illumination, and the two examples chosen here are to a degree arbitrary. The aim in the following is to explore the imaginary landscapes of Sebald's work a little more fully. They are imaginary in that they are presented in works of literature, but also because they derive from and lead into the world of the human imagination – that of the solitary observer of the devastation of the storm, or the writer who meditates on the affairs of the heart of his predecessor, Gottfried Keller.

After Nature – Abandon Every Hope – The Nature Theatre of Oklahoma

In *After Nature* a storm is described that has at least one thing in common with that of October 1987 in England: those who experienced them, Sebald as the narrator of *The Rings of Saturn* and the crew of Vitus Jonassen Bering's ship, have never known anything like it. The ship stands alone on the high seas:

> For almost a quarter of a year
> the ship was tossed hither and
> thither, by hurricanes of a force
> none of the team could recall
> ever having experienced, on the Bering Sea
> where there was nothing and no-one but they.
> All was greyness, without direction,
> with no above or below, nature
> in a process of dissolution, in a state
> of pure dementia. (NN: 63/56)

This image of an entropic landscape is enhanced and reinforced throughout the narrative of Georg Wilhelm Steller's expeditions, where the effects of the Arctic land and seascapes on men is to make them introspective and melancholy, no longer wishing to perceive anything outside their own souls. Man is a beast, as Bering's state of mind witnesses, and his only salvation is in the blank emptiness inside his own head. In Matthaeus Grünewald's art the landscapes have a similar blinding effect. It is not just that the visions of human cruelty that Grünewald includes in his landscapes are a sign of human depravity and injustice. The whole natural world is corrupt and fallen, merely experimenting with man to see what further aberrations are possible – and botching the experiment. The facial expressions and upturned heads in Grünewald's pictures are interpreted as:

> the extreme response of our bodies
> to the absence of balance in nature
> which blindly makes one experiment after another

and like a senseless botcher
undoes the thing it has only just achieved.
To try out how far it can go
is the sole aim . . . (*NN*: 27/24)

The theory of evolution, and the progress inherent in it, are inverted here, and again the landscape leads to an entropic, dead and barren scene – this section of the poem ends with darkness, and the land is covered with yellow and grey dust. Sebald is not projecting human sentiment onto the landscape; this is not anthropomorphism, nor is it a form of gruesome pathetic fallacy. This is a baroque metaphysics of landscape, wherein there is nothing behind the scenes but the empty grin of death.

There is a case for arguing that Sebald's *After Nature* is a work informed by late twentieth-century ecology, the knowledge that humankind's expansionism into nature, that is landscape itself, took on ever more menacing forms from the mid-nineteenth century onwards. There could even be a case for arguing that Sebald is mourning the damage inflicted on nature by industrial civilisation, and for seeing this poem as a protest. This would be supported by the final chapter, which concludes with Sebald himself dreaming he is flying over the industrial wastelands of Europe by night. Then the biblical, apocalyptic tone returns emphatically, as Sebald invokes Albrecht Altdorfer's *Alexanderschlacht*. If this is a book about the environment, then it is so only as an allegory, in that the unremitting destruction of nature by nature stands in for man's own destructiveness. The title of this book can be read as 'after the end of nature', signalling that all is destroyed, but 'formed after nature' makes more sense. Humankind's endeavours end in melancholy, barren emptiness and death, because humankind is just one further experiment undertaken by nature on its inexorable path to self-destruction. It is not primarily that we destroy nature, but that nature, using us as one of its agents, destroys itself.[1]

This poem contains many motifs that Sebald later developed more fully, from the city of Jerusalem to the air raids on German cities, and also a large number of literary and artistic allusions. One of these is the oblique reference to Kafka's nature theatre of Oklahoma, in the final chapter of *America*, which appears in *After Nature* in the form of a poster advertising the theatre, hanging in the deserted Jewish quarter of Cheetham Hill in northern Manchester, behind Strangeways prison (NN: 99/86). The door that leads there is still open. The nature theatre of Oklahoma is a place where anyone is welcome and the angels play out of tune, a gently ironic allegory of the promise of redemption. For Sebald it is one of those places where the lost end up, as he writes in his foreword to *Die Beschreibung des Unglücks*, his first collection of essays on Austrian literature (*BU*: 10). The nature theatre of Oklahoma is another of those empty spaces in Sebald's work, where hopes converge and disappear.

ENTROPIC LANDSCAPES – *VERTIGO* – PETER WEISS AND KAFKA

If *The Emigrants* covers the landscape of exile, then *Vertigo* is centred on entropic landscapes of the dissolution of identity. In both of these books dark, gloomy landscapes figure prominently. They are monotonous and unwelcoming, and the people who experience them primarily in the act of travelling through them are like lost souls in one of the circles of hell. In many cases these people are Sebald's narrators or Sebald himself, and in other cases characters in exile. In 'All' Estero', East Anglia is described as consisting of 'great wheatfields which in the autumn are transformed into a barren brown expanse' (*V*: 48/58). The narrator takes a train from Vienna to Venice, and the dark mountains of the Alps, in which there is no light, remind Sebald of a painting by Tiepolo, showing a landscape shrouded in ashen light: 'The light diffused through the picture seems to have been painted as if through a veil of ash' (*V*: 51/62). This is just one more landscape of death in Sebald's works: the painting shows the town of Este stricken by the plague. In *The Emigrants* similar barren and obscure landscapes recur, and they are always incomprehensible to the exiles who cannot relate to them. Uncle Kasimir, in the story 'Ambros Adelwarth', has no memory of the German countryside he travelled through by train as he left for the United States, other than its being unfamiliar and incomprehensible (*E*: 81/118), just as Max Aurach recalls his own train journeys in the land of his exile in terms of a distressingly foreign landscape: 'Waiting at stations, the announcements on the public address, sitting in the train, the country passing by (which is still quite unknown to me), the looks of fellow passengers – all of it is torture to me' (*E*: 169/252). Sebald visits Uncle Kasimir in the USA, and they drive through a deserted landscape to the coast: 'One might indeed have thought that night was falling, so low and inky black was the sky. The streets were deserted' (*E*: 86/126). It comes as no surprise that when Sebald leaves Aunt Fini and Kasimir for the last time the light is fading, although it is still morning: 'The morning I left Cedar Glen West was icy and dark' (*E*: 104/152).

The frequency with which oppressive, dark landscapes are invoked in Sebald's prose indicates a very deliberate technique whereby landscape, and particularly the journey through it, invoke not merely alienation or disorientation, but death. This is at its most apparent, perhaps even overdone, in 'Il ritorno in patria', the tale in which Sebald, coming from Italy, visits W. in the Allgäu, the town where he grew up. As the use of Italian in the title suggests, the narrator is apprehensive about this return, and attempts to keep a distance from his past – he comes as a 'foreign correspondent'. He comes on foot, through a dark, mountainous landscape. It is snowing. He rests in a chapel in the mountains – 'and presently it seemed to me as if I were in a boat on a voyage, crossing vast waters' (*V*: 179/203). This image of crossing the water is not just a stock image for death; it is reinforced here as the first of a number of allusions to Kafka's 'Der Jäger Gracchus' in this tale (explicitly prepared for in the preceding story in the volume, 'Dr K. Takes the Waters at Riva', which ends with a direct mention of Gracchus). Like K. in Kafka's *Castle*, the narrator of 'Il ritorno in patria' walks in unannounced, a stranger in a dark wintery landscape; he is exhausted before he arrives, and he puts up at the inn. Unlike K., Sebald survives to leave the town – but the story of the death of the hunter Schlag that is central to this tale is related in place of the death of the narrator. Sebald's own interpretation of Kafka's *Castle* is centred on motifs of death (*BU*: 78–92), and his reading of Kafka has clearly influenced what is going on in the stories of *Vertigo*.[2]

The snowstorm that Sebald sees as the threat of 'entropic contingency' in Stifter's *Aus dem baierischen Walde* might just as well be from 'Il ritorno in patria':

> 'The forms . . . were no longer visible. It was a mixture of impenetrable grey and white, light and dusk, day and night, incessantly pitching and thrusting, all-consuming, and infinitely large . . .' In view of the dissolution of reality, the narrator, in a state of panic, is only able to 'stare into the confusion'. He himself is in acute danger of bodily disintegration . . . In the dissolution of space and time in the whirling snow the identity of the author also dissolves . . . (*BU*: 174–5)

The danger of entropic dissolution is indeed acute in 'Il ritorno in patria' – it is also a key to the title of this book: *Schwindel. Gefühle*, or *Vertigo*, and to Sebald's narrative technique. In his work on Stifter, Sebald notes that Stifter was writing at the moment when capitalism's encroachment into the landscape was becoming virulent – a development he registered in the work of Gottfried Keller. Stifter records the loss of the natural environment, but glosses this over with his utopian landscapes, and the ideological process whereby harmony between man and nature is projected as an image of landscape onto landscape.[3] The moments of entropy are those moments when the impossibility of the ideological project is suddenly apparent, and the cracks appear. In terms of narrative rhythm, these are moments of vertigo. Sebald begins his essay on Stifter and Handke with a description of a Biedermeier print showing four people and a dog standing above a precipice in the mountains: 'There is a dog too, and they are all leaning slightly forwards and gazing into an apparently bottomless abyss that gapes directly beneath their feet. It has often been noted that Stifter's prose frequently takes its readers past such places' (*BU*: 165). Vertigo as a narrative method corresponds to the shock insight that lurking behind nature, behind history and behind narrative is death, or rather a vertiginous hiatus, into which everything collapses: 'The . . . ambivalence of the emotions when confronted with the beauty of natural and also artistic images reaches its point of indifference in the sensation of vertigo' (*BU*: 165–6).

Sebald's work is replete with literary references – he himself said that he came to writing late, after many years as a critic, and that the furnishings of the mind cannot be ignored. Kafka plays a key role in *Vertigo*, Nabokov in *The Emigrants*. The complex system of referencing that characterises Sebald's prose is not just literary. Critics have looked at the role of photography in Sebald (Harris 2001; Long 2003; Boehncke 2003), and Sebald's use of painting and fine art will surely attract closer attention (Weber 2003). Particularly in *After Nature* and *Vertigo*, works of art are described in detail, but many lead to the same conclusion: they are allegorical records of great suffering and pain. There is another important literary model for this in Peter Weiss, on whom Sebald published a critical essay in 1986 (Sebald 1986; *NHD*: 173–95). Monolithic blocks of prose are punctuated only by the moment of painful insight beyond language, the pause of vertigo.[4] Whereas in *Die Ästhetik des Widerstands* [The Aesthetics of Resistance] Weiss provides the theoretical framework of a Marxist history, Sebald leaves his readers with no such interpretative reassurance. There is one scene in Sebald's 'Il ritorno in patria' which directly follows a similar scene in an early prose work by Weiss, and may be 'lifted' from there.[5] In the closing scene of Weiss's novel *Der Schatten des Körpers des Kutschers* [The Shadow of the Body of the Coachman] the narrator witnesses sexual intercourse between the coachman and the housekeeper as a game of shadows. A very similar play of shadows in the dark is witnessed by Sebald, as a boy, and he recalls the sex in the yard between the hunter Schlag and Romana, who helps in the inn. In both cases the scene is both distinct and indistinct – it takes place in the dark, and the observer has no direct view, and yet the bodily movements and the act of copulation are as clear as day. In each case the scene concludes with vertigo, in Weiss with the narrator closing his tale by saying that he was unable to sleep for three nights – the reader can infer whatever reasons he will. In Sebald's prose there are two subtle pauses at the end of the scene in the yard, one between the 'one single indivisible form' of the two lovers and the shift to the narrator's 'I do not think', and the other before the sentence that describes what is probably the destructive reaction of the landlord to Schlag's 'taking' of Romana. The prose is deceptively simple, for between these two breaks, there is a further break, but on another level: the hunter's dog, a mute witness, excluded from the action like the narrator himself, and a symbol of sexuality, melancholy and death:

> From deep in the hunter's chest came a heavy moaning and panting, his frosty breath rose from behind his beard, and time after time, when the wave surged through the small of his back, he thrust into Romana, while she, for her part, clung closer and closer to him, until the hunter and Romana were but one single indivisible form. I do not think that Romana or Schlag had any idea I was there. Only Waldmann saw me. Fastened as

always to his master's rucksack, he stood quietly behind him on the ground and looked across at me. That same night, around one o'clock, the one-legged Engelwirt landlord Sallaba destroyed the entire furnishings and fittings of the bar. (*V*: 239/271–2)

SEBALD'S VOICE – *THE RINGS OF SATURN* – FIXED UNALTERABLE CARE – INVOLUNTARY COMEDY

This glassy stream, that spreading pine,
Those alders quiv'ring to the breeze,
Might sooth a soul less hurt than mine,
And please, if any thing could please.
But fix'd unalterable care
Forgoes not what she feels within,
Shows the same sadness ev'ry where,
And slights the season and the scene.
                          (William Cowper)

According to the doctrine of modernism, good writers have their own distinctive or unmistakable voice. The prose of Thomas Bernhard, for example, is immediately recognisable, and this is also true of Sebald's prose, which bears certain resemblances to Bernhard's. A better definition of what makes Bernhard so distinct, if not stylistically and formally, then in terms of the fundamental essence of his world-view, would be harder to find than Sebald's own. The ideological concept of nature creates a dichotomy between nature and society, and projects onto nature a corrective for what is awry in society, as in Stifter, for example. Bernhard will have nothing to do with this:

> Bernhard's criticism of the ideological concept of nature contains the insight that nature has always been a rather unpleasant institution, and that it was only possible for man to see in it a kind of paradise because society, to cite Chamfort, made its own chapter to the 'malheurs de la nature'. In reality, and this is what Bernhard's texts drive home relentlessly, nature is an even greater madhouse than society.[6]

This is also an apt description of Sebald's own view of nature, at least up to and including *The Rings of Saturn*. There is no distinction between human nature and the natural, non-human world, nor between these and society. In 'Dr K Takes the Waters at Riva' love is seen as a natural disaster, and art (the opera) the expression of the same:

> Final contortions of this kind, which regularly occur in the opera where, as Dr K once wrote, the dying voice aimlessly wanders through the music, did not by any means seem ridiculous to him; rather he believed them to

be an expression of our, so to speak, natural misfortune, since after all, as he remarks elsewhere, we lie prostrate on the boards, dying, our whole lives long.[7]

This is Sebald's voice, his unmistakable melancholy, tinged with often involuntary humour.

There is no alleviation to be found in nature, as the ideological view is discounted. The melancholic knows too much, and like Sebald in *The Rings of Saturn*, he sees through the gloss to the darker history beneath. Even clearly historical and political events are given the sheen of natural disaster: the air war over Germany and the destruction of German cities, which Sebald lectured on in 1997, feature in both *After Nature* and *Vertigo* as a quasi-natural disaster.[8] In *After Nature* the burning city of Nuremberg is given a mythological setting in the context of an Altdorfer painting showing Lot and his daughters before a city in flames (*NN*: 84–5/73–4). *Vertigo* recalls the perspective of Sebald the boy on the post-war ruins, mediated through cinema newsreels:

> almost every week we saw the mountains of rubble in places like Berlin or Hamburg, which for a long time I did not associate with the destruction wrought in the closing years of the war, knowing nothing of it, but considered them a natural condition of all larger cities. (*V*: 187/213)

Finally, after finding many of his own ideas confirmed or inspired by Kafka, Stifter, Bernhard and others from the Austrian tradition, Sebald discovers a seventeenth-century English writer who provides a summary of his own melancholic view of human nature:

> On every new thing there lies already the shadow of annihilation. For the history of every individual, of every social order, indeed of the whole world, does not describe an ever-widening, more and more wonderful arc, but rather follows a course which, once the meridian is reached, leads without fail down into the dark.[9]

Following this reading of Thomas Browne, Sebald sets out on an overcast day in August 1992 on his walking tour of the English landscape. The reader is presented with the 'traces of destruction' (*RS*: 3/11) that Sebald uncovers, the fruits of his labour under the sign of Saturn. His unrelenting, wholesale perception of human history and human nature as the history of destruction need not be recapitulated here: in essence it does not differ from what is already known of *After Nature* and *Vertigo*, whereas of course the details of Sebald's historical research and arrangement of material differs from these earlier books.

The few negative critical opinions on Sebald have noted his use of obscure language (Ayren 1998) or his involuntary comedy.[10] In fact, the latter amounts to the probably inevitable result of the author's insistence on melancholy, for keeping this up over long distances requires a great amount of tact. The risk of running into platitudes or contrivance is high, as is the risk of ridiculous hyperbole, and Sebald is often too close for comfort. When in 'Beyle' it is noted that the young man walked around Paris in his new clothes for several days with an erection (*V*: 11/15), or when Sebald's enthusiasm for the author Robert Walser leads him to claim several times that there is no equal in the space of just a few pages (*LL*: 129–68), then it would seem that his desire to keep the show going has somewhat dulled common sense. There is a certain vanity and coquetry in Sebald's view that writing is a pathological act, a view which may have been more acceptable as an approach to a volume of essays on Austrian literature before the author himself was known as a writer[11] than when presented in the foreword to the much later volume of essays, in which Sebald pays his respects to eminent colleagues:

> The arc spans nearly two hundred years, and it shows that in the course of this time not much has changed in respect to that peculiar behavioural defect, which is forced to transform each and every feeling into letters on a page, just missing the point of real life with remarkable precision. (*LL*: 5–6)

Every time the author emerges to resume his travels from a gloomy interior, he is greeted by a darkening sky at daytime, a landscape empty of life, be it in *Vertigo*, *The Emigrants* or *The Rings of Saturn*. Sebald's method is not realist, but it does not take an inveterate realist to find this and other features of his work forced. Alan Bennett wrote of *The Rings of Saturn*:

> I persevere with Sebald but the contrivance of it, particularly his unpeopling of the landscape, never fails to irritate . . . Sebald seems to stage-manage both the landscape and the weather to suit his (seldom cheerful) mood . . . Once noticed Sebald's technique seems almost comic . . . The fact is, in Sebald nobody is ever about. This may be poetic but it seems to me a short cut to significance. (2003: 5)

There are often a few too many such short cuts to significance in Sebald's work. Take his meal in Lowestoft, a town that is completely run down, and which Sebald approaches after walking past the local prison. A quarter of the population is illiterate, he writes, then continues to describe the shabby town centre and the Victoria Hotel, where he will stay the night. The place is totally deserted, but for one woman at reception, who avoids looking Sebald in the eye, and later serves him with the ridiculous meal, which Sebald so overloads with short cuts to significance that it is worth quoting at length:

> That evening I was the sole guest in the huge dining room, and it was the same startled person who took my order and shortly afterwards brought me a fish that had doubtless lain entombed in the deep-freeze for years.

> The breadcrumb armour-plating of the fish had been partly singed by the grill, and the prongs of my fork bent on it. Indeed it was so difficult to penetrate what eventually proved to be nothing but an empty shell that my plate was a hideous mess once the operation was over. (RS: 43/58)

This is not the end of the plaice and chips: the terrible sight ('furchtbarer Anblick') on the plate is described in some detail. If Sebald was aware of how incongruous language and subject are in this passage, and others, then the question would have to be asked as to the real function of the comedy. Rather I suspect that this kind of stylistic faux pas is what happens when the melancholic gaze has to be upheld at all costs, even when there is nothing for it to fix itself upon.

THE NETWORK – MAPPING HISTORY – NABOKOV – THE MODERNIST MELANCHOLIC

The Rings of Saturn introduces an idea that is latent in Sebald's prior work, and comes to fruition in *Austerlitz*. This is the notion that the whole world, including the material and physical world, history, and the realm of coincidence and mystery, represents a network that spreads out before our eyes, without our ever being able to make sense of it.[12] In *The Rings of Saturn* Sebald recalls a flight from Amsterdam to Norwich, and the view from the plane down over the network of industry and human activity below – an image already employed in *After Nature*. It leads him to consider the human networks across the globe – 'networks of a complexity that goes far beyond the power of any one individual to imagine' (RS: 91/113–14). The notion is put only a little more prosaically in *Logis in einem Landhaus*, when the author remembers the first time he read Robert Walser's text *Kleist in Thun*, and concludes:

> Slowly since then I have come to understand how everything is linked to everything else across space and time, the life of the Prussian author Kleist with that of a Swiss writer of prose, who claims he was in the employment of a brewery in Thun, the echo of a pistol shot over the Wannsee with the view from the window of Herisau clinic, Walser's walks with my own excursions, the date of birth with the date of death, happiness with unhappiness, the history of nature with the history of our industry, the history of home with the history of exile. (LL: 162–3)

This notion of the network is essentially paranoid (Sebald knew that well enough from his study of the work of Elias Canetti), but to recognise the network also amounts to the potentially liberating moment of enlightenment. This dialectic takes on its own twentieth-century form, with our ever increasing global totalitarian networks. Jacques Austerlitz lives within this paradigm, for, after living in darkness for so long, he finally discovers the complex network of his own history, which he will never completely comprehend. He is able to shed *some* light on it, whilst at the same time living through increasingly traumatic experiences of fear that it has taken him a lifetime of involuntary suppression to release. *Austerlitz* contains the same hellish landscapes of Sebald's earlier works, but here they are historically more tangible and real, being the bunkers in Belgium where the Nazis tortured their victims, and Theresienstadt, where Austerlitz's mother died. In *Austerlitz* Sebald's narrative of the survivor is given its best expression, and what was already powerful in *The Emigrants* is allowed to develop into a much fuller, and ostensibly far more authentic, account of the survivor filling in the gaps.[13] After *The Rings of Saturn* and *Logis in einem Landhaus*, *Austerlitz* is refreshingly free of Sebald's own confessional, first-person accounts, and the narrator's role is reduced to that of witness and orderer of material – there is much less vertigo, or personal emotion for the narrator himself, and more space for the more reserved voice of Austerlitz.

There is also a utopian landscape in *Austerlitz*, in and around Andromeda Lodge. Before Austerlitz arrives there for a brief happy period in his life, he dreams up his own ideal landscape, in lieu of any notion of home or origin, based on his reading in the school library at Stower Grange:

> My mind thus created a kind of ideal landscape in which the Arabian desert, the realm of the Aztecs, the continent of Antarctica, the snow-covered Alps, the North-West Passage, the river Congo, and the Crimean peninsula formed a single panorama, populated by all the figures proper to those places. (*A*: 85/89)

This panorama has something of the nineteenth century about it, the age of the eccentric naturalist, as does Andromeda Lodge with its eminent connections to the natural sciences of the nineteenth century. Here, there is hope in Sebald, but (like the effect of reading Stifter today) it is projected back before the calamity of the Holocaust, before everything began to go downhill.

Vladimir Nabokov, or his double, appears in a number of guises in Sebald's works as a figure of hope, the butterfly man in a world before the disaster.[14] In Sebald's tale 'Die Alpen im Meer: Ein Reisebild', there is a butterfly catcher in the ideal landscape in Corsica, contrasted with the hunting and the destruction of the Corsican forests that took place in the nineteenth century.[15] The butterfly man will never stay long, but will linger on in the mind, the contradictory image of hope that is lost – for Sebald there can be no postmodern synthetic view of man moulding nature and nature moulding man, a new form of coexistence and optimism with technology and nature enmeshed. Sebald is a modernist melancholic: his works are based on a critique of the history of progress – and enlightenment – that cannot conceive of a world in which progress is no longer a category. In order to criticise the negative dialectic, you have to believe in enlightenment in the first place.

Austerlitz is faced with the ruins of progress, but the only response available to him is to look back on those ruins, doing what he can to discover their sense. Great lacunae remain: Austerlitz can only wonder – and fail to comprehend – that a Russian exile can remember the snow that fell on his grandmother, who loved to powder herself with talcum, while she slept in peaceful oblivion under an open window, and that the same Russian exile need never ask himself whether the memory is reliable or not.[16]

NOTES

1. In his book on Alfred Döblin one of Sebald's political criticisms was that Döblin's philosophy of nature is irrational and reactionary. It would be fair to ask at least whether, applying the same political criteria, Sebald himself cannot be read this way. See Sebald 1988: 101–4. The truth about melancholy is, however, that it traverses the division between protest and resignation (Sebald 1988: 112). Thomas Kastura (1996: 211) suggests that Sebald's view of nature is an eighteenth-century one, in that without the destruction brought about by human intervention, nature would regenerate. On the contrary, there is no fundamental difference between human destruction and the workings of nature.
2. Kafka is not Sebald's only point of reference. His early stories, up to and including *The Emigrants*, all make use of motifs and techniques that are discussed in his first volume of essays on Austrian literature, published in 1985.
3. 'Bis an den Rand der Natur: Versuch über Stifter' (*BU*: 15–37).
4. Adorno and Horkheimer write about this method in *Dialektik der Aufklärung* in their discussion of Homer's treatment of violence. They write of a narrative gesture that holds up the narrative and respects the victims: 'By cutting short the account, Homer prevents us from forgetting the victims, and reveals the unutterable eternal agony of the few seconds in which women struggle with death' (1997: 79–80). The use of the caesura may, of course, be applied to any moment when the narrative has a point to make.
5. The same scene in Sebald is also a reference to Kafka's *Castle*, by dint of the subversive clandestine sexuality of the maid in the inn in an otherwise oppressive male-dominated world.
6. *BU*: 108. This essay also treats entropic disarray in Bernhard.
7. *V*: 152/174–5. On Kafka Sebald writes of 'the play of love not only as a bourgeois fantasy but also as a self-perpetuating debacle of natural history' (*BU*: 87). In his critical essays Sebald frequently concludes that a view of the world and of humanity as nature under decay is at the base of the work of the author under discussion – Sebald's own interests as a writer are clearly evident.
8. It becomes a natural disaster in his lectures also. Gently taking issue with Alexander Kluge's materialism (and missing the irony that comes from Kluge's use of Marx and a photograph of Halberstadt in ruins), Sebald writes 'This is the history of industry as the open book of human thought and feeling – can materialistic epistemology or any other such theory be maintained in the face of such destruction? Is the destruction not, rather, irrefutable proof that the catastrophes which develop, so to speak, in our hand and seem to break out suddenly are a kind of experiment, anticipating the point at which we shall drop out of what we have thought for so long to be our autonomous history and back into the history of nature?' (*NHD*: 67).
9. *RS*: 23–4/35–6. The ideas on anatomy, dissection and decay linked to Thomas Browne in *The Rings of Saturn* can be found in Sebald's own essays on Peter Weiss and Thomas Bernhard.

10. Less critically Thomas Kastura writes of involuntary comedy: 'Dry humour unfolds on the margins, and derives from the involuntary banality of what is depicted' (Kastura 1996: 209).
11. In *Die Beschreibung des Unglücks* one of Sebald's interests was in 'the unhappiness of the writing subject'. He makes the following unintentionally funny statement: 'Now those people who assume the profession of the writer are not as a rule the more carefree among us' (*BU*: 11).
12. This is better described as a network, not a labyrinth, as Thomas Kastura saw it. A network is more rational, more political, and holds the promise of emergence. See Kastura 1996: 201–5.
13. Sebald's debt to William G. Niederland's pragmatic case studies in *Folgen der Verfolgung* (1980) is surely greater than that to Freud's theory of trauma.
14. That Nabokov is a figure of hope, contrasting with all Sebald's exiles, has been noted before. See Korff 1998: 189–90, and Schuhmacher 1998: 69 and 83. Nabokov features in Andromeda Lodge by dint of the photograph of butterflies in a cracked display case, which in fact stands in St Petersburg Zoological Museum. The butterfly catcher is in truth another image of the dialectic of enlightenment.
15. Sebald, no date: 18–26.
16. Compare *A*: 86–7/90–1 and Nabokov 1967: 155.

5

ECOCENTRISM IN SEBALD'S
AFTER NATURE

Colin Riordan

Sebald's *After Nature*, first published in German as *Nach der Natur* in 1988, but not in English until 2002, calls itself in the original version 'Ein Elementargedicht': an elemental poem. The self-classification is important, for there is a sense in which this work concerns itself with the fundamentals as well as with the elements. Life, death and the struggle for existence, not only of the individual but also of the species, emerge against the backdrop of a variety of hostile environments. Elemental, then, though not elementary, for the poem itself is multilayered and highly structured, being a literary triptych composed of three separate but thematically interlinked narratives, each focusing on a different character. The first is the sixteenth-century painter Matthaeus Grünewald, the second is the eighteenth-century naturalist and explorer Georg Wilhelm Steller, the third being Sebald himself. When the poem was published in English, at least one reviewer found the three narratives connected in ways which were 'at best obscure' (Romer 2002). In fact, as will become apparent below, the connections are all too clear if one considers the heavy hint supplied by the title. The ways in which those connections are made, the Sebaldian techniques of history by association, of minute exegesis of the by-ways of the past, of moving through time by moving through space, are all familiarly present here. So, of course, is nature: the glory and pleasure in nature revealed through a detailed understanding of its manifestations is something which permeates the whole of the Sebald oeuvre. But themes in Sebald rarely appear in isolation; rather, they emerge as part of a complex interweaving. It is that technique of connection by association which raises the question of ecocentrism.

I do not mean ecocentrism in the political ecological sense, as a strand of activism, but rather as a question of values. How do we value the world around us and how does that value relate to the way we value ourselves, our history, our perception of the world? As Carolyn Merchant puts it, an ecocentric ethic implies that: 'The whole environment, including inanimate elements, rocks and minerals along with animate plants and animals, is assigned intrinsic value' (1992: 74–5). Ecocentrism is a holistic ethos: context, connections and process are the foundations of an ecocentric understanding of the world and our place in it. The unmissable strengths of Sebald's approach, the ability to see ourselves in context, to think in terms of connective processes, are in essence ecocentric. Sebald's narrative techniques which rely on connections – 'only connect'[1] – have as an inevitable consequence the effect that the natural world, which is the ultimate context, becomes a central object of textual inquiry. The intensity of *After Nature* makes this process particularly apparent.

The poem is constructed such that nature makes an appearance only gradually, but so that the dynamics of the lyric and the narrative all inexorably point and pull in the same direction: cumulatively, the poem amounts to an ecological critique which is explicitly linked to German culture. Surprisingly, given Sebald's richly descriptive and contemplative style, nature is not represented as a primarily aesthetic object; that is, it derives its value not solely from the perceptual impact it makes on the observer, but from within itself. The question of nature's intrinsic value, however, presupposes some notion of what that concept actually encompasses.

Raymond Williams's remark that nature is 'perhaps the most complex word in the language' (1988: 219) has become a thoroughgoing cliché. Yet it is easy to forget the implication, which is that intuitively the word nature is also one of the most uncomplicated in the language. After all, everybody experiences trees, grass, rivers, mountains. In consequence, the term continues to be used in the most uncritical way, not least by environmentalists. The reason for the straightforward assumptions which one often finds is clear enough; when the fate of species, wilderness areas, or the planet itself is at stake, apparently metaphysical discussions of what we mean by nature seem hopelessly irrelevant. When dealing with nature in literary discourse, however, it quickly becomes apparent that the need for a definition of what we mean when using the term is more than a theoretical necessity. This is not a question of the historical or other specific conditioning of the term. What people understand by nature clearly depends heavily on historical context, national-cultural factors and a host of other variables. It is rather a question of the principles underlying our understanding of nature, the factors which need to be taken into account when considering the meanings of nature. And that is an important question, for it is not going too far to say that in discussing textual perceptions, conceptions, constructions or representations of nature we are actually discussing nature itself, and simultaneously human society and our relationship with the world around us. That is, nature does not exist separately from us, but only as a necessary pendant to human society and human identity. The argument runs in three main ways: first, that everything we regard as nature is in fact transformed by human action; secondly, that nature is a social construct and the environment is constituted by human social practices (see Vogel 1996: 171); and thirdly, that nature is meaning in the sense that representations of nature constitute its actuality. Nature, then, 'exists only as a mental and linguistic construct' (Coates 1998: 9).

There is an important qualification to be made here. Nobody seriously suggests that plants, rain or rock are the products of human creation, or that human beings, as natural, have created themselves. However, all of these arguments have in common a rejection of the understanding of nature alluded to above as being commonly held by environmentalists, and which Gernot Böhme terms 'traditionally a dominant concept', namely, 'the order established by nature versus that installed by human beings' (1992: 57). That is, nature is everything which is not human artefact; it is that which is outside us, that which is not human. Though this distinction is indeed 'central to Western thinking about nature' (Soper 1995: 37), the problems it raises are immediately apparent. First, it leaves open the question of how such a distinction may be drawn. At what point in our interaction with non-human nature is the natural transformed into the artificial or the cultural? Is there an 'unbridgeable divide' between nature and culture, or is the difference one of degree rather than kind (Soper 1995: 42)? This leads us to the first of the arguments outlined above. The history of cultivation, especially since ancient human beings began using fire as a tool, has transformed the landscape in ways which modern human beings are only able to appreciate through detailed scientific and historical analysis. This point is elucidated at length by Clive Ponting in his *Green History of the World* (1991), and indeed in practically any history of the countryside. Is this grounds for denying the existence of nature? It rests on the Rousseau-derived assumption that the natural is only that which is either untouched or virgin or wilderness. Though, as mentioned above, this has been and is still a common assumption among some environmentalists and even theorists such as Robert Goodin (1992: 32) it does not stand close scrutiny. For even apparently untouched nature bears the physical evidence of human activity, and, in a metaphysical sense, it is transformed into 'nature' by our mere perception of it.

Theories of the social construction of nature can broadly be divided into those deriving from Georg Lukács and those deriving from the Frankfurt School. While both of them understand nature as a product of social practices, they differ in their analysis of how nature is constructed. Horkheimer and Adorno postulate the existence of a 'natural' nature from which human beings become alienated as their ability to dominate the natural increases. They therefore forget their position as part of the nature from which they separate themselves in the quest for domination and in the move from 'magic to science, from ritual to technology' (Vogel 1996: 52). Yet the success of this enlightenment project can only be achieved through an inevitable dialectic of the return of nature: 'the separation from the past and from nature, the autonomy of the rational self from the external, can be assured only by a willing (if cunning) submission to externality, to nature' (61). Nature is thus re-created as an object to be feared, leading to ever greater efforts to overcome it. Lukács, on the other hand, understands nature entirely as the product of social practice (172).

This brings us to the third argument on the invention of nature: nature as a linguistic construct. Culture, in this view, defines rather than reports what exists. Cultural practices and contexts crucially shape our perceptions of the world: 'nature's meaning is thus not inherent but varies according to context and derives from convention' (Coates 1998: 10). This means that the representation of nature – for example, writing about nature – is inseparable from nature. Since we assume that the representation of nature is related to the way in which society behaves with respect to nature and to itself, writing about 'nature' must have some objective parallel in the way in which human beings relate to the non-human world. 'Constructed nature' *is* nature, because it cannot be separated from what human beings do to nature (including representing it).

Sebald's poetic musings on nature are thus not merely descriptive or representational, but constructive. That is why, both by implication and explicitly within the text itself, representation, and the crisis of representation, are so frequently at the forefront. The modern crisis of nature is simultaneously a crisis of representation. It is in the fifth section of the first (Grünewald) narrative that nature is explicitly represented for the first time: not as static and passive, but as an active, dynamic system. The famous altar at the hospital chapel in Isenheim (now in a museum in Colmar) bears on its right-hand leaf a picture by Grünewald representing St Anthony being dragged off by demons:

> shark- and dragon-like
> maws, rows of teeth, pug noses
> from which snot flows, fin-shaped
> clammy limp wings, hair and horns,
> skin like entrails turned outwards,
> excrescences of an entire life,
> in the air, on land and in water.
>   (NN: 26/23)

Hamburger's translation chooses to render the German 'des ganzen Lebens' as 'of an entire life'. A better version in this context would be 'the whole of life', for it is subsequently suggested that the painter is actually representing the essence of nature, or of creation, as he would have understood it. The very elements of life on earth engender not some harmonious nature, perfectly in balance, but evolutionary chaos, a 'pathological spectacle' (*NN*: 26/24). To Grünewald 'this is creation, / image of our insane presence / on the surface of the earth' (*NN*: 26/23), a creation to which he himself, and his art, belonged. The follies, madnesses and perversities of human existence, in this view, actually shape nature. An utterly unsentimental image of nature as a series of devastating experiments emerges:

> The panic-stricken
> kink in the neck to be seen
> in all of Grünewald's subjects,
> exposing the throat and often turning
> the face towards a blinding light,
> is the extreme response of our bodies
> to the absence of balance in nature
> which blindly makes one experiment after another
> and like a senseless botcher
> undoes the thing it has only just achieved.
> (*NN*: 27/24)

This is a striking analysis for its concentration on process; it is a bitter critique of evolution and our place within it. We are as much its victims as other organisms. Nature is far from some beneficent maternal figure, but instead a terrifyingly nihilistic process over which we have, or had (in Grünewald's world) no control. Its sole aim is to test the limits of its own self-reproduction:

> inside us also and through us and through
> the machines sprung from our heads,
> all in a single jumble,
> while behind us already the green
> trees are deserting their leaves and
> bare'
> (*NN*: 27/24)

This interpretation of Grünewald's painting implies that in representing the natural order (or disorder) we are not only recognising but shaping the ultimate fate of the human species. It is our very intellectual ability which makes it impossible for humanity, ultimately, to survive. The section ends with a devastating vision of apocalypse:

> The black bird that in its beak
> carries a break-time meal

to St Anthony on his site
in the desert may be the one with
the heart of glass, the bird
flying ever closer to us,
of which another prophet
of the last days announces
that it will shit into the sea
so that the water boils itself out,
that the earth trembles and the great city
with the iron tower stands in flames,
whilst the Pope squats in a barge
and darkness comes and
with it a yellow dust
that covers the land.

(NN: 27–8/25)

In the context of 1988, when this text was written, the prospect of a final global catastrophe was all too immediate. Images of catastrophe were common in German literature of the period, as Axel Goodbody (1997) has shown. This apocalyptic myth, then, concludes a view of the possibilities of nature which is profoundly pessimistic, if in its temporal context not unusual. What is at issue here is not so much the extent to which we value nature, but the reverse: that nature has no need whatever to value us. Indeed, despite our subjective position which draws us inexorably to deny the evidence, the question of our value in nature is a meaningless one.

In the light of this, what are we to make of the title of Sebald's poem? The immediate reference in both the translated title *After Nature* and the original *Nach der Natur* is not to nature but to art – to the representation of nature, and the extent to which authenticity can be achieved. Once, however, as argued above, the distinction between nature and its representation is eroded, the further implications of the title, that we live in a post-natural environment, become apparent. The explanation of the title comes in a passage at the very outset of Section VI of the Grünewald narrative, just after the apocalyptic images which populate the ending of Section V. The description is of a picture of the crucifixion of 1505:

On the Basel *Crucifixion* of 1505
behind the group of mourners
a landscape reaches so far into the depths
that our eyes cannot see its limits.
A patch of brown scorched earth,
whose contour like the head of a whale
or an open-mouthed Leviathan

> devours the pale green meadow plains
> and the marshily shining stretches
> of water . . .
> Most probably Grünewald painted
> and recalled the catastrophic incursion
> of darkness, the last trace of light
> flickering from beyond, after nature . . .
>
> (NN: 29–30/26)

Again the translation is perhaps not as pellucid as it might be; the sense of 'nach der Natur' in this context is 'from nature', as in a scene painted through direct observation of nature. The translation problem is tricky, however, for the English also needs to convey the temporal sense inherent in the German. The scene Sebald has in mind that might have been the model for the 'catastrophic incursion of darkness' is a solar eclipse that took place on 1 October 1502, and which Grünewald may have experienced and perceived as a vision of apocalypse. It is this, the poetic voice speculates, that may have led Grünewald to depict a barren landscape redolent of the future. The emotional despair of the figures in the painting is expressed through the very topography, in the form of:

> the mountain landscape of weeping,[2]
> in which Grünewald with a pathetic gaze
> into the future has prefigured
> a planet utterly strange, chalk-coloured
> behind the blackish-blue river.
> Here in an evil state of erosion
> and desolation the heritage of the ruining
> of life that in the end will consume
> even the very stones has been depicted.
>
> (NN: 31/27–8)

Sebald here creates a link between the biblical apocalypse with which Grünewald would have been intimately familiar and ecological apocalypse, the prospect of which was so prominent at the time this poem was composed in the 1980s, but of which Grünewald could have known or suspected nothing. Yet he does so by poetically depicting a representation of nature, itself conditioned (in the poetic world at least) by a rare and spectacular natural event which at the time of its occurrence must have been profoundly ominous. By making a connection in this way between a natural event, its representation and its modern reading as alluding to future environmental depredation, Sebald is poetically depicting the relationship between the way we think about nature (the way we construct nature) and our assumption of its objective existence. Nature stops being 'out there', and instead adopts a central position in human affairs. Merely recognising that centrality is a long way from recognising the intrinsic value of nature, however. For, as becomes apparent in the succeeding two narratives, in refusing to acknowledge the value of the non-human world, we are simultaneously devaluing ourselves.

If Grünewald's concern was the artistic representation of nature, then one might expect that the protagonist of the second of the three poems, the eighteenth-century botanist and explorer Georg Wilhelm Steller, would, as a trained scientist, take a more detached view. Yet even as he is taking and passing his examinations with glowing success, he is, the poetic voice speculates, thinking about

> the shapes of the fauna and
> flora of that distant region
> where East and West and North
> converge, and of the art and skill
> required for their description.
>
> (NN: 44/38)

The representation of nature, then, is central to Steller too, and the beginnings of a pattern emerge. Again the future appears gloomy; the Archbishop of St Petersburg, Theophon, by whom Steller is employed as a personal physician, extrapolates from his own experience of aging to the way in which all things change with age:

> But all things, Theophon says,
> all things, my son, transmute
> into old age, life diminishes,
> everything declines,
> the proliferation
> of kinds is a mere
> illusion, and no one
> knows to what end.
>
> (NN: 50/43)

Hamburger's translation of 'Arten' by 'kinds' would surely be better rendered by 'species', for Sebald is imagining Theophon here denying the scientific representation of nature embodied in the naturalist and botanist who is his personal physician. Again the concerns of the 1980s about the dangerous decline in biodiversity glimmer through, as does an awareness that even today we have no real idea of what the effects of such decline might be.

In Steller, Sebald creates a character (albeit one based closely on the historical figure)[3] whose fascination with the natural world leads to an erosion of the borders between the human and the non-human. By implication, their intrinsic value becomes more evenly distributed. When his wife refuses to accompany him on expeditions, he replaces her with two ravens that possess the power of speech, making ominous predictions. When meeting Bering for the first time, he is moved to observe:

> What is this
> being called human?
> A beast, shrouded
> in deep mourning,
> in a black coat
> lined
> with black fur.
>   (*NN*: 56/49)

While the original is less declamatory than resignedly assertive ('Ein Tier / ist der Mensch, in tiefe / Trauer gehüllt . . . '), the sentiments remain broadly similar. Humanity, deprived of its special place in creation, faces future catastrophe; grief and despair are the only adequate reactions.

Section XI of this second narrative poem consists of a brief account of the first weeks of the Bering voyage, in which the explorers mistook a dead whale for land. The subsequent section speculates that there must have been live whales present too, which by association leads to a reference to a later voyage by Otto von Kotzebue, financed by Count Romanzoff, on which the soldier, poet and scientist Adalbert von Chamisso (1781–1838) was the naturalist. In their search for a North-East passage, the later explorers retraced the wake of Bering, passing indeed through the Bering straits. Steller and Chamisso, then, must have been confronted with similar scenes. Sebald notes that in his account of the voyage, Chamisso not only set out a scheme to use whales to tow ships but also suggested that the steam engine was the first warm-blooded animal to be created by human beings. This is a little unfair to the eminently sensible and learned Chamisso, for in Sebald's source he is merely reporting the words of a 'naturalist of genius' ('genialer Naturforscher', Chamisso 1900: 100). It is, however, significant that Sebald forges a link via the topography of the region coupled with its wildlife (the whales), which then allows reference to a scheme to extend the dominion of human beings over nature by exploiting the contents of the sea, and, further, however ironically, allows the comparison between the steam engine and a creature engendered by human beings. Here is an example of Sebald's narrative technique (which applies just as much to this form of poetic narrative as to his prose) of creating associations through places and objects to other times, thereby allowing a complex, layered picture to be built up. The implication here is that the distinction between nature and culture has in the past been broken down: Sebald erodes the distinction which O'Riordan would draw between the technocentric and the ecocentric (O'Riordan 1976: 3–19).

Once Steller sets foot on land, using the ten hours granted to him by Bering for scientific investigation, he is confronted by wilderness. The poetic voice speculates on his reaction:

> He came close to simply proceeding
> towards the mountains, into
> cool wilderness, but the constructs
> of science in his head,
> directed towards a diminution
> of disorder in our world,
> ran counter to that need.
> (NN: 61–2/54)

The association of chaos with virgin nature, as opposed to order with scientific training, is an indication of a problem which plagues human attitudes to nature to the present day. Because we construct nature as the other from which we distinguish ourselves, we lose the ability to recognise ourselves in context. The poem at this point is beginning to focus not, as the blurb to the German paperback edition says, on 'the conflict between mankind and nature' but on the real problem at issue. That is, the egocentricity which is our key individual survival trait tends to counteract the ecocentricity which is the key collective survival trait of humanity. Our ability to make judgements assigning value where it is due is perverted by our self-obsession.

Yet immediately, in the next section, the characters in the narrative are forced physically to recognise the context in which they find themselves, as they are caught in tempest after tempest of ferocious proportions:[4]

> For almost a quarter of a year
> the ship was tossed hither and
> thither, by hurricanes of a force
> none in the team could recall
> ever having experienced, on the Bering Sea
> where there was nothing and no one but they.
> All was a greyness, without direction,
> with no above or below, nature
> in a process of dissolution, in a state
> of pure dementia.
> (NN: 63/56)

The anthropomorphisation of nature in this extract is especially telling. Our tendency to ascribe to nature moods, emotions, a will to destroy, is the most eloquent possible evidence of the way in which we construct nature as a part of our identity even as we are in the grip of the most terrifying physical manifestation of its indifference to us. As Max Frisch puts it in *Der Mensch erscheint im Holozän* [Man Appears in the Holocene]: 'There are no catastrophes for nature. There are only catastrophes for people' (1979: 103). As death approaches, this sentiment becomes all too clear to Steller:

> Such are you, *doctores*,
> spilt lamps,
> thus nature has her way
> with a godless
> Lutheran from Germany.
> (NN: 75/67)

The third and final element of the poetic tryptych adopts the perspective familiar to readers of Sebald's later work. Through the poetic narrative voice the writer explores his own position in context, beginning with his grandparents' marriage, and using the techniques of describing photographs which are so characteristic of Sebald's later fiction, as well as themes such as the aerial bombardment of Germany which figure prominently in his more widely known work. Even as he was growing up, we learn, the minor accidents of childhood brought with them an awareness of potential 'silent catastrophe that occurs / almost unperceived'. Although the unidentified catastrophe is associated, bizarrely, with a 'stunted Tatar / with a red headcloth' (NN: 87/77), the reader schooled both in 1980s catastrophism and in the cumulative references to apocalypse and nature that have characterised this poem so far cannot surely overlook the apparent allusion to Rachel Carson's ground-breaking work *Silent Spring* (1962), which was one of the first texts to alert the world to the impending but largely unnoticed ecological crisis. Indeed, this contemporary section harnesses the earlier references to nature, its representation and gloomy prospects in the service of a more explicitly ecological critique. Yet the narrative is recounted internally – our perceptions are those of the poetic voice, and little explanation is given of the circumstances. The solipsism is emblematic of the plight of humanity itself: fearfully aware of some apparent impending disaster, the subject is unable to identify let alone counteract its occurrence. As in the case of Grünewald, the future is a repository not of hope but of dust.

Sebald's move to Manchester in 1966 provides fertile material for the fourth section of this third element of the triptych. The city revered by Disraeli as the new Jerusalem is at this point an industrial wasteland, still majestic perhaps, but shot through with

> mythical rivers now dead,
> which in better times
> shone azure blue.
> (NN: 96/83)

This post-industrial landscape sets the tone and mood for the poem, but it is the fifth section which considers more fully the consequences of the industrial age. This section is nothing less than an elegy for nature. In Zurich in the summer of 1987 (we surmise) the narrator of the poem visits an engineer acquaintance who has lost his faith in science, and who seeks solace in nature writing of the eighteenth century. Rather than Steller and Chamisso, he is comforted by the work of Hölderlin and the eighteenth-century Swiss poet and naturalist Albrecht von Haller. The engineer, having devoted his life to science and, we must presume, to the shaping of the natural world, persuades the first-person narrator to waste no time, because the crisis is now:

> So you'd better be off,
> said Engineer D, this very day.
> The country's on fire already and everywhere
> the forests are ablaze, there's a crackling
> of fire in the fanned leaves
> and the African drought plains
> are expanding.
>
> (NN: 103/90)

There is, it seems, still some hope that there will be fresh and unspoiled landscapes available: 'a golden coast, / a land veneered with rain' (NN: 103/90), but still the fate of nature hangs in the balance. A lyrical image of the flight of Icarus, imagined over Germany, raises the prospect of disaster for the human race as a whole, and for the natural beauties of Germany and Switzerland in particular:

> The shady shore of a lake
> emerges, the water's surface,
> the ribbons of rocks and
> on the highest summit the dragon's
> many-coloured plumage, Icarus,
> sailing in the midst of
> the currents of light. Beneath him,
> time divides the Rhine glacier
> into two mighty branches,
> the Churfirsten peaks emerge,
> the Säntis range rises,
> chalk islets, glowing
> bright in drifting ice.
> If his eyes are now
> lowered, if he falls
> down into the lake,
> will then, as in Brueghel's
> picture, the beautiful ship,

the ploughing peasant, the whole
of nature somehow turn away
from the son's misfortune?
(*NN*: 103–4/90–1)

The contemplation of these matters, and perhaps the beauty of their description, leads the narrator into a personal crisis. But the passage is important from another point of view. Again it implies an anthropomorphism of nature, and is emblematic of a tension between the explicit and the implicit representation of nature in this work, one which represents the tension which exists more generally in ecological ideas. On the one hand nature is represented as malleable and subject to human whim, and on the other as elemental, eternal, unconcerned with the fate of human beings and easily able to outlive us. This is no polemic in favour of environmental protection, but a subtle attempt to place nature in the context of human history and to accord it the status it deserves. More than a mere backdrop, it is crucial to the way we perceive everything about ourselves. Despite the dichotomy between nature and society which the poem superficially expresses, the implication is that we are inseparable from nature, and that since in our egocentricity we can do no other than to place ourselves at the centre of things, we have no choice but to place nature there as well. As the final section lyrically puts it:

Now I know, as with a crane's eye
one surveys his far-flung realm,
a truly Asiatic spectacle,
and slowly learns, from the tininess
of the figures and the incomprehensible
beauty of nature that vaults over them,
to see that side of life that
one could not see before.
(*NN*: 112/98)

NOTES

1. E. M. Forster's dictum 'only connect', originally conceived with human relationships in mind, is as true of ecology as it is of culture.
2. 'Weeping' is a rendering of the German 'Beweinung', which here in this scene of the crucifixion refers to 'die Beweinung Christi', the Mourning of Christ. 'Mountain landscape of mourning' might thus be more apposite.
3. The account is based mainly on Steller's journals of the voyage, readily available in the original German. They were published in English translation in 1988 (Steller 1988).
4. This is drawn from chapter 6 of Steller's journals, entitled 'Storms at Sea' in the English translation. See Steller 1988: 109–22.

6

RUINS AND POETICS IN THE WORKS OF W. G. SEBALD

Simon Ward

There is a continual danger of misrepresenting the complex and subtle self-reflexive style of Sebald's work. In *The Rings of Saturn*, Sebald cites Chateaubriand on the problem of doing justice to one's subject: 'I was troubled by the question of whether in the writing I should not once again betray and lose Charlotte Ives, and this time forever' (*RS*: 254–5/302). Any examination of the content and themes of Sebald's works has to take into account that this content is continually disrupted and placed in question by Sebald's formal strategies. In an attempt to do justice to these complexities, this chapter follows the 'thread' of the ruin through the labyrinths of *The Emigrants* and *The Rings of Saturn*, arguing that the ruin is central to both the content and the form of Sebald's literary production.

The architectural historian Robert Harbison has proposed that the ruin represents a 'way of seeing': the spectator's perspective is always constitutive of the meaning of the ruin (Harbison 1991: 99). Peter Geimer, writing on the attitude of artists and aestheticians in the second half of the eighteenth century, observes that the ruin was the 'empty space ("Leerstelle") par excellence', and enabled them to insert 'texts, images and imagination into those empty spaces' (Geimer 2002: 8). Both Geimer and Harbison emphasise the ruin as a site for projection, where narratives can be constructed to fill in the gaps in the material. Sebald's ruins are an investigation of ways of seeing, a central concern of his works. From that central concern, following the thread of the ruin leads us into other important areas of Sebald's labyrinthine work. In terms of content, the topos of the ruin allows both a consideration of a 'metaphysics of nature' that haunts the text (Huyssen 2001: 84), and a consideration of those ruins specific to Sebald, the cities whose post-war ruinous appearance seemed to him their natural condition (E: 30/46). In terms of form, it enables the elucidation of a tradition of the ruin in which Sebald's writing can be placed, while starting from a close reading of textual sequences that illustrate his complex and subtle self-reflexive style.

When looking at the presentation of ruins in Sebald's work, the potential complexity of these suggestions begins to reveal itself. Four different sites of ruin are considered in the following – Jerusalem, Orfordness, Berlin and Manchester – with as great a focus on the similarities in their formal presentation as on their thematic significance for differing narratives of ruination, since they illustrate in part Georg Simmel's suggestion that the ruin 'creates the present form of a past life, not according to the contents or remnants of that life, but according to its past as such' (Simmel 1959: 265). These ruins are, fundamentally, the presence of the past in the present.

Jerusalem is the archetype of the ruined city, although it also appears as a reconstructed model in Sebald's works. The depiction of Jerusalem in *The Emigrants* is mediated through Ambros Adelwarth's diary. Jerusalem is initially presented through a detached aesthetic gaze which highlights the effect of the light and the framing effect of the landscape: 'A rosy glow lay upon the valley, and through an opening in the mountainous terrain we could see the promised city in the distance – a ruined and broken mass of rocks, the Queen of the desert' (E: 136/202). The final remarks enshrine two ways of seeing the ruin: as a 'meaningless' mass of material and as an ideal construction. This sense of distance is also found in a passage highlighting the gaze that constructs the ruinous landscape. Ambros and Cosmo travel out to the Mount of Olives and look across from the Josaphat valley to where the 'silent city rises from the white limestone with its domes, towers and ruins': 'Over the rooftops not a sound, not a trace of smoke, nothing. Nowhere, as far as the eye can see, is there any sign of life, not an animal scurrying by, or even the smallest bird in flight' (E: 141/208).

The depopulated nature of Sebald's landscapes of ruin has been commented on before (Juhl 1995: 653; Kastura 1996: 209). On the surface, this is paradoxical, given that his works are very much about individual human stories.[1] This depopulation is a function of a perspective that views the ruin as a building or buildings (apparently) without human use or function. The perspective from which the ruin is seen (and thus constructed) is the 'high vantage-point' (a phrase which recurs in Sebald's work), an almost impossible, 'inhuman' perspective where the observer is not part of the landscape.[2]

The process of Jerusalem's ruination is told not through this gaze upon the ruins, nor is it directly narrated, but is mediated through a guidebook bought in Paris. 'The age of destruction' was a project that was for years deliberately organised by the Caesars, and thus has echoes of the premeditated planning that lay behind the bombing campaigns of the Second World War. As the archetype of the ruined city, Jerusalem's ruination is the result of planned human destruction. What remains of Jerusalem is nothing but 'dry stone and a remote idea in the heads of its people, now dispersed throughout the world' (E: 142/210).

In the ruination of the city, the idea and the material have become separated, as was suggested in the double description in Ambros Adelwarth's diary quoted above. The construction of the (ruined) idea can be conjured up only from a distance, in the models of the city and of the temple that recur in Sebald's texts (E: 176/263; RS: 247–9/292–4), or from the perspective of the (uncommented) image of Jerusalem which spans pages 138–9/206–7 in *The Emigrants*. The text surrounding the image offers a commentary about 'foul puddles and cesspits', for the sensory experience of Jerusalem is full of physical unpleasantness. It is also a disorientating experience, something repeated at Orfordness (RS: 136/203). The exterritorial space of the ruin causes the time–space continuum to be suspended. The ruins of Jerusalem thus illustrate the problem of perspective and the need for artifice: it is Max Ferber who describes the model of the (intact) Jerusalem as giving him a sense for the first time of what 'a true work of art' was (E: 176/263). At the same time, the textual discussion of a bird's-eye perspective of the model of the Jerusalem temple in *The Rings of Saturn* is undercut by the fact that the photograph with which the reader is presented is taken from within the model, and is so blurred as to render it almost meaningless (RS: 248/293).

If Jerusalem represents the original ruin, then Orfordness in *The Rings of Saturn* appears as the final ruin at the end of the earth. In Orfordness, we are in another of those 'extraterritorial' regions that recur in Sebald's work. The geological formation of Orfordness is the result of a process of natural history, as it had been shifted to its current location 'stone by stone, over a period of millennia' (RS: 233/280). The buildings on Orfordness seem initially to belong to this prehistorical narrative: 'From a distance, the concrete shells . . . looked (probably because of their odd conical shape) like the tumuli in which the mighty and powerful were buried in prehistoric times' (RS: 235–6/281). Through the inscription of his distance from the object, the spectator constructs this prehistorical narrative as his projection onto the ruin. This narrative is apparently corrected from a different, closer perspective: 'But the closer I came to these ruins . . . the more I imagined myself amidst the remains of our civilization after its extinction in some future catastrophe' (RS: 237/282). As indicated by the 'imagined', this is a further projection, in this case of the future onto the ruin. As the narrator comments that he felt 'out of time' and 'out of place', these projections can be read as establishing a parallel between the prehistoric and the futuristic modern in a continuity of, or return to, natural history. The ruin as a site for projection is underlined by the conclusion of this chapter, as the narrator looks back to Orford: 'There, I thought, I was once at home. And then, through the growing dazzle of the light in my eyes, I suddenly saw, amidst the darkening colours, the sails of the long-vanished windmills turning heavily in the wind' (RS: 237/283). The inclusion of 'I thought' creates distance between the moment of narration and the moment being narrated, when the spectator was becoming increasingly blinded, and projecting the images of the (ruined) windmills which we had encountered at the beginning of the journey: 'some ruined conical brick buildings, like relics of an extinct civilization. These are all that remains of the countless wind pumps and windmills . . . Sometimes I think, when I look over there, that everything is already dead' (RS: 30/42–3; the final sentence is missing from the published translation).

The windmills are a reminder that the perception of ruined technology is indeed a matter of perspective. The passage suggests not only a historical continuity of technological rise and fall, but also a literary continuity of projection into the extraterritorial ruined space that is also the space of the imagination, the space for a literary stylisation of the narrator as a Quixote tilting against the (imagined) windmills of progress. So while it is possible to read Orfordness as a site of natural-historical processes from the prehistoric past to the catastrophic future, all these perspectives are marked as projections, as possible, but not definitive, ways of seeing.

Orfordness in *The Rings of Saturn* is the projection of a self-stylising narrator, while Jerusalem in *The Emigrants* is mediated, in principle at least, through the perspective of Ambros Adelwarth. A similar process is at work in the representation of the ruins of post-war Berlin in *The Rings of Saturn*, for here the remembrances belong to Michael Hamburger. These recollections, or rather Hamburger's attempts to recall his childhood in Berlin before his family's emigration to the United Kingdom, are situated within a meditation on the workings of memory:

> Whenever a shift in our spiritual life occurs and fragments such as these surface, we believe we can remember. But in reality, of course, memory fails us. Too many buildings have fallen down, too much rubble has been heaped up, the moraines and deposits are insuperable. (RS: 177/211)

This passage is concerned with the impossibility of accessing memories. In the context of our thread, however, the deployment of an architectural metaphor to illustrate the process of sedimentation is significant because it *precedes* reference to the actual 'buildings' and 'rubble' of post-war Berlin. Important too is the use of the passive, a technique that Sebald often employs in the context of the ruin, and that implies the absence of, or at least a refusal to name, an agent in the process of ruination, something underlined by the use of natural-historical metaphors.

While the passage does not clarify the nature of this 'memory-fragment', the following excerpt gives us an inkling:

> If I now look back to Berlin, writes Michael, all I see is the darkened background with a grey smudge in it, a slate pencil drawing, some unclear numbers and letters in a gothic script, blurred and half wiped away with a damp rag. Perhaps this blind spot is also a vestigial image of the ruins through which I wandered in 1947 when I returned to my native city for the first time to search for traces of the life I had lost. (*RS*: 177–8/212)

On the one hand, this fragment is the (extinguished) trace of a piece of writing, perhaps on a blackboard; on the other it may be a blind spot which is the 'after-image' of the ruined landscape. In other words, it is not the ruins themselves, nor the original image of them, but the retinal trace thereof. This section sets at several removes the material of the ruins themselves, the 'facades . . . smoke-blackened brick walls and fields of rubble' (*RS*: 178/212) through which Hamburger wandered 'like a sleepwalker', first, by means of the metaphor which precedes them; second, due to the fact that they have actually become a blind spot written over other, earlier memories; and third, because these are Hamburger's recollections, and not those of the narrator.

Given that the ruins are experienced in a kind of sleepwalk, it is not surprising that the image of the ruined Berlin that does remain is a hallucinatory one of an empty site filled with 'bricks retrieved from the ruins'. Hamburger's vision, not of ruins, but of the preparatory stage to reconstruction, shares many characteristics of the 'ways of seeing' we have already noted:

> If I now think back to that desolate place, I do not see a single human being, only bricks, millions of bricks . . . a deathly silent image of the onset of winter, which I sometimes suspect may have originated in a hallucination, especially when I imagine that out of that endless emptiness I can hear the closing bars of the *Freischütz* overture, and then, without cease, for days and weeks, the scratching of a gramophone needle. (*RS*: 179/213–14)

Like the other ruined sites in Sebald's work, this landscape is emptied of people. Throughout the description of Berlin, the accessibility and authenticity of the act of remembrance is called into question. The past is retrievable only in fragmentary form, and can be perceived (only) through a hallucinatory state of mind in which the mediated fragments of a ruined culture repeat themselves endlessly. The ruins of Berlin are the inaccessible memories overlaid with the 'blind spot', that is, the afterimage, of the ruin landscape.

It has become clear from a consideration of the three ruin landscapes thus far depicted that these are sites of broken narration, realms where the imagination actively engages with, indeed transforms, the material environment, filling in the gaps in the manner of the Korsakow syndrome, a condition described in *The Emigrants* by Aunt Fini as 'an illness which causes lost memories to be replaced by fantastic inventions' (*E*: 102/149). The location of cultural production in *The Emigrants* is also such an environment. The narrator's arrival in Manchester in 1966 sees him take a taxi ride through the city from the airport. Once again, the gaze of the observer is highlighted in the construction of the ruined landscape:

> Day was just breaking, and *I looked out in amazement* at the rows of uniform houses, which *seemed* the more run-down, the closer we got to the city centre. In Moss Side and Hulme there were whole blocks where the doors and windows were boarded up, and whole districts where everything had been demolished. *Views opened up* across the wasteland towards [what . . .] had once been the hub of one of the nineteenth century's miracle cities. (*E*: 151/222; my emphases)

As with the other sites, these ruins too have the appearance of being uninhabited, as though they had been left as a necropolis or a mausoleum (*E*: 151/223), and laid open to the spectator. The narrator wanders through the deserted streets, shaken by the way the city 'displays' (*E*: 156/231) the signs of impoverishment and degradation. This sense of detachment is supplemented by aspects of the hallucinatory and fictional. As he considers not only the monumental Victorian buildings but also the post-war constructions, the narrator considers these might be 'mysterious facades or theatrical backdrops' (*E*: 157/231),[3] while his experiences in Manchester are described as completely unreal. As the narrator wanders through the industrial ruins to Ferber's painting studio, the unreliability of memory is highlighted through the addition of the sub-clauses, 'if I remember correctly' and 'as I now think I remember' (*E*: 158/231).

One further aspect of these deserted ruins distinguishes them from the others we have looked at thus far: the narrator remarks on the traces of those who had lived there:

> By way of a sign that someone really had once been there, the barely decipherable brass plate of a one-time lawyers' office, bearing names that *had a legendary ring to my ear*: Glickmann, Grunwald and Gottgetreu . . . All that was left to recall the lives of thousands of people was the grid-like layout of the streets. (*E*: 157/233; my emphasis)

The Manchester that is evoked or constructed in Sebald's final story in *The Emigrants* is a space of the past that bears traces of a life that has disappeared. As the engagement with the traces of disappeared lives can be described as the operating principle of *The Emigrants*, this can be read as an emblematic space. In the studio at the centre of this space, the artistic process that goes on there is described as follows:

> Work on the picture of the butterfly man had taken more out of him than any previous painting, for when he started on it, after countless preliminary studies, he not only overlaid it time and again but also, whenever the canvas could no longer withstand the continual scratching-off and reapplication of paint, he destroyed it and burnt it several times. (*E*: 174/260)

Whereas the environment reveals (only) traces of past lives, the danger of the art work lies in its claim to representation. This is made evident by the narrator as he reproduces Ferber's 'method' in describing the difficulty of writing Ferber's story:

> These scruples concerned not only the subject of my narrative, which I felt I could not do justice to, no matter what approach I tried, but also the entire questionable business of writing. I had covered hundreds of pages with my scribble, in pencil and ballpoint. By far the greater part had been crossed out, discarded, or obliterated by additions. (*E*: 230/345)

This repetition of Ferber's method might seem a little self-conscious if one takes Ferber's approach to be the method of the master at whose hand the narrator learns his trade. But both 'methods' have been presented within the text of which Sebald is the author.[4] As with all the 'models' of production presented in the text, in trying to describe Sebald's poetics through these models, we are in the position that Nietzsche describes with reference to things in the mirror: 'If we try to observe the mirror itself, then we discover nothing but things upon it. If we want to grab hold of the things, then in the end we come across nothing other than the mirror again' (Nietzsche 1966: 1172).

It is more profitable to consider these models as potential descriptors of a process of literary production (and a literary product) that is consciously in search of its own analogies. That process leaves the *artistic representation* in a state of ruin, rather than the traces of the thing that was to be represented. Whereas time or some other process of destruction has ruined the material, the artist sets about destroying his signifiers in order to arrive at an approximation of the trace. The motto of the first story of *The Emigrants*, 'Zerstöret das Letzte / die Erinnerung nicht' ['And the last remnants memory destroys' in Michael Hulse's translation], is ambiguous, and can also be read as an injunction not to destroy the last thing, memory. Paradoxically, a process of destruction becomes the aesthetic strategy of 'preserving' the signified once it has entered the realm of the textual. What presents itself to the reader is a document of that simultaneous process of destruction and preservation.

The four ruin landscapes discussed here, when viewed from the 'spectator' position (as in a theatre), are seldom experienced directly. They are spaces of projection and hallucination. As the 'present form of a past life', these are locations where the time–space continuum is suspended, spaces where the process of ruination is invisible or presented through passive constructions. The exception is Jerusalem, but in order to tell that history, there is need for recourse to another text, a historical study.

In the light of these observations, it is time to turn more directly to the thematic elements of Sebald's writing on ruins, and in particular the historical narratives that underpin the depictions of the ruins. Andreas Huyssen draws our attention to the fact that a major part of Sebald's lectures on the representation of the air war was a revision of a scholarly article that Sebald had published in 1982 under the title 'Zwischen Geschichte und Naturgeschichte' ['Between History and Natural History']. Huyssen opines that, whereas Sebald's position in 1982 was 'in between' these poles, in the Zurich lectures, Sebald comes down on the side of 'natural history', as demonstrated in the following quotation:

> This is the history of industry as the open book of human thought and feeling – can materialistic epistemology or any other such theory be maintained in the face of such destruction? Is the destruction not, rather, irrefutable proof that the catastrophes which develop, so to speak, in our hands and seem to break out suddenly are a kind of experiment, anticipating the point at which we shall drop out of what we have thought for so long to be our autonomous history and back down into the history of nature? (*NHD*: 67/79)

For Huyssen this is a 'discourse of a natural history of destruction' that 'remains too closely tied to metaphysics and to the apocalyptic philosophy of history so prominent in the German tradition'.[5] Huyssen understands this belief in 'natural history' to be a resignatory attitude that sees human destructive actions as part of an inevitable natural cycle, even if this goes beyond the so-called 'natural' to a point where nature can no longer recover. This, for Huyssen, is Sebald's metaphysics of nature operating behind the physical phenomena that resulted from the bombing strategy of the Allies in the Second World War or, if we look back to *The Emigrants*, the planned destruction of Jerusalem. Huyssen's critique is based on a rhetorical polarity between 'natural history' (negative, resignatory, mystificatory) and 'history' and 'politics' (positive, critical, enlightening). This ignores the fact that, at the end of his essay on Hebel's 'Rheinischer Hausfreund' in *Logis in einem Landhaus*, Sebald distinguishes between two kinds of ruination. He contrasts Hebel's finding consolation in the way in which nature is reclaiming the decaying Basel with the view from the Milky Way down onto the blackened burnt-out ruin of the earth. This is not just eschatology but the vision of a new era that, while still dreaming of the pursuit of happiness, is setting the wheels of destruction in motion (*LL*: 39). These are the ruins of the dialectic of the Enlightenment, in that the process of enlightenment already contains the seeds of its own destruction. As such,

Hebel's position (and by extension Sebald's) can be understood as a critical engagement with modernity.

Nevertheless, Huyssen's is a serious accusation, given the critique Sebald makes of those works that do actually attempt to represent the destruction of the Second World War. Huyssen accuses Sebald of repeating 'exactly that type of discourse' which he rejected in 1982 and, ostensibly, again in 1999. Sebald's disapproval of the 'key text', Kasack's *Die Stadt hinter dem Strom*, derives from the fact that such works cause 'the real terrors of the time to disappear through an art of abstraction and metaphysical swindle/vertigo'.[6] For Sebald, the construction of a 'presumptive metaphysical meaning' out of the experiences of those 'who had come away with nothing but their lives' (1982: 57), the 'production of aesthetic or pseudo-aesthetic effects out of the rubble of a destroyed world' is 'a process through which literature revokes its right to exist' (1982: 59).

If Huyssen is correct, then Sebald's own works would be ruled out of court by the standards set in his 1982 essay, but it can be argued that Sebald's work is a complex engagement with this insight into the dialectical ruins of modernity. Whereas the works of the immediate post-war period destroy (i.e. make disappear) the traces of reality, his own works are concerned with representing, in an appropriate aesthetic form, the fragments of a destroyed past.

One of the major contextual differences between the scholarly article of 1982 and the published lectures of 1999 is Sebald's development of an aesthetic strategy of fictionalised documentary in which, as suggested above, the traces of the past are of necessity aesthetically appropriated, but that the process of appropriation is signalled, or even placed in question.[7] Believing he has discovered Sebald's 'blind spot', Huyssen suggests that *On the Natural History of Destruction* gives us 'a re-inscription of the trauma (of the air raids) through quotation' (Huyssen 2001: 89), but Sebald's book also sees and reflects on precisely this danger. Sebald continually foregrounds the mediated nature of transmitted experience, even in the third section of *On the Natural History of Destruction*. Amongst the many responses to his lectures is a twelve-page letter from Harald Hollenstein, who had grown up in Hamburg under the National Socialists and had experienced the first air attacks on the Hanseatic City. However, Sebald immediately interrupts this report with a recollection (and citation) from Chateaubriand's description of the burning of Moscow. But, Sebald points out, this description was 'not an eyewitness account but a purely aesthetic reconstruction' (*NHD*: 87/93), and such a 'retrospective' description of the German cities was presumably impossible, suggests Sebald, 'probably because of the horrors so many experienced and perhaps never really overcame'. He then contrasts Chateaubriand's panorama with Hollenstein's report of the destruction of a bunker during an air attack. Hollenstein is not reporting directly as an eyewitness, but re-telling what his mother had told him. Indeed, in a style reminiscent of Sebald's own, the report ends: 'Many could not help vomiting when they saw the scene, many vomited as they trampled over the dead, others collapsed and lost consciousness. So my mother told me' (*NHD*: 88/93).This is, as Sebald comments, a 'second-hand memory going back over half a century' (*NHD*: 93–4).

Here we have the selective quotation of a textual representation of the memory of a memory, interrupted by the selected reproduction of a 'purely aesthetic reconstruction' of a real event by a canonical writer.[8] An important word here is 'purely' ('rein')', and it is also a key word in Sebald's 1982 critique of 'a purely natural-historical interpretation of recent historical developments'. Rather than being purely one thing or another, Sebald's texts move dialectically between the details (in which they threaten to lose themselves) and the high vantage point above the material that offers insight but also induces vertigo. Similarly, in place of any 'purely natural-historical' interpretation, Sebald maintains an unresolved tension in his texts, even in *On the Natural History of Destruction*, where his rereading of Alexander Kluge's *Neue Geschichten* (whose documentary form he evaluates positively in the 1982 article) indicates a change in his own position, in a different way to that which Huyssen suggests. Citing one of Kluge's sources, Sebald comments that it might well be one of Kluge's famous pseudo-documentary devices (*NHD*: 25/32), a remark that would have been out of place in the scholarly argument in 1982. Similarly, at the end of the second part of *On the Natural History of Destruction*, he reconsiders the perspective from which Kluge views his destroyed hometown:

> Here Kluge is looking down, both literally and metaphorically, from a vantage point above the destruction. The ironic amazement with which he registers the facts allows him to maintain the essential distance of the observer. Yet even Kluge, that most enlightened of writers, suspects that we are unable to learn from the misfortunes we bring on ourselves . . . For all Kluge's intellectual steadfastness, therefore, he looks at the destruction of his home town with the horrified fixity of Walter Benjamin's 'angel of history'. (*NHD*: 68/73)

Sebald rereads Kluge's work as a dialectic between a 'natural-historical' perspective and an intellectual analysis – though both tellingly share the same vantage-point. It is a reconsideration of Kluge's 'pseudo-documentary art' which allows Sebald to draw a line of tradition from his own contemporary aesthetic back to Walter Benjamin's angel of history, whose perspective is likewise a high (albeit tempest-blown) vantage point above the ever-more mountainous rubble of history.

In Benjamin we also have a thinker who actively engages with traditions of 'natural history'. For it was Benjamin who, in his study of the Baroque tragedy, made precisely this point that anyone studying the ruins of history had to acknowledge the complexities of the scholar's vantage point. Benjamin writes of the 'necessity of a sovereign attitude', but also concedes:

Even then the danger of allowing oneself to plunge from the heights of
knowledge into the profoundest depths of the baroque state of mind, is
not a negligible one. That characteristic feeling of dizziness which is
induced by the spectacle of the spiritual contradictions of this epoch is a
recurrent feature in the improvised attempts to capture its meaning.
(Benjamin 1977: 56)

The quotation at the end of the second section of *On the Natural History of
Destruction* of Benjamin's thesis about the angel of history is not simply there
to give Sebald's metaphysics some intellectual respectability, as Huyssen (2001:
84) claims, but to pose the question about a 'natural history of destruction' and
the relationship between progress and ruination, and to suggest an aesthetic
and philosophical tradition.

The problem of the author/critic's relationship to his material is a recurring
issue to which Sebald's work offers an eloquent if unsettling response. The question revolves around the author's sovereignty over his material, a question which
Sebald drives to the point of crisis, the point at which this particular reader was
truly unsettled. It is the conclusion of *The Emigrants*.[9] It is that point where
Sebald's chain of correspondences comes full-circle: Manchester was after all
described (by Ferber) as an industrial Jerusalem, but now we are in a hotel room
in Manchester, where the narrator feels as if he were 'in a hotel somewhere in
Poland' (*E*: 233/350) but is looking at photographs of Lodz, once known as
'*polski Manczester*' (*E*: 235/352). Before we arrive at the photographs, the narrator piles layer upon layer of fictionalisation in Borgesian fashion, where, of
course, the theatre motif also recurs: it is as if he hears ('though it was utterly
impossible') an opera singer in the nearby Free Trade Hall:

The sound came from so far away that it was as if he were walking about
behind the wing flats of an infinitely deep stage. On those flats, which in
truth did not exist, I saw, one by one, pictures from an exhibition that I
had seen in Frankfurt the year before. (*E*: 235/352)

The objects that the narrator sees through the many layers of projection are
photographs. The point is, however, that the 'knowledge' in these photographs
does not, cannot lie on the surface, because, on the surface, they lie. First, there
are pictures of merry Germans in the (newly named) Litzmannstadt. Secondly,
there are photographs of the ghettos that resemble the highly self-reflexive
images of the ruins in that scarcely one of them showed a 'living soul' (*E*:
236/354). And thirdly there are the images of the 'ghetto factories', highly constructed images of workers, 'who looked up from their work (and were permitted to do so) purposely and solely for the fraction of a second that it took to
take the photograph' (*E*: 236–7/354). Given that this kind of photography
might be considered diametrically opposed to Sebald's aesthetic, it is important

to realise that the narrator's engagement with the photographs is ambivalent. At first, he admits that he does not know who the young women in the photograph are: 'but I sense that all three of them are looking across to me, since I am standing on the very spot where Genewein the accountant stood with his camera' (*E: 237/354*). This is a central event, because in taking up Genewein's position, his eye is (imagined as) the 'organ for seizing control and taking possession' (*BU: 26*), thus entering into the most high-risk dialectic of the book. His perspective may be equivalent to Genewein, but his feelings are not, for the women objectified in the picture are subjects, albeit (and very importantly) within the narrator's own subjectivity:

> whilst the woman on the right is looking at me with so steady and relentless a gaze that I cannot meet it for long. I wonder what the three women's names were – Roza, Luisa and Lea, or Nona, Decuma and Morta, the daughters of the night, with spindle, scissors and thread. (*E: 237/355*)

The final scene of *The Emigrants* tests the ethical limits of seeing. Since Sebald's prose continuously offers itself as self-commentary, this moment is where he drives the antinomy of the allegory to the point of collapse, because the need to discover meaning in the object also leads to the betrayal and devaluation of the object. The process of ruination never stops, not even at the conclusion of the book. This is a most disconcerting but also productive way of avoiding closure. Ruth Franklin has expressed how this passage unsettled her, since, through certain factual parallels, the young woman could have been her own grandmother. For Franklin this illustrated the dangers of the 'illusory workings of art against memory', for her grandmother is a real person 'whose experiences during the Holocaust cannot be subsumed in the cycle of life's sorrows'.

> [M]y imagining her behind Sebald's loom, like Sebald's invocation of Altdorfer or Virgil to describe Nuremberg, merely substitutes an artistic image for a blank space. The blankness, however, is closer to the truth. When it seeks to do the work of memory, art may be a source of illusion. (Franklin 2002)

Franklin's own response is a striking demonstration of the potential that art (and Sebald's art in particular) has to provoke both the imagination and the conscience of the reader, but 'the workings of art against memory' are, as I have suggested, precisely what Sebald is writing towards and against. Franklin understands art as artifice here, but art is, in Sebald's presentation of it, not only a conscious construction. Let us return to Max Ferber's studio:

> the floor was covered with a largely hardened and encrusted deposit of droppings, mixed with coal dust, several centimetres thick at the centre and thinning out towards the outer edges, *in places resembling the flow of*

lava. This, said Ferber, was the true product of his continuing endeavours and the most palpable proof of his failure. (*E*: 161/237–8; my emphasis)

The process of artistic production is a conscious act of destruction, but also a natural eruption of material; a self-conscious art that is also, in part, a natural product. And so, while Sebald's texts may contain a metaphysics of the natural history of destruction (with the dangers of relativisation and mystification that implies), his response to that metaphysics is not resignation, but is to be found in the production of an art which understands itself as part of nature, but only partly, and thus able to offer resistance through its conscious process of simultaneous construction and ruination. Such a conception can be fruitfully related to another German thinker about the ruin. In Georg Simmel's essay 'The Ruin' (1911), the ruin is emblematic of the relationship between human desire to form material ('the will of the spirit' – 'der Wille des Geistes') and the natural process of decay ('the necessity of nature' – 'die Notwendigkeit der Natur'), as well as of an ambivalent attitude towards formal perfection which was indicative of a decadent era: 'The aesthetic value of the ruin combines the disharmony, the eternal becoming of the soul struggling against itself, with the satisfaction of form, the firm limitedness, of the work of art' (Simmel 1959: 265).

Whereas Simmel, with an aesthetic sensibility formed at the birth of modernism, reads the art work as something static, completed and perfectly formed, Sebald's aesthetic practice might, metaphorically, be read through Simmel's observation about the attraction of the physical ruin: '. . . it is the fascination of a ruin, that here the work of man appears to us entirely as a product of nature' (Simmel 1959: 261).

The ruination involved in the process of representation leads to an ambiguous aesthetic of ruination and construction. This aesthetic leaves the reader wandering through a highly constructed artifice, maybe even an edifice, that is also a ruin, but which bears the traces of reality. But then Sebald the narrator, reporting the voice of Austerlitz experiencing Liverpool Street Station, has offered a more subtle commentary than my own:

> I remember, said Austerlitz, that in the middle of this vision of imprisonment and liberation I could not stop wondering whether it was a ruin or a building in the process of construction that I had entered. Both ideas were right in a way at the time . . . in any case, the crucial point was hardly this speculation in itself, which was really only a distraction, but the scraps of memory beginning to drift through the outlying regions of my mind. (*A*: 191–2/195)

NOTES

1. Williams (2001: 82) has noted this fact without investigating the paradox.
2. This sovereign perspective (and its correlative, the loss of perspective in the detail) is

prevalent in Sebald's work (see Williams 1998: 103), and frequently results in a feeling of dizziness.

3. The 'perspective' of remembrance is often likened to a theatre in both *The Rings of Saturn* and *The Emigrants*, and here it is as if the narrator is moving through the theatre-set of the past.

4. Juhl: 650, sees simply an analogy 'on the level of narrative' with Sebald's 'poetic strategy'. In his otherwise insightful reading of these passages, Williams discusses the writer's self-doubt and artistic production before presenting Ferber's, which in fact comes first (1998: 100–3).

5. (Huyssen 2001: 89.) If one examines this passage closely, the assertion is posed as a question and the 'unvermittelt ausbrechenden Katastrophen' are not simply that; their eruption is 'anscheinend', that is to say, subject to the perception of the person who interprets the event (just as the 'gewissermaßen' stands as a question mark before the 'unter unserer Hand sich entwickelnden Katastrophen'). In other words, this philosophy of history is bound up in paradoxes in a way that is not the case with other epistemologies as represented in this passage.

6. (Sebald 1982: 56.) The German is 'metaphysischen Schwindel'. The choice of words appears self-conscious, if one recalls the German title of Sebald's earlier book, *Schwindel. Gefühle.*

7. This 'natural-historical' understanding of the ruins of modernisation is perhaps the reverse of the positivistic 'natural' reading of free-market capitalism which has become paradigmatic (both in and outside academia) over the last two decades

8. Sebald's position as a member of the 'second generation' enables him to develop an aesthetic that is appropriate to his situation, and that simultaneously allows his works to appear to do justice to the 'realen Schrecken'. See also Huyssen 2001: 82.

9. For other readings of this passage, see: Williams 2000: 108; Parry 1997: 425.

PART III
TRAVEL AND WALKING

7

READING ROOM: EROSION AND SEDIMENTATION IN SEBALD'S SUFFOLK

John Beck

The East Anglian coast is notoriously vulnerable to erosion caused by the insistent embrace of the North Sea. While defences are periodically updated, those who live by the sea tend to accept the ultimate claim the water has upon the land and the inevitable decomposition of the line that separates notionally solid ground from the encroaching sea. A fragile coastline and the efforts to fortify it provide powerful metaphors for, depending on one's point of view, the hubris or stoicism of human enterprise in the face of insuperable non-human forces. Likewise, the representational structures built to describe natural phenomena strive to contain the chaos of nature by locating patterns, laws, constants. In human affairs similarly, philosophical and social theories seek to represent generalities that might contain the contingency of experience. A mark of a sophisticated civilisation, one might say, is its capacity for system-building. Yet just as a culture is busy celebrating its triumph over the unknown, the tide invariably comes in again.

Erosion is the subject of Sebald's *The Rings of Saturn*. The book is about the erosion of confidence in the power of representation to record a knowable world adequately and thereby control it. It is about the arrogance of a rapacious European capitalism that built its empires too close to the water. Along the Suffolk coastline the text finds everywhere the ruins of a great power: in the 'silent oblivion' of industrialist Morton Peto's Somerleyton Hall (*RS*: 36); in the decrepitude of the once-rich port of Lowestoft; in the decaying Victorian manor houses scattered between Woodbridge and Orford; and in the remains of the

Ministry of Defence installation at Orfordness that looks like 'our own civilization after its extinction in some future catastrophe' (*RS*: 237/282).

The sediment of history litters the coastline; all that is left of so many grand schemes is the residue of their extravagant expenditure of natural and human material. The exploitation of nature for profit in *The Rings of Saturn* is usually figured as mindlessly cruel, and the text's narrator finds examples of near-sighted greed to be synecdoches for the brutality of empire-building. Catching herring, for example, the industry that fuelled Lowestoft's expansion in the nineteenth century, involves, we are told, snaring the fish by the gills in nets followed by an eight-hour throttling before they are finally hauled from the water (*RS*: 56/73). Similarly, the production of silk, used, among other things, to make fishing nets, involves the steaming of the cocoon in order to kill the pupa. The Victorian fashion for shooting and fishing also reveals a thirst for mass annihilation, as shooting parties regularly gunned down thousands of fowl, hares and rabbits in a single day (*RS*: 223/266). Arguments that humanity exploits only a fraction of nature's bounty and that, in the case of the fish, at least, fear and pain are not felt, are dismissed with the admission that 'we do not know what the herring feels' (*RS*: 57/75).

Not knowing what the herring feels acknowledges the otherness of the non-human and the limitations of any system of representation that claims to offer categorical knowledge of its subject. While the examples above suggest a victimised nature, Sebald's text does not posit a benign non-human world entirely at the mercy of human violence. The viciousness of capitalist extravagance is matched by nature, and the book is full of floods, sandstorms, hurricanes, fires, Dutch Elm disease. It is difficult to tell whether human destruction is considered part of a cosmic tendency to annihilation or whether, in order to survive the contingencies of life on earth, human beings have been defensively driven to ever more desperate acts of retaliation.

The Rings of Saturn invites such speculation as its narrative cocoon thickens. The intensely local gives rise to considerations of global and cosmic scale as the narrator finds correspondences and analogues everywhere. Nothing is accidental; everything confirms the narrator's view of history as a story of universal decomposition. The text is critical of arrogant system-builders in its exposure of the folly as well as the violence of acquisition and accumulation, yet it appears tragically resigned. Nothing is straightforward about Sebald's work, however, and its labyrinthine self-reflexivity demands that we consider not just the claims made by the text regarding its subject but also the position of the narrator and the form of the text itself. For if this is, as I believe it is, a book that is sceptical about representational truth-claims, stable viewpoints, and the authority of rational argumentation, then the evidence it provides – references, quotations, manuscript reproductions, photographs – must be greeted with a similar scepticism.

The Rings of Saturn is placed in precarious relation to the real. The reader is asked to embrace the textuality of this constructed world fully in complete awareness that it must always already be radically unreliable. Reading the text leads us further into doubt even as we are seduced by the plausibility of the book's content. This interpretive uncertainty – is the narrator Sebald himself? Did the events described really take place? Are the references and characters genuine? Is evidence of decay and depravity 'really' there or the paranoid product of a sick narrator? – is crucial to the text's ambitious objective. This aim is to challenge Enlightenment rationality, and the imperial and capitalist projects it legitimised, through the creation of a counter-system, a mirror world that reflects back the deformed 'truth' of historical experience. In this, the text maintains a faith in the authority of literature even as it appears to discredit it. The complex power of reading and writing defended and exemplified by this text produces systems of thought that are not necessarily logical but do make sense, once sense is allowed to include non-rational, associational and non-verifiable intuitive leaps. The book, then, does not seek to offer another theory of history; instead, it is a poetics of history that contains even as it deforms the modes of domination it seeks to reject. *The Rings of Saturn* is a space of and for reading.

The text opens with its narrator looking out of a hospital window which is draped in black netting, hoping to assure himself that a reality he feared 'had vanished forever' still exists (*RS*: 4/13). The final lines of the book tell of the old Dutch custom of draping black mourning ribbons over mirrors and pictures of landscapes, people and fruits of the field, in order that the departing soul should not be distracted by reflections of things 'now being lost forever' (*RS*: 296/350). As the text closes, then, we are reminded of the beginning, the intervening pages retrospectively understood as the record of a final passage from this world to another. Certainly, *The Rings of Saturn* is distracted by landscapes, people, fruits of the field and by reflections of the self. It is, more particularly, concerned with the uncanny deformations produced by representations of these things: reflections, paintings, photographs, catalogues, ledgers, letters, poems, fictions. As landscapes are transformed by natural and cultural intervention, so too do industries and empires rise through environmental and human exploitation only to collapse, usually because of a rapacious will to destroy. What persists are the representational traces of this process of exhaustion, the granulated evidence of realities now 'vanished forever'. This scattered archive of remains works as a deformed testimony of the world it has left behind. A glimpse of this ghost world of texts behind black drapes that tells the monstrous truth of the 'real' is accessed by Sebald's narrator through careful reading, by following trails in dead worlds. It is this work of reading that appears to have made him ill; *The Rings of Saturn* emerges from reading, walking and sickness as a book that pieces together a delirious understanding of both a vanished reality and the textual sediment left behind.

The coastal walk along Suffolk's North Sea margin that *The Rings of Saturn* records precedes the narrator's hospitalisation owing to 'almost total immobility' (*RS*: 3/12) by precisely a year; the 'freedom' and 'horror' experienced during the journey seem somehow to be the cause of this undiagnosed sickness. While the black netting signals mourning, the narrator does not die but survives to assemble the notes presented now as evidence. The text offered walks, as it were, through death, wandering between the 'real' and its representations, the past and the present, the dying and the dead, as if the narrative is itself in transit between worlds. The narrator has journeyed toward death, perhaps, to return with a message from the other side.

This is a book, then, that insists upon reading as the necessary condition for understanding what has been lost. While nothing appears to be safe from violence, and while all forms of knowledge and industry seemingly do little but produce elegant descriptions that confirm the grinding down of the universe, the text still persists in its conviction that there is a kind of melancholy necessity to interpretive pattern-making that makes it the most serious business of the culture. The reading of textual remains, however, is never put forward explicitly as a way of preventing a repetition of past calamities. Nevertheless, the failure or refusal to read the signs of the past is seen as a denial of responsibility and the wilful ignorance of a debased culture.

The narrative is driven by the physical movement of the narrator through space, by his stuttering progress along the coast, and by the ostensibly arbitrary digressions triggered by often the most accidental of events and discoveries: a scrap of newspaper, a television programme's droning while the viewer teeters at the edge of sleep, the expression of a shopkeeper, the positioning of fishermen along the beach, chance meetings with strangers in pubs. Walking, in Sebald's text, leads to readings, as all experience becomes freighted with intertwined significances that invite interpretation. Reading, likewise, becomes for Sebald a kind of walking, a wandering into the thicket of writing. Somewhat surprisingly, it is in Southwold that reading is most forcefully defended.

Situated between the atrophied port of Lowestoft and the Sizewell nuclear power station, between a relic of England's past seafaring prowess and the humming carbuncle of the future's half-life, in Southwold dray horses still haul hops and barrels for the Adnams brewery, retired Cambridge dons while away the afternoons in the Swan hotel, and beach huts are sold for prices that make the national news. Southwold is militantly resistant to the encroachments of modernity, making it an attractive refuge for conservatives and pessimists seeking a location congenial to a particular kind of English historical amnesia. Among Southwold's attractions, especially for the romantically inclined, is the old Sailor's Reading Room, one of the few places in *The Rings of Saturn* where the narrator does not detect signs of catastrophe. If Southwold might be said to profit from the amnesia that rewrites history as 'heritage', it is provocative that Sebald identifies within the town a site that activates a turbulent interpretation of history. Within the text, the Reading Room offers a position from which to meditate on the futility but also the necessity of literature in the face of universal ruin. Significantly, in a text that spatialises mental processes, reading has a room of its own. Here, reading remains the designated purpose of the space.

Elsewhere in *The Rings of Saturn*, intellectuals are perceived as eccentric exiles who die alone in a culture where 'most people have constantly to be shopping in order to survive' (*RS*: 6/15). In this world the aspirations of European civilisation have been reduced to 'nothing but amusement arcades, bingo halls, betting shops, video stores, pubs that emit a sour reek of beer from their dark doorways, cheap markets, and seedy bed-and-breakfast establishments' (*RS*: 42/57). A room for reading is, then, rare, and even in Southwold the Reading Room serves 'principally as a kind of maritime museum' which attracts, at best, 'a handful of visitors during the holidays' (*RS*: 92/115). The few who do 'cross the threshold leave again after they have taken a brief look around in the uncomprehending way characteristic of such holidaymakers' (*RS*: 92–3/115). The narrator's contempt for the fairweather visitors' incomprehension when faced both with history and such a thing as a reading room is cause for both disappointment and relief. The Reading Room is 'almost always deserted but for one or two of the surviving fishermen and seafarers', who mercifully sit in silence (*RS*: 93/115). For the narrator, the Reading Room is 'by far' his 'favourite haunt' when in Southwold.

The Reading Room's redundancy, then, is also its main asset. Elsewhere, intellectual labour has become the activity of a handful of social misfits whose arcane concerns are tolerated only as a form of eccentricity, outside the orbit of philistine convention. In the Reading Room the narrator crosses the threshold into a museum world of discarded significance, a world he enters to check whether anything has changed (*RS*: 93/116). Of course, it has not, and, as on earlier visits, he begins by perusing the log of the Southwold patrol ship, 'astounded that a trail that has long since vanished from the air or the water remains visible here on the paper' (*RS*: 93/116). This 'pondering [of] the mysterious survival of the written word' might be said to be the most vital practice that *The Rings of Saturn* undertakes. For, like the academic devotions of Janine Dakyns, who shores up 'a virtual paper landscape' (*RS*: 8/17) in her office during a lifetime studying Flaubert, Sebald's text produces a topography and a geology of forms from mapping the paper landscape of a lost world.

Dakyns's paper, in the course of time, takes over her office, advancing 'imperceptibly towards the centre', flooding the carpet and 'climbing from the floor' until, 'like the snow in the fields', it settles as high as the top of the door frame (*RS*: 8–9/17–18). Dakyns – and here again we might say the narrator also – resembles 'the angel in Dürer's *Melancholia*, steadfast among the instruments of destruction' (*RS*: 9/18–19). Curiously, though, Dakyns claims that 'the apparent chaos surrounding her represented in reality a perfect kind of order, or an order which at least tended towards perfection', a landscape within which she could easily find her way (*RS*: 9/19). Documents are figured here as both the means of destruction and the materials of order, overlaying actual space through a process of sedimentation that erases the real and provides an alternative foothold in the world, a space of writing within which each scribbled note, like the grain of sand in Emma Bovary's gown, contains the 'whole of the Sahara' and 'weighs as heavy as the Atlas mountains' (*RS*: 8/17). The apparent chaos of this paper world represents, in fact, a dense kind of order, an order of the sort that requires sustained and meticulous scrutiny. The Reading Room, like Dakyns's office, is both literally a roomful of reading matter and a space that enables reading, a physical site that is produced by and conducive to literary activity.

The notion of a reading room, then, emphasises the spatial dimension of documents: the printed matter of history takes up space, it is shored up and deposited in the present. People like Dakyns and Sebald's narrator – intellectuals – effectively dwell in a paper world that no longer represents the 'real' world but has replaced it. While this might be considered a withdrawal from worldly responsibility, in *The Rings of Saturn* this is not the case. For the interrogation of the authority of constructed worlds and how representations shape, influence and legitimate material facts and events – how narratives make and unmake the world – is a direct confrontation with the technology of linguistic power in the modern world.

More than once, *The Rings of Saturn* returns to the Borges tale 'Tlön, Uqbar, Orbis Tertium'. This story concerns the production of the entirely fictitious world of Tlön by experts in every field, an 'orderly planet' (1972: 42) that makes so much sense on paper that humanity, enchanted by its rigour, is willing to forget that Tlön is made up and substitutes the horrors of real uncertainty with the coherence of the imagined. Eventually, we are told, the world 'will be Tlön' (43). As with Dakyns's paper landscape, the disciplines that create Tlön are both 'instruments of destruction' (they dismantle the real) and the means toward a 'perfect kind of order' (by substituting form for contingency). The narrator of Borges's tale tells us that 'any symmetry with a semblance of order – dialectical materialism, anti-semitism, Nazism – [used to be] sufficient to entrance the minds of men. How could one do other than submit to Tlön, to the minute and vast evidence of an orderly planet?' It is useless, he goes on, to answer that

> reality is also orderly. Perhaps it is, but in accordance with divine laws – I translate: inhuman laws – which we never quite grasp. Tlön is surely a labyrinth, but it is a labyrinth devised by men, a labyrinth destined to be deciphered by men. (42)

Borges's characters have been discussing 'the composition of a novel in the first person, whose narrator would omit or disfigure the facts and indulge in various contradictions which would permit a few readers – very few readers – to perceive an atrocious or banal reality' (27). This might serve as a definition of *The Rings of Saturn*. Sebald himself has said that facts are 'troublesome'. The point of his writing, he explains, 'is to make it seem factual, though some of it might be invented' (Atlas 1999: 282). The major challenge of Sebald's text is this disfiguring of facts, their refusal to disclose themselves as fiction or non-fiction. Sebald's Suffolk is a Borgesian world where the visible universe may well be an illusion 'or (more precisely) a sophism' (Borges 1972: 28). Like Dakyns, Sebald appears to have produced out of 'apparent chaos' a reading room that represents 'a perfect kind of order', a textual world that might enable a few readers – sophisticated readers like Sebald rather than uncomprehending tourists – to 'perceive an atrocious or banal reality'.

If Southwold represents a simulacrum of pre-war England and is, like Tlön, a kind of orderly refuge from the disorder of historical contingency, *The Rings of Saturn* might be seen likewise as an uncanny representation of the 'real' reconfigured as the orderly labyrinth devised and deciphered by man. If this is so, one danger for the text is that the semblance of order it produces aligns it with the other systems 'sufficient to entrance the minds of men'. *The Rings of Saturn* thus presents a knotty problem. On the one hand, the text is clearly contemptuous of a debased contemporary culture of historical amnesia, the orderly simplicity of its narratives of leisure and consumption, and in favour of a radical scepticism that refuses to ignore the historical conditions that have produced the current cultural blight. On the other, in defending intellectual labour and textual interpretation, the text appears to favour yet another form of self-legitimised order: the enclosed world devised according to the scholar's own preoccupations. The pursuit of a representational strategy commensurate with historical contingency, then, threatens to merge with the rage for order to produce a labyrinthine system that replicates the system of control it seeks to overthrow. This view would position the author of *The Rings of Saturn* 'steadfast' among his 'instruments of destruction', replacing Sebald with 'Sebald', Suffolk with 'Suffolk', piling up inscriptions until the ground of the 'real' is obliterated, covered like 'the snow in the fields' by its textual doppelgänger. The text does indeed create an orderly simulation of the 'non-fiction' world of history, yet it does so, I would argue, in full awareness of the perils of such representational tyranny. Indeed, like Borges's tale, *The Rings of Saturn* is a mode of metacommentary that produces order with a view to dismantling it from the inside. The text, so sensitive to processes of decomposition, piles up the sediment of history not in order to fill sandbags against the tide, but so that it can be scrutinised for signs of the processes that made it. As such, reading and writing, as conceived

ⴰⴰald's book, are not part of the machinery of domination because they make plain their partiality and because they increase instability rather than reduce it.

The narrative is, nevertheless, one of melancholy despair: the universe is grinding down and humanity is bent on accelerating our eventual demise. This, for the narrator, is the truth of the world, the facts. Yet the facts here are, as I have suggested, disfigured. In the monstrous reality of the text, the world is careering toward destruction. If we continue to follow Borges, this is the 'atrocious and banal reality' Sebald's text allows us to glimpse. The gap opened up between the 'real' and the monstrous textual reflection of it, however, makes it impossible to tell what the world outside its representations would be like. As such, the reader is exiled from the text's putative 'truth' and left to wander uncompassed with the narrator along the coastal threshold between the solid and the fluid, between the seductions of order and the rapture of chaos. This is not a dialectical movement that trundles toward some telos of understanding; it is a particular kind of destabilising orderly disorder that trawls time and space – 'haunts', like Sebald in the Reading Room – in a perpetual state of melancholy that teeters on the edge of oblivion: order is sophistry, chaos is indescribable, a kind of death. As a kind of counter-enlightenment joke, the book piles up the 'facts' – the biographies of eminent figures, local history, natural history, arcane industrial techniques, international relations, imperial adventures – only to demonstrate that the increasing volume of interconnected information does not build toward an organised structure of control but to further instability and disappointment. 'Advances' in scientific knowledge and technological capacity since the Enlightenment have not, on the evidence provided, enlightened but only facilitated domination and destruction. Historical time for Sebald is not the narrative of progressive linear unfolding associated with Enlightenment conceptions of history, including literary modes of representation – the novel, biography, or autobiography – that rely upon the teleological structure of a unified, unidirectional time, but is a tidal temporal ingress and egress. Late twentieth-century cultural collapse is not, then, the end-time of an apocalyptic reading of linear history but a phase of decay that repeats and monstrously mirrors other such phases. It is no accident, then, that central to Sebald's narrative is another master of cultural pessimism, the Renaissance writer Thomas Browne.

'One of the momentous effects of the Renaissance', writes George Williamson, 'was to give new life to the idea of the decay of the world by planting mutability in the heavens and by stimulating admiration for Antiquity' (Williamson 1935: 121). Paradoxically, this sense of decay is generated by new knowledge. Astronomy following Copernicus revealed a universe of 'corruption and change' in what had been believed to be the 'incorruptible and changeless heavens' (Williamson 1935: 123). Previously unknown stars were discovered only to burn out, spots were found on the sun, planetary orbits found to be irregular, Jupiter's satellites proved the earth was not the only centre of motion. Each new discovery appeared to reconfirm cosmic instability and decline. While the concept of progress finally 'subdued the vapors of melancholy that rose from a decaying world' (Williamson 1935: 133), for many during the early seventeenth century optimism was rare. Old certainties were now mere points of view, leaving the imagination, as William Drummond observed in 1623, in 'a thousand Labyrinthes. What is all wee knowe compared with what wee knowe not?' (Williamson 1935: 145).

Browne's *Urn Buriall,* described by Williamson as 'that great funeral sermon on the decay of the world' (1935: 147), is an important source in Sebald's bricolage of historical pessimism and the book that Borges's narrator in 'Tlön, Uqbar, Orbis Tertium' is busy translating at the end of that story. Everywhere in nature Browne observed endless and inexorable mutation that tended toward disorder. Browne looked upon the world, Sebald writes, 'with the eye of an outsider, one might even say of the creator' (*RS*: 19/29). To create, then, is to be outside, to have a vantage point. Browne's creations are encyclopaedic collections, wrought

> out of the fullness of his erudition, deploying a vast repertoire of quotations and the names of authorities who had gone before, creating complex metaphors and analogies, and constructing labyrinthine sentences that sometimes extend over one or two pages, sentences that resemble processions or a funeral cortege in their sheer ceremonial lavishness. (*RS*: 19/29)

This is clearly another self-reflexive moment in Sebald's prose, for his own work follows this very process of sedimented analogy, his own sentences carrying an effect of ceremonial mourning.

Sebald's prose is also that of the outsider and the creator, a repetition of Browne's lament that it is too late for ambition, but reconfigured for the fallen subject under postmodernity: there are no new forms, no singular self to articulate an uncorrupted identity, no utterance that is not a repetition. The narrative position in Sebald's text is always already secondary, even as it insists on calling upon itself by name (we are offered Saint Sebolt, Seybolt the keeper of silkworms). There is a barely submerged longing for an originary self here, an undivided voice. The text, however, refuses that indulgence even as it appears to yearn for it. *The Rings of Saturn* does not just allude to or quote from its sources, it lifts lines and phrases verbatim, binding its precursors into its own structure. Once we know this, it becomes clear that the text never intended to speak as one voice, as one traveller's tale. It becomes impossible, in a sense, to 'trust' the text and its narrator. Our own yearning for a unified narratorial 'presence' is lost forever and, as Sebald dissolves, so we are hurled into the tidal pull of the text.

Andre Aciman (1998) has suggested that Sebald

> is so thoroughly woven into what he's read that he is no longer able to think about his dislodgement or anything else for that matter without also thinking of the terms that have made such thoughts possible. Exile may be a condition, but it is also a metaphor for something that had less to do with a homeland and far more with how one slips out of oneself or how in thinking about identity all one does, really, is run circles around oneself.

I believe Aciman is correct and that the 'Sebald' of the text is the monstrous mirror reflection of an inaccessible 'real' Sebald. The representation, like Tlön, has replaced the world, substituting homelands, individuals and uncertainties with the homelessness of the text.

Browne's awareness of cosmic deterioration made him, like Sebald, sceptical of human desire for the memorialisation of the individual, a desire, notably, that lay behind many an imperial adventure and stately pile. Since there is merely a 'remaining spark of futurity', Browne accepts, there will be no one to remember us, even if we were worth remembering. The 'bare Inscriptions' of our names upon the world are worthless folly, for names are lost and we will doubtless be given new ones 'like many of the Mummies' (Browne 1958: 46). Individuals who project their names into the heavens in the hope of immortality do so in vain for the

> various Cosmography of that part hath already varied the names of contrived constellations; Nimrod is lost in Orion, and Osyris in the Dogge-starre. While we look for incorruption in the heavens, we finde they are but like the Earth; Durable in their main bodies, alterable in their parts. (Browne 1958: 48)

Words here do not confer identity but confirm arbitrariness: all descriptions – of individuals and of planets – are historically contingent and infinitely revisable.

The Copernican 'new science', while it shattered one set of certainties, eventually gave rise to a new set grounded in the rational power of the human mind to harness the powers God had put into motion. Narratives of progress helped assuage the fears articulated during Browne's era. By the twentieth century, however, more than one wave of new 'new science' served to erode the sea defence of reason. Relativity theory, quantum mechanics, Heisenberg's uncertainty principle, Bohr's theory of complementarity and so on exploded the mechanical universe just as the First and Second World Wars laid waste to the great nineteenth-century empires and ate away at the totalitarian logic latent in the discourse of instrumental rationality. Yet again, like poor William Drummond, we are, with Sebald, left in a thousand Labyrinthes.

The pessimism of Sebald's narrative thus chimes with that of Browne's. In *The Rings of Saturn* the day is, as it was in the 1620s, at an end. We are again, it appears, in the winter of our years cowed by the giant achievements of the past, our energies sapped, resources exhausted, habitat crumbling. We are a culture bullied by yet obsessed with the past; we are a generation of antiquaries and archivists, preserving the relics of our wasted civilisation against we know not what. In this world, Southwold is not so much a quaint holiday destination but hideous evidence of cultural ossification. New science has again contributed to a pessimistic outlook as old certainties are exposed as mere opinion. For Sebald's narrator, though, the new indeterminacy provides an apt model for the sort of sceptical eccentricity his text celebrates. Perversely, then, science still shows the way, but now the model is not exactly of orderly control but one that embraces contingency.

One of the epigraphs of *The Rings of Saturn*, from the *Brockhaus Encyclopaedia*, gives some indication of the significance of the book's title. The particles that make up the rings of Saturn, we are told, are probably 'fragments of a former moon that was too close to the planet and was destroyed by its tidal effect'. Sebald's epigraph cross-references the Roche Limit, but a definition of this term is not given. The particles independently orbiting Saturn do not, strangely, accumulate to form a single satellite. This is due to the relationship between the gravitational tension of the planet and the particles and the attraction between the particles themselves. While the planet is trying to pull the particles apart, their own gravity is pulling them together. Particles far from the planet will pull together to form satellites. Closer in, they will be prevented from joining together by the planet's gravity. The borderline which separates the area of rings and the area of satellites is known as the Roche Limit, a threshold marking the point at which resistance to tidal disruption is impossible. Classical geometry cannot describe such a phenomenon, but new forms of scientific representation can.

The mathematician Georg Cantor created a monster. He removed the middle third of a line and then removed the middle third from the two remaining sections. Repeated many times, the resulting geometrical pattern has become known as Cantor dust: the dust of points is infinite, but their total length is zero. Cantor dust is a fractal, a monstrous or pathological phenomenon that wanders outside classical geometry. Cantor dust, claims Katherine Hayles, 'can be used for a model of distribution of galaxies in the universe. When the horizontal lines are made to flow vertically into one another to form two draped curtains, the figure models the breaks in Saturn's rings' (Hayles 1990: 166). This kind of geometry has also, famously, been used to measure coastlines. The typical coastline, Benoit Mandelbrot has observed, 'is irregular and winding, and there is no question that it is much longer than the straight line between its endpoints'. Indeed, 'coastline length turns out to be an elusive notion that slips between the fingers of one who wants to grasp it' (Mandelbrot 1991: 449). Sebald's text thus links the rings of Saturn with the Suffolk coastline as two natural forms of apparently indeterminate dimensions and ostensibly random organisation which can, using fractal geometry, however, be seen to have a deep order in their disorder.

Sebald's length of Suffolk coastline curves gently to the southwest; its beginning and end points are Lowestoft and Orfordness, a distance of just under thirty miles. It is a short journey but certainly much longer than the straight line between its endpoints. The narrative, too, is 'irregular and winding'. Henry David Thoreau wrote famously that the shortest walk should be undertaken 'in the spirit of undying adventure', the walker 'prepared to send back our embalmed hearts only as relics to our desolate kingdoms' (Thoreau 1994: 2079). That which is closest to home is perhaps most distant, the distance multiplying in complexity the closer we look. But how do we measure that distance in Sebald's text? Between beginning and end is a proliferating middle of increasing density that sends us further from any perceivable destination. Sebald is interested, I believe, in fractal forms that are distinguished by recursive symmetries across scales: the closer in or further out you look, the pattern remains the same. This might be said about the formal patternings of *The Rings of Saturn*, which confirm the sinister spiral of decay and deterioration, whether we are considering individual lives, towns, empires, geographies, universes, theories of representation, time, and history. In all cases, one scale echoes and contains all other scales; each phenomenon repeats and confirms the others. Joseph Conte explains that the 'paradox – and the pathology – of a shape that describes an infinite perimeter within a finite area disturbs the conventional understanding of dimensionality' (2002: 171). Euclidean points, lines, and planes are only sufficient for the description of regular forms. Coastlines and history – space and time – are irregular and contingent. Such a method of fractal description, James Gleick writes, represents qualities 'that otherwise have no clear definition: the degree of roughness or brokenness or irregularity in an object' (1998: 98). In other words, it measures disorder, that which lies beyond the world regulated by conventional systems of order. The decay of the world Sebald's narrator identifies around him is confirmed at all levels, across time and through space. While the 'new' science of non-linear dynamics provides a model of the universe, it is a labyrinthine model that is irregular, broken and winding, a model in which we are lost. The latest 'true' representation of the world does not master the universe but confirms only the elegance of its precarious existence. All the observer can do is walk through and read the signs.

Sebald's walk – and his documentation of it – is governed by the irregularities of the terrain and the unpredictable impulses of the walker:

> If one obeyed one's instincts, the path would sooner or later diverge further and further from the goal one was aiming to reach. Simply walking straight ahead cross-country was out of the question on account

of the heather, which was woody and knee-deep, so that I had no choice but to keep to the crooked sandy tracks and to make mental notes of even the least significant features, even the slightest shift in perspective. (*RS*: 172/205)

Contingent circumstances lead Sebald to walk, and write, toward the dying of the light, moving southwest. 'Eastward I go only by force', Thoreau wrote, 'but westward I go free' (1994: 2086). To go west is to follow the sun into darkness. Thoreau is thinking of Berkeley, no doubt, in his yoking of solar movement and imperial destiny. The freedom the west offers however, is also the walk toward the end, as Sebald realises, again signalling a recursive symmetry across scales: 'All that is certain is that night lasts far longer than day, if one compares an individual life, life as a whole, or time itself with the system which, in each case, is above it' (*RS*: 154/186).

At this point, Sebald approaches the ancient town of Dunwich which, suffering the perpetual onslaught of the sea, also moves increasingly westward, following 'one of the fundamental patterns of human behaviour'. The east, claims the narrator, 'stands for lost causes. Especially at the time when the continent of America was being colonized, it was noticeable that the townships spread to the west even as their eastern districts were falling apart.' In North America to this day, the narrator notes, echoing Thoreau,

> countless settlements of various kinds, complete with gas stations, motels and shopping malls, move west along the turnpikes, and along that axis affluence and squalor are unfailingly polarized. I was put in mind of this phenomenon by the flight of Dunwich. (*RS*: 159/191–2)

The earth, it seems, is rushing westward toward night, and it is not the sun that sets on us but the world that turns into darkness. The 'system' that is above life and time is the cosmic network of force and counterforce; the orderly disorder of matter spinning, unobserved and meaningless. While such a system is intuited in *The Rings of Saturn*, the kind of God's-eye-view necessary to perceive the way the parts work together is persistently refused by the narrative as an Enlightenment vanity. Certainly, issues of perspective are active in the text; this is the flatland of East Anglia, after all, where it is easy to fall into Euclidean reveries of line and plane. But such overviews are revealed by the narrative as part of the process of amnesiac fiction-making that makes Tlön so inviting: a world where things can be seen as of a piece. Contemplating the Waterloo Panorama, the narrator concludes that such a representation of history 'requires a falsification of perspective. We, the survivors see everything from above, see everything at once, and still we do not know how it was'. If the horizontal view is a fiction of optical containment, what of the vertical?: 'Are we standing on a mountain of death? Is that our ultimate vantage point? Does one really have the much-vaunted historical overview from such a position?' (*RS*: 125/152).

This last question is clearly rhetorical. Sebald has already had occasion to question the truth of omniscient representation. Discussing Jacob van Ruisdael's *View of Haarlem with Bleaching Fields*, the narrator explains that although the scene is understood to be viewed from the dunes, the vantage point is, in fact, 'an imaginary position some distance above the earth. Only in this way could he see it all together' (*RS*: 83/103). Again, Sebald's stress is on the priority of the imagined over the 'truth' of empirical observation. Like the physicians in Rembrandt's painting of the Guild of Surgeons, the preference for the inscription over the real, for the artificial order of Tlön over the disorder of actuality, is a form of invention as domination. Sebald is right that viewers of Rembrandt's masterpiece, and Rembrandt himself, see what the surgeons do not – the corpse – yet it is also true that the painting is not a body but itself a representation, a text which refuses 'Cartesian rigidity' by disfiguring the facts: the dead man's hand is deliberately out of proportion and the wrong way round (*RS*: 16–17/26–7). Like Rembrandt's picture, *The Rings of Saturn* destabilises even as it utilises the strategies of 'accurate' representation.

What we are left with is a document that consistently and visibly repeats the crimes it also exposes: *The Rings of Saturn*, as the deforming power of representation, is the carrier of catastrophe and also its historian. Representation leans toward order even at its most disordered – if order is not apparent, then go up or down a scale and a pattern will eventually emerge. A trip to the reading room for *Urn Buriall*, Borges, information on Saturn's rings, or any of the other documents and places referred to in the book does produce a sense of order, but an order that is as precariously held in position as the particles suspended either side of the Roche Limit: any slight gravitational wobble and some things will collide, others fall apart. *The Rings of Saturn* is a Borgesian labyrinth, and like other labyrinths the objective, once you are inside, is simply to work out how to escape.

8

TEXTUAL WANDERINGS: A VERTIGINOUS READING OF W. G. SEBALD

Massimo Leone

A paradox springs from the reading of W. G. Sebald's travelogues (the legitimacy of using this word will be discussed later). It springs primarily from the opposition between the reader's traditional and conventional process of identification with the narrative hero of a literary text – which is also encouraged by the interpretative cues contained in the text itself (Eco 1979) – and the strategies of semantic isolation, alienation and dismantling which constantly frustrate the reader's ingenuous and naïve longing for an effortless and transparent textual coherence.[1]

Within the conceptual framework that typically characterises the physical activity of travelling, this paradox could be described in an oxymoron of companionship: Sebald's literary alter-ego would be an ideal Amphitryon in the complex world of postmodern travel; he would be capable of poetically deciphering the apparently meaningless space of the many anonymous urban 'non-places' (Augé 1995) which surround the contemporary Ulysses, endowing them with visual, historical and exegetical significance, and projecting onto them the shadows of his own hallucinations.[2] Yet, this quasi-shamanic power (since only shamans can perceive and evoke the gods that hide in ostensibly amorphous and meaningless objects) stems precisely from the extreme solitude of the traveller Sebald.[3] This aloofness is stylistically embodied by the lack of dialogue in its most typical typographical appearance: there are no quotation marks; whenever dialogue does take place, it is always incorporated into the narrator's monologue. The reader's relationship to Sebald could be summarised by the following paradoxical and frustrating aphorism: everyone would like to travel with Sebald, because Sebald travels alone. On the one hand, the writer's narrative alter-egos immediately become a model for those who wish to recover (or discover) their relationship with reality. On the other hand, as soon as readers seek to emulate Sebald's travellers, they realise that solitude, which consists precisely in the *absence* of guides or models to follow, is the source of Sebald's original mode of being in the world.

Nevertheless, I should like to emphasise that the impossibility of physical companionship does not exclude the opportunity for theoretical friendship. Resisting Sebald's literary charisma and trying to describe and understand the textual devices through which it is built may cast more light on the relation between (Sebald's) literature and travel than would a slavish process of entrapment in empathic identification or aesthetic fascination. Instead of travelling with Sebald, we should understand why and how his travelogues trigger the desire to travel with him. In particular, I argue that the analytic tools of semiotics can explain the literary mechanisms through which he builds his poetics of travel. Sebald's travelogues are linked in a circular fashion to the disciplinary area which I shall tentatively call the 'semiotics of travel'. This circularity stems from the deductive-inductive method of semiotics in general: semioticians analyse and interpret texts within pre-existent theoretical and analytical frameworks, but the insights they gain from this operation retroact on the shape of the theoretical system itself (and so on ad infinitum). So not only does semiotics provide a highly suitable method of tackling the many interpretative problems raised by Sebald's travelogues; Sebald's texts themselves can be invaluable for the development of a semiotics of travel.

Many features of Sebald's poetics and aesthetics of travel call for semiotic attention, but I shall deal exclusively with two elements: the patchwork nature of Sebald's style and the labyrinthine topology of his semantics. As regards the first element, the urgent need for a semiotic appraisal of Sebald's writing resides mainly in the difficulty of classifying his works in terms of genre, style, discourse or even medium.[4] Semiotics is perfectly equipped to analyse fictional stories imbued with autobiographical fragments, essays whose verisimilitude is mingled with far-fetched details, realistic travelogues peppered with dreams and hallucinations, intertextual references or pseudo-references, words that caption images and images that illustrate words. As regards the second element, the labyrinth in which Sebald entraps his reader throws up another paradox: on the one hand, Sebald's prose juxtaposes various semantic particles (by which I mean fragments of knowledge belonging to disparate cultural contexts) without following any particular system of rules; on the other hand, the writer is so skilful in erasing his own organising function that his continuous and systematic digressions flow in an apparently steady stream, the voice of the narrator discreetly intervening only in order to guide the reader from one micronarrative to the next. Sebald is not simply a writer, he orchestrates a multiplicity of voices and text-types in order to produce his own coherent discourse. An important consequence of this is that one can easily perceive the meaningfulness of Sebald's works, but one cannot as easily describe or explain it.

If semiotics provides an ideal framework through which Sebald's works can be analysed, Sebald's writings can, at the same time, function as a useful case study in the development of a semiotics of travel. Many semioticians are currently turning their attention to the semiotic interpretation of this fascinating anthropological phenomenon and its (literary) representations. While a comprehensive overview of developments in this field falls outside the scope of this chapter, I should like to point out some of the reasons why travel should be studied through a semiotic lens. First, travel can be interpreted as a textual genre with its own discursive conventions; secondly, it can be studied as a matrix of possible signs; thirdly, its representations can be considered as a form of lie, as nothing more than a form of narrative fiction. According to a famous and witty definition of Umberto Eco (1976), the lie is the main object of semiotics, which is 'the discipline which studies everything that can be used to lie'. If one could not construct a lie, he argues, there would be neither the occasion nor the necessity for interpretation, and hence no possibility of building a semiotic theory. Sebald's travelogues are a lie in the sense that they express much more than the mere description of a journey: they are the particular narrative shape into which the author moulds his stories.

I use the word 'travelogue' here not as a simplistic generic label, but because it designates, simultaneously, the two distinct meanings that are implied by its etymology: 'logos' as 'word' (the verbal representation of travel), but also 'logos' as 'innermost principle' (the centre of both the anthropology and ontology of travel). In what follows, I shall illustrate the intertwining of these two levels in Sebald's major prose works, focusing on six points: (1) the semantics of dizziness in Sebald travelogues; (2) the incipit; (3) wandering; (4) hallucinations; (5) Sebald as the reincarnation of Walter Benjamin; (6) space and language as mutual metaphors.

None of Sebald's works provides a better occasion for an inquiry into the writer's poetics of travel-dizziness than *Vertigo*. This is immediately evident in the title itself (notwithstanding the considerable semantic slip between the German title *Schwindel. Gefühle* and the English *Vertigo*). It is confirmed by the frequency with which Sebald's prose dwells on the description of dizziness, giddiness and vertigo as emotional states. At the same time, it is undeniable that the narrative structure of *Vertigo* can be seen as an exploration of, and a challenge to, the traditional patterns of travel literature. This is nowhere clearer than in the wording of the headings of the four chapters which constitute the book. While the title of the first section – 'Beyle, or Love is a Madness Most Discreet' – does not address the thematics of travel, the three subsequent chapters bear titles that contain an explicit reference to it. Furthermore, they outline a classical circular topographical and narrative path: the Italian locution '*All'estero*', 'abroad', not only suggests that Italy will be the main setting of both the writer's journey and its representation but also succinctly designates a state of displacement, as if this was the result of an embarkation that had already taken place in the first chapter. The third heading, 'Dr K. Takes the Waters at Riva' seems to allude to a prolongation of the voyage. Finally, the last title (another Italian locution, '*Il ritorno in patria*', 'Return to one's homeland') appears to close the circle of travel in the most conventional manner. Ironically, however, the assumption of a circular narrative evoked by Sebald's choice of chapter headings is destined to be undermined by the text itself: the reader is gradually forced to strip locutions such as '*all'estero*' and '*in patria*' of their conventional semantic content, and to replace them with the new meanings constructed by Sebald's text.

The aforementioned headings do not openly refer to the semantic field of dizziness, yet this or analogous feelings are frequently described in *Vertigo* (as well as in Sebald's other works). As I have shown elsewhere, the concept of vertigo is an important one in the humanities, and especially in semiotics and travel studies (Leone 2004a, 2004b). With regard to the physiology of vertigo, medical treatises that deal with this subject are generally of little interest to the semiotician. They tend not to take into account the aesthetic dimension of the vertigo phenomenon, and restrict themselves to explaining its anatomical causes. Nevertheless, some interesting philosophical meditations on vertigo can be found in the branch of medicine known as 'semeiotics', or the science of symptoms, which is usually considered as a specific part of general semiotics, at the junction between natural and human sciences. Physiologists Guerrier and Bassères, for example, in their essay *Le vertige et le vertigineux* ([Vertigo and the Vertiginous], 1984), make a point which is relevant to semiotics or to a semiotically oriented phenomenology: equilibrium, such as we would associate with the average human body, cannot and must not be perceived. This means that sensing one's own equilibrium only ever happens negatively, as an absence, as a lost property of the body. This simple observation can have significant philosophical consequences. First of all, it reveals that what is called equilibrium is nothing but a zero degree of the awareness of the body in a given space. It is, however, only through a pathological condition, an alteration of normality, that this point of departure of perception can itself be perceived. Second, this medical remark can lead us to argue that all those circumstances and practices that provoke a feeling of vertigo could be an occasion (or a voluntary strategy) through which the human body seeks to develop a full awareness of itself.

For the existentialists, sensations of vertigo are inextricably linked to feelings of *Angst* and are passively suffered by the subject. In Sartre and Kierkegaard, for example, vertigo functions as a powerful metaphor for the shiver of theoretical awareness before the abyss of the human condition. Yet this existentialist paradigm is not applicable to Sebald's texts, for in Sebald vertigo is not only passively endured but also actively sought. Such voluntary vertigo is best explained with reference to Roger Caillois's essay on games (Caillois 1961). Caillois classifies games according to four categories, the last of which is *ilinx*, a term derived from the Greek for 'vertigo'. For Caillois, games belonging to this category consist in the pursuit of vertigo, that is, the attempt to destroy – even if only for a single instant – the stability of perception. Among the countless games of this kind mentioned by Caillois, the most relevant are the Dervish *tourneurs* and the Mexican *voadores*. In these games, there is a close relationship between vertigo and trance. Vertigo can thus be considered as a by-product of an active bodily strategy whose purpose is to achieve a state of trance.

This point is important for a reading of vertigo in Sebald's travel literature. I wish to suggest that the vertigo of both travel and the literature that represents it is an important component of the writer's mystical quest for the annihilation of space and language through, respectively, a specific type of movement and a particular kind of semiosis. Both language and space (especially urban space) are complex structures, networks of distinctive characteristics which can, however, be destabilised through two parallel processes: wandering, and above all *flânerie*, produce the fading-away of the features that define the quality of the objects constituting and delimiting space, while the language of Sebald's travelogues tends to erase the traditional distinctions between meanings, for example through the rhetorical devices of synaesthesia or repetition. In *Austerlitz*, the smell of soft soap is associated with the locution 'Wurzelbürste', a favourite of the narrator's father:

> But I do remember that there in the casemate at Breendonk a nauseating smell of soft soap rose to my nostrils, and that this smell, in some strange place in my head, was linked to the bizarre German word for scrubbing-brush, *Wurzelbürste*, which was a favourite of my father's and which I had always disliked.[5]

This strange association of fragments of meaning reveals the abyss of memory lurking behind an apparently common and inoffensive expression. As in language, so also in space, the discovery of this unexpected profundity and the memory it evokes trigger a feeling of dizziness: 'Black striations began to quiver before my eyes, and I had to rest my forehead against the wall, which was gritty, covered with bluish spots, and seemed to me to be perspiring with cold beads of sweat' (*A*: 33/41). On another occasion, it is the narrator's abnormal concentration on a single detail of reality that provokes a vertiginous experience. A passage of *Austerlitz* is particularly revealing of Sebald's peculiar obsession with discovering new meanings through the apparently insignificant repetition of the signifier. (This is analogous to the spatial strategy of the wanderer: the repetitive exploration of a territory allows the walker to transcend its superficial appearance and to discover the secret meanings of things):

> [Novelli's] main subject, depicted again and again in different forms and compositions – *filiforme, gras, soudain plus épais ou plus grand, puis de nouveau mince, boiteux* – was the letter A, which he traced on the coloured ground he had applied sometimes with the point of a pencil, sometimes with the stem of his brush or an even blunter instrument, in ranks of scarcely legible ciphers crowding closely together and above one another, always the same and yet never repeating themselves, rising and falling in waves like a long-drawn-out scream. AAA. (*A*: 35–6/43–4)

As in Hesychasm, where an infinitely repeated word or prayer loses its original meaning in order to become the expressive receptacle of another, mystical, significance, so in Sebald the current meaning of words is often modified in order to reveal the heterodox relationships that constitute the writer's imaginary. Thus, the annihilation of space and language does not produce a void of meaning, but a new configuration of it, a phenomenon which is close to the estrangement effect described by the Russian formalists. A close reading of Sebald's texts will help to clarify this point.

In *Vertigo*, feelings such as dizziness, giddiness and discontent are announced on the very first page. Both the first image and the first paragraph of verbal text evoke a sense of unease which is frequently associated in Sebald with a sensation of lack of bodily equilibrium: 'In mid-May of the year 1800 Napoleon and a force of 36,000 men crossed the Great St Bernard pass, an undertaking that had been regarded until that time as next to impossible' (*V*: 3/7). Thereafter, a feeling of vertigo is rapidly instilled in the reader by means of two narrative techniques that Sebald adopts frequently in his prose. The first is the abrupt connection, within the discourse, of remote temporal or spatial dimensions, for example, Beyle's military experience as a seventeen-year-old youth and 'the notes in which the 53-year-old Beyle, writing during a sojourn at Civitavecchia, attempted to relive the tribulation of those days' (*V*: 5/8). The second is the sudden juxtaposition of different planes of the framework of narrative enunciation.[6] This second point deserves closer attention. One consequence of Sebald's citing and reproducing the multiplicity of exterior objects and personae within the claustrophobic framework of his monologues is that his texts appear to be constituted of complex hierarchies of narrative levels, which results in the emergence of an intricate and labyrinthine syntax, even more striking in the original German than in English translation. This strategy, as well as the fact that Sebald manages to combine extreme hypotaxis with impressive lexical precision, is closely connected with Sebald's philosophy of memory and writing, but is also an important source of the vertiginous reception which characterises the reading of Sebald's work: he obliges the reader to follow him while he rapidly scales between different (and often remote) levels of enunciation, between different planes of his interior narrative discourse.

Furthermore, when vertigo is explicitly mentioned, it frequently originates from the spectacle of the temporal abysses (those of memory, for example) which Sebald's texts manage to build within themselves, as in the following passage:

> The difference between the images of the battle which he had in his head and what he now saw before him as evidence that the battle had in fact taken place occasioned in him a vertiginous sense of confusion such as he had never previously experienced. (V: 17/21)

The lack of equilibrium triggered by the discontents of human existence can be healed only through the act and strategy of writing, which in Sebald often possesses a curative effect: 'not until he determined to set down his great passion in a meditation on love did he recover his emotional equilibrium' (V: 20/25). Through writing, Sebald tries not simply to recover the ineffable complexity of reality but to place it within another, completely different and extremely personal, network of relations. This process could be schematised as follows: existential melancholy – a perpetually frustrated nostalgia for the unity and plenitude of being – triggers the desire to recover this plenitude through the frantic exploration of space. Yet confrontation with the swarming and elusive complexity of the urban landscape and the memory it contains provokes a feeling of confusion and dizziness, which the writer can master only by recounting it, by replacing the (uncontrolled) vertigo of travel with a (systematic) representation of vertigo. Likewise, readers following the circumvolutions of Sebald's prose are seized by a temporary bewilderment, which is nevertheless constantly soothed by the measured perfection of Sebald's linguistic constructions. However, it is only through a titanic effort that literature can reorganise the scattered fragments of life into a coherent whole, as Sebald underlines through the tragic story of Jacques Austerlitz, whose prose is unable to perform such a redemption of reality.[7]

The theme of vertigo is only metaphorically evoked in the first chapter of *Vertigo*, while the second one contains a meticulous and systematic exploration of it. Here the analysis of Sebald's semantics of dizziness requires an inquiry into textual beginnings (the second focus of the present paper), since they are the place where the feeling of vertigo usually arises. The way in which Sebald begins his stories, and especially his travelogues, is characterised by a programmatic regularity. As Susan Sontag argues, the centrality of travel in Sebald's poetics is evident especially in the incipit of his works ('often the narrator begins to travel in the wake of some crisis. And usually the journey is a quest, even if the nature of that quest is not immediately apparent', 2002: 43). According to most structural theories, the beginning of a narrative plays a particularly important role in shaping the tone of a text.[8] The beginnings of Sebald's works share some common features. First, the incipit of the book almost always coincides with the beginning of a journey. Second, travels are undertaken in order to soothe a previous feeling of discontent. Third, travel gives rise to a state of trance, whose main bodily manifestations are wandering and vertigo, topoi that correspond to a diminution in exterior and interior equilibrium respectively.

In *Vertigo*, the section entitled '*All'estero*' begins with the following words:

> In October 1980 I travelled from England, where I had then been living for nearly twenty-five years in a county which was almost always under grey skies, to Vienna, hoping that a change of place would help me get over a particularly difficult period in my life. (*V*: 33/39)

This passage refers to travel as to a therapeutic activity, and is followed by a disquieting description of how the narrator's wandering through a precise area of Vienna leads him to a state of hallucinatory trance. '*All'estero*' is paradigmatic for Sebald's narrative beginnings, almost all of which are characterised by the coexistence of vagueness and precision. Sebald's incipits are vague for several reasons. They do not reveal the innermost motives of the traveller's distress, and the reasons for travelling become blurred: 'I literally did not know where to turn' (*V*: 33/39). This uncertainty is embodied by the narrator's ostensibly aimless wandering: 'early every morning I would set out and walk without aim and purpose through the streets of the inner city' (*V*: 33/39). At the same time, however, Sebald's incipits are precise since they usually situate the beginning of the travelogue in a remote but determinate time ('in October 1980', *V*: 33/39) and describe both the narrator's wandering and the feeling of vertigo that springs from it with the customary profusion of concrete detail. Moreover, wandering itself, which is usually characterised precisely by its randomness, turns out to be governed by precise rules, which are even geometric in their obsessive rigour: 'I saw to my astonishment that none of my journeys had taken me beyond a precisely defined sickle- or crescent-shaped area'.[9] The most important effect of this juxtaposition of vagueness and precision is that Sebald's travelogues almost immediately plunge into a sort of day-dream, but without completely losing their realistic potential, so that they can function as both a representation of travel and a reflection on it.

The same elements that I have singled out in the incipit of *Vertigo* recur also in Sebald's other works, for example, in the beginning of *The Rings of Saturn*:

> In August 1992, when the dog days were drawing to an end [precise temporal indication], I set off to walk the county of Suffolk [allusion to aimless wandering], in the hope of dispelling the emptiness that takes hold of me whenever I have completed a long stint of work [distress which triggers the desire of travelling, vague mention of discontent]. (*RS*: 3/11)

In this case, the state of trance into which the narrator falls as a consequence of his wandering is so acute that it culminates in a form of paralysis: 'a year to the day after I began my tour, I was taken into hospital in Norwich in a state of almost total immobility' (*RS*: 3/11–12). Similarly, the opening of *Austerlitz* follows the same schema: 'In the second half of the 1960s [precise temporal indication] I travelled repeatedly from England to Belgium, partly for study purposes, partly for other reasons which were never entirely clear to me [motivational vagueness]' (*A*: 1/9). Here the paradoxical fusion of vagueness and precision reaches its apex, above all in the skilful depiction of the feeling of dizziness (and of wandering as its external counterpart). On the one hand, symptoms of unease progressively invade the narrator's perception of reality:

> I still remember the uncertainty of my footsteps as I walked all round the inner city, down Jeruzalemstraat, Nachtegaalstraat, Pelikaanstraat, Paradijsstraat, Immerseelstraat and many other streets and alleyways, until at last, plagued by a headache and my uneasy thoughts, I took refuge in the zoo by the Astridplein, next to the Centraal Station, waiting for the pain to subside. (*A*: 1–2/9–10)

On the other hand, the semantics of confusion is counterbalanced by what I should like to call the rhetoric of the collector, which in Sebald's prose attains its most spectacular peak in the quasi-scientific denomination of plants and animals:

> I cannot now recall exactly [!] what creatures I saw on that visit to the Antwerp Nocturama, but there were probably bats and jerboas from Egypt and the Gobi Desert, native European hedgehogs and owls, Australian opossums, pine martens, dormice and lemurs. (*A*: 2/10)

The eye of the collector sees things in a different way: objects that are totally insignificant for a profane observer suddenly become meaningful, because they are placed within a series of analogous objects. Sebald often resorts to this strategy in order to attribute a specific meaning to an otherwise insignificant description. Components of reality that commonly either go unnamed or are subsumed beneath broad generic labels here receive a specific denomination, as in a collector's cabinet of curiosities. From this point of view, the lexicological precision of Sebald's prose produces a maieutic effect: it helps reality to come into existence.

It is also interesting to note what happens when the phase of wandering is over. As Rebecca Solnit points out in her intriguing history of walking (2000), wandering – especially its Benjaminian variant, *flânerie* – requires an urban setting. It is thus no coincidence that the narrator dispels his feeling of unease (or even anguish) by meandering hypnotically and aimlessly through the urban labyrinth of Vienna or Antwerp. This movement is then followed by a period of stasis, during which the narrator reclines in a particular posture of bodily relief: 'How often, I thought to myself, had I lain thus in a hotel room, in Vienna or Frankfurt or Brussels, with my hands clasped under my head' (V: 63/72). This passage possesses intertextual significance, for the kind of setting in which Sebald's narrative alter-ego rests after the soothing physical exhaustion provoked by vertiginous wandering is exactly the same as the domestic scenery which, according to Benjamin, receives the *flâneur* after he has completely wrecked his body by frantically chasing the vital lymph of the city (1982: 525). This is not the only connection between Sebald and Benjamin; Sebald's literary works are steeped in Benjamin's aesthetics. Sometimes the reference is explicit, as in the title of *The Rings of Saturn* (an allusion to Benjamin's essay: 'Der Saturnring oder Etwas vom Eisenbau' ([The Ring of Saturn or Notes on Cast-iron Construction], 1982: 1060–3). More often, subtler connections link Benjamin and Sebald, as is evident, for example, in the hallucinations which pervade Sebald's prose.

The presence of visions, epiphanies, déjà-vu and other abnormal perceptions in Sebald's vertiginous urban wandering is particularly evident in *Vertigo*, where the narrator, at different moments of his meandering, experiences somnambulistic encounters with Dante, Ludwig II of Bavaria and Kafka (cf. Sontag 2002: 45–6). There are two ways of shedding new light on this particular narrative idiosyncrasy: on the one hand, the analogy between Sebald's hallucinations and Benjamin's philosophy of similarities; and on the other, the presence of aqueous elements in Sebald's prose. In his fragments on *flânerie*, Benjamin argues that similarity is a matter of gradations, and exemplifies this by pointing out how hashish moves one to perceive multiple superimpositions of slightly different faces. Sebald's dizziness, a by-product of his alter-ego's *flânerie*, is a feeling whose effects on the narrator's sensibility are the same as the effects of hashish in Benjamin's theory: wandering allows the traveller to blur the conventional distinctions between fragments of space and time and to reveal secret connections between them. This is probably the main reason why Sebald's stories are peppered with references to aquatic landscapes. Water, as psychoanalysis has frequently emphasised, is the element of dreams, since its most important physical features, such as transparency, shapelessness and mobility, perfectly convey the idea of the existence of a different reality, contiguous to the reality of dry land, and sometimes visible from it, but governed, at the same time, by completely different rules (cf. Bachelard 1983). Similarly, when Sebald introduces aqueous details into his prose, he does so in order to transform his narrator's sensibility into a sort of membrane, connecting different ontological realities: 'the memories . . . rose higher and higher in some space outside of myself, until, having reached a certain level, they overflowed from the space into me, like water over the top of a weir' (V: 82/93–4).

From this perspective, Sebald is a mystical writer, and the obsessive walking of his narrative alter-egos (but also of many of his characters, especially Jacques Austerlitz) bears conspicuous similarities to the various techniques of bodily trance discussed by Caillois (1961) and Eliade (1964). The strategy of using space and, by extension, travel and travelogues, as a means of transcending phenomena in order to attain the kernel of reality and, therefore, of experience and language, becomes strikingly apparent in the relation that Sebald establishes between geographical vertigo and linguistic dizziness. This is best exemplified in *Austerlitz*. The anguished historian of architecture whose tragic life constitutes the plot of the text starts his nocturnal wanderings through the city of London with exactly the same aim as Sebald's literary narrators in *Vertigo* or *The Rings of Saturn*: to dispel sorrow through physical meandering. The random exploration of geographical space is a bodily therapy through which Austerlitz tries to map another – lost – geography: that of a language that he can no longer recognise as his own. First of all, Austerlitz compares his linguistic dizziness with the loss of one's bearings that one experiences in an unknown or imperfectly known urban space:

> If language may be regarded as an old city full of streets and squares, nooks and crannies, with some quarters dating from back in time while others have been torn down, cleaned up and rebuilt, and with suburbs reaching further and further into the surrounding country, then I was like a man who has been abroad a long time and cannot find his way through this urban sprawl any more, no longer knows what a bus stop is for, or what a back yard is, or a street junction, an avenue or a bridge. The entire structure of language, the syntactical arrangement of parts of speech, punctuation, conjunctions, and finally even the nouns denoting ordinary objects were all enveloped in impenetrable fog. (*A*: 174–5/183)

It is in order to dissipate the fog that veils the truthfulness of language that Austerlitz starts his nocturnal wanderings:

> It was then, after my work of destruction in the garden and when I had turned out my house, that I began my nocturnal wanderings through London, to escape the insomnia which increasingly tormented me. For over a year . . . I would leave my house as darkness fell, walking on and on. (*A*: 178/186)

The result of this systematic *flânerie* (to use a somewhat oxymoronic expression) is similar to the by-product of the wanderings of Sebald's narrators: a wave of hallucinations is produced:

> In fact at this time, usually when I came home from my nocturnal excursions, I began seeing what might be described as shapes and colours of diminished corporeality through a drifting veil or cloud of smoke, images

from a faded world: a squadron of yachts putting out into the shadows over the sea from the glittering Thames estuary in the evening light, a horsedrawn cab in Spitalfields driven by a man in a top hat, a woman wearing the costume of the 1930s and casting her eyes down as she passed me by. (*A*: 179–80/187–8)

The hypnotic rhythm of walking, as well as its hallucinogenic properties, transform Austerlitz's nocturnal wandering into a mystical exercise, through which the exploration of space replaces an impossible exploration of time and memory.

Travel is a fundamental element in Sebald's literary works, from several points of view: the narrative structure of the travelogue provides Sebald with an extremely flexible and nevertheless coherent device for the organisation of extremely multifarious material. The extraordinary mélange of genres (autobiography, biography, apologue, fiction, essay), which characterises Sebald's texts, would probably appear chaotic without the thread of travel. At the same time, travel is not a mere literary expedient for the formal amalgam of Sebald's prose, but its thematic centre. By travelling, and especially through those particular forms of aimless walking – wandering and *flânerie* – Sebald explores not only a given space but also the (otherwise scattered and unintelligible) fragments of time and memory that are contained in it. A semiotic framework of interpretation allows the reader to realise how Sebald transforms a reality made of things into a reality constituted of signs, each one of which becomes the origin of a complex network of cultural and personal references. The result of such an amplification of meanings is sometimes unbearable, so that, like the depth of an abyss, it triggers a fearful feeling of vertigo. Thereafter, it is only through a meticulously sculpted language that Sebald succeeds in mastering this exuberant complexity, replacing the disordered vertigo of travel with the systematic labyrinth of his literature.

NOTES

1. According to Umberto Eco's semiotic theory, every text implicitly contains a model of the intended reader, whose inferences are guided by the narrative and stylistic structures of the text itself. The reader's interpretative activity is not totally free, but must follow the lines proposed by the text (unless the reader consciously decides not to 'cooperate' with the text and its rules, so wilfully misinterpreting it). Besides an *intentio lectoris* – the meaning that the reader attributes to a given text, and an *intentio auctoris* – the meaning that authors wish to embody in their texts, Eco's semiotic theory has shown the possibility of an *intentio operis*, 'the intention of the work' – the meaning that the very structure of a text seeks to express.

   The term 'semantics' and its derivatives (such as the adjective 'semantic') are used here according to Greimas's theory of language. Every text can theoretically be separated into expression and content. Semantics refers to everything that can be related to the second of these elements, that is, to the sphere of meaning. 'Semantic isolation' takes place when the reader's attempt to penetrate the meaning of a text fails. The text becomes like a remote island, whose exterior shape can be perceived but whose interior cannot be directly explored.

2. The term 'exegetical' is used here instead of the more common adjective 'interpretative' because it indicates the possibility of deciphering cultural artefacts whose matrix is scarcely known (as happens in exegesis, which, taken literally, is the interpretation of ancient sacred texts).

3. Solitude allows Sebald to escape from the *conventional* (social) meaning of things, and to explore the hidden significance of reality, as happens in animistic rites.

4. A confirmation of the fact that Sebald's extremely heterogeneous and idiosyncratic prose resists any attempt to classify it relates to the impossibility of denominating Sebald's works precisely: are they novels? Travelogues? Essays? Biographies? Autobiographies? Given the inappropriateness of adopting each one of these definitions, one has to have recourse to more general terms such as 'works', 'literature', 'prose' or 'texts'. I would argue that this last label is the most appropriate, since it conveys the sense that Sebald's prose is an intricate structure of interwoven elements like a textile or tissue. Furthermore, in semiotics the term 'text' designates not only a verbal artefact but also everything that *can be studied as a text*, that is, as an entity whose structure can be described according to the same general principles that are used to describe language.

5. *A*: 33/41. It is notable that associations of meanings are expressed through topological relations (places in one's head).

6. Enunciation is the theoretical framework of space, time and actors constructed by a text (for example, through the choice of adverbs, the morphology of verbs, the use of pronouns). On the semiotics of enunciation, see Manetti 1998.

7. The fact that Austerlitz writes in an alien language is one cause of his defeat. In this sense, W. G. Sebald, as an exiled German writer who re-appropriates his own language, can be seen to succeed where his protagonist fails.

8. On the relevance of textual beginnings in the history of literary criticism, see the lecture on 'beginnings' in Calvino 1992.

9. *V*: 33/39. The shape of the area could also embody precise symbolic meanings (the sickle as a symbol of death).

9

SEBALD'S UNCANNY TRAVELS: THE IMPOSSIBILITY OF GETTING LOST

John Zilcosky

Susan Sontag has correctly identified W. G. Sebald as a travel writer: journeys, she claims, form the 'heart of all Sebald's narratives' (2002: 43). But it is important to add that Sebald is also a textual traveller within the European travel-writing tradition: his journeys follow in the footsteps of others (Stendhal, Kafka, Casanova), or take place only in his head, when he reads travel stories (Conrad's, Diderot's, Grillparzer's). The goal of this chapter is to delineate precisely how Sebald's travels fit into the tradition of travel writing he so richly evokes. Specifically, I am interested in the way that Sebald reconceives what may well be travel writing's master trope: the fear of getting lost and the desire to find one's way. Sebald obsessively returns to this ancient paradigm, and, as I argue here, overturns its basic structure. Whereas traditional literary travellers get lost in order ultimately to find their way back home, Sebald undermines this narrative, but not as we might expect: he does not claim that we are all hopelessly lost and thus unable to come home. Rather he demonstrates how our disorientations never lead to new discoveries, only to a series of uncanny, intertextual returns. In this sense, I am working against the grain of what has already become a recurring argument in Sebald criticism: that Sebald's heroes are postmodern nomads, figures of disorientation desperately lost at the turn of our twenty-first century.[1] I maintain – in an investigation of his three travel narratives from the early 1990s (*Vertigo* [1990], *The Emigrants* [1992], *The Rings of Saturn* [1995]) – that Sebald sustains a decidedly modernist (*not* postmodernist) tension within this model of lost-and-found. Instead of providing accounts of nomadism, Sebald tells stories in which subjects can never become sufficiently disoriented, can never really lose their way. Like Freud, Sebald thus views modern travel as primarily uncanny. Emblematic is the title of Sebald's essay collection from the same period, *Unheimliche Heimat* (unhomely/uncanny home), whose word-play closes the gap, as I attempt to, between travelling and dwelling, thereby producing the sensation that the traveller, no matter how far away he journeys, can never leave his home.[2]

LOST-AND-FOUND: ROMANTIC AND POSTMODERN PARADIGMS

Before discussing Sebald's texts, I will briefly outline the literary history of getting lost. From *The Odyssey* onward, disorientation has usually implied its opposite: the hero will eventually find his way home. This economy of return gained special prominence in the Romantic period, especially in Goethe's *Italian Journey*, where Goethe deliberately repeated the Odyssean story in order to inscribe himself in the pantheon of heroic homecomers: Goethe loses his way in Italy so that he can return triumphantly to Germany. We witness this larger project in microcosm during Goethe's September 1786 description of getting lost in Venice.[3] Venice is, of course, still famous today as a confusing place where it is very easy to lose one's way. But most tourists are aware of this and, unlike Goethe, take a map along when leaving the hotel. Goethe, however, intentionally discarded his guide and map, and 'noting only the points of the compass, plunged into the labyrinth of the city' (Goethe 1994: 59).

Goethe entered the labyrinth again the following evening, this time continuing his wanderings ('again without a guide') all the way to Venice's poorer, 'remoter quarters':

> I tried to find my way in and out of this labyrinth without asking anyone, again only directing myself by the points of the compass. Finally one does disentangle oneself, but it is an incredible maze, and my method, which is to acquaint myself with it directly through my senses, is the best.

Typically for the Romantic traveller, Goethe gave up control by deliberately losing his way because only by doing this could he eventually gain a new, more robust sense of self. Goethe 'disentangle[d]' himself from the urban maze, as he claimed, by relying only on his senses and can thus return to his hotel with a higher regard for his subjective powers ('my method . . . is the best'). Only after successfully concluding this game of lost-and-found did Goethe (who seemed to need it no longer) purchase his map of Venice (1994: 60).

Using a model from Freud's *Beyond the Pleasure Principle*, we can observe how this lost-and-found game exemplifies the traveller's attempt to shield himself from anxiety. Like Freud's World War I amputees who dreamt over and over again of their injury in order to inoculate themselves psychologically, Goethe preventatively loses himself in Venice in order to protect himself against the real trauma of self-loss. This strategy is, in terminology supplied by *Beyond the Pleasure Principle*, a kind of 'fort/da' game: Goethe substitutes his own body for the Freudian spool, which the child repeatedly throws behind a curtain and then reclaims (Freud 1920: 15). Goethe similarly hurls his body behind the exotic city's curtain only to retrieve it victoriously. This 'fort/da' game forms what we might term a traveller's insurance policy. Goethe underwrites his own worst apprehensions by realising them; that is, he gets lost in order to make sure that he will never suffer the agony of *really* losing his way.

As I have argued elsewhere, this Romantic lost-and-found game repeats itself – however subtly – in postmodern figurations of travel (Zilcosky 2004). Even though Gilles Deleuze and Félix Guattari's urban 'nomadism' claims to resist all forms of return and recuperation,[4] other postmodern narratives of disorientation such as Roland Barthes's *Empire of Signs* (1982) reconnect directly to Romantic models. Barthes claims that the final goal of his Tokyo wanderings is to 'disturb' his 'person', but he, like Goethe, gets lost in a bewildering foreign city with the precise goal of discovering the travel writer in himself. His Tokyo disorientations, he claims, offer him inspiring 'flashes' that afford him a 'situation of writing' (4). Barthes's lostness thus ultimately grounds him as an author: he gets lost in order to find himself as – in a neo-Romantic twist – a writing nomad. How does Sebald – an author acutely aware of contemporary literary theory – react to this postmodern conceit?[5] Sebald resists this disingenuous attempt to turn the margin into a new centre (i.e., making disorientation into a new form of orientation) by deconstructing the traditional opposition between 'home' and 'away'. More interesting than the fact that we might always be lost is, for Sebald, the fact that we might always know where we are, whether we like it or not: when we find ourselves in the same hotel in a city we have already visited; when we become disoriented only to keep circling back to the same spot; when we move away from our homes only to see our pasts creeping in everywhere around us. It is this persistence of the familiar, this *unheimlich* (uncanny) *in*ability to lose one's way that haunts Sebald's travel narratives.

VERTIGO: *UNHEIMLICHKEIT* AND SEXUAL (DIS)ORIENTATION

Against the backdrop of travel stories from antiquity to postmodernity, Sebald develops a late twentieth-century (post-postmodern?) paradigm that raises the stakes of disorientation to new heights. In his earliest prose fiction, *Vertigo*, this issue of lostness occupies the writer-narrator, 'Sebald', as well as his friend, Ernst Herbeck. Herbeck was committed and released from mental institutions several times throughout World War II before being permanently committed because of a series of topographical disorientations: his goalless 'wandering the streets of Vienna at night' (*V*: 38/45). But even more upsetting than Herbeck's insane disorientation is the narrator's – 'Sebald's' – *inability* to lose his way. Sebald leaves his home in England for Vienna, hoping that travelling will help him to get over a particularly difficult period in his life. He, like Herbeck, drifts through Vienna's streets each day. But unlike Herbeck the narrator *wants* to get lost: he walks 'without aim or purpose', 'wander[s] aimlessly', is 'aimlessly wandering about the city' (*V*: 33, 35, 36/39, 41, 42). This juxtaposition of Herbeck's and the narrator's wanderings outlines the risks and rewards of getting lost. On the one hand, getting lost implies madness (*die Irre* meaning lostness, *der Irre* meaning madman) and is precisely what gets him irrevocably institutionalised.[6] On the other hand, getting lost suggests, for the narrator, a traditionally Romantic possibility of rebirth: it will, he hopes, both dissolve his psychological difficulties and free him from the literary ghosts – Dante, Casanova, Grillparzer, Kafka – that continue to haunt him.

By *trying to get lost* – that is, seeking out that proximity to madness that ancient travellers feared – the narrator situates himself within a specifically post-Enlightenment, touristic discourse of lostness that extends from Goethe to Barthes. Lostness, here, means diverging from (literary) tourism's 'beaten track' and, in so doing, discovering what Goethe calls the 'new'.[7] But the narrator's attempt to escape the mortifying effects of the past (the ghost of Dante brings on his 'mental paralysis') fails (*V*: 36/42). Unlike Goethe in Venice, who effortlessly loses his way in 'remoter quarters', the narrator is uncannily unable to move beyond Vienna's well-defined city centre:

> Early every morning I would set out and walk without aim or purpose through the streets of the inner city . . . Later, when I looked at the map, I saw to my astonishment that none of my journeys had taken me beyond a precisely defined sickle- or crescent-shaped area, the outermost points of which were the Venediger Au by the Praterstern and the great hospital precincts of the Alsergrund. If the paths I had followed had been inked in, it would have seemed as though a man had kept trying out new tracks and connections over and over, only to be thwarted each time by the limitations of his reason, imagination or will-power, and obliged to turn back again. (*V*: 33–4/39–40)

Whereas Goethe successfully got lost in Venice's peripheries, Sebald's narrator cannot escape Vienna's centre. The narrator's problem, then, is neither the typically Romantic one (how to find one's way after deliberately getting lost) nor the typically postmodern one (how to celebrate a world in which one is always lost). Whereas Barthes's Tokyo has an 'empty centre', Sebald's Vienna has an empty margin.[8] Correspondingly, the narrator cannot get lost at all. And this inability has devastating symbolic importance for the narrator: it brings into relief the miserable limits of his mind (his 'reason', 'imagination' and 'will-power') and of his writing (the 'ink[ing] in' of his wanderings). Whereas Barthes's lostness finally allows him a neo-Romantic moment of literary self-discovery (giving him a 'situation of writing'), 'Sebald's' wanderings reveal only that he cannot leave literary history's well-worn path (Barthes 1982: 4). Just as he cannot get lost in Vienna, he cannot develop a Romantic situation of writing peculiar to himself: he can only walk/write in the footsteps of Dante, Kafka and Grillparzer.[9]

Goethe's controlling 'fort/da' game thus gives way, in Sebald, to an uncanny paradigm, in which the subject is always, against his will, returning to familiar places. Sebald's precursors, in this regard, are neither the Romantics nor the postmodernists but rather the modernists: Aschenbach, in Thomas Mann's *Death in Venice* (1912), for example, follows Tadzio through Venice's labyrinthine alleys, eventually losing his bearings, but never gaining the triumphant feeling of going off-course and finding his way back; rather, Aschenbach inexplicably appears in exactly the same forsaken square he had sat in weeks earlier, where he now finishes the tainted strawberries that bring on his death. Similarly, we read of Sigmund Freud travelling in 1919 to a town in Italy where he loses his way – only to keep returning against his will to the same spot. Kafka's Josef K. from *The Trial* (1914–15), too, loses his way in the attics behind the painter Titorelli's bed, only to find these attics leading inexorably to the all-too-familiar hallways of the Courts. In each of these cases, getting lost leads not, as in Goethe and Barthes, to the excitingly strange, but rather to the unsettlingly known. Lostness, it seems, is impossible.

Such uncanniness determines *Vertigo*'s form, which stages travel alternately as textual and physical returns: *textual* in sections 1 and 3, where the narrator repeats the journeys of his literary precursors by reading their travel diaries; *physical* in sections 2 and 4, where the narrator either literally follows in their footsteps (Section 2) or returns, Odysseus-like, to his home town (Section 4). In the textual returns (1 and 3), 'Sebald' reads the Northern Italian notes of Stendhal and Kafka, both of whom have already repeated their own journeys (Stendhal going twice to Milan, Kafka twice to Lake Garda). In the first example of physical return (Section 2), the narrator consciously retraces the steps of Stendhal and Kafka, and, like both of them, leaves and returns to the same cities, even staying twice, like Aschenbach, in the same hotel and returning a second time over exactly the same route. The final physical return (Section 4, 'Il ritorno in patria') ironically repeats the ancient topos of the homecoming: the extravagant Italian title towers over the narrator's Odyssean journey to an insignificant village in Allgäu, which may or may not be his 'patria'. The Italian title deliberately puts the narrator's 'fatherland' in question. Is it Allgäu? Or is it England, where he now lives and whence he finally 'returns' in the very last pages of *Vertigo* (V: 257/280)? Or is it Italy (as 'patria' suggests), the spiritual homeland of the German writer-in-training from Goethe onward? The narrator's 'patria' is all three of these. Thus what appears to be the narrator's homelessness turns out, rather, to be an uncanny surplus of homes: the returns multiply, overwhelming the narrator, as we shall see, in the final sentences.

This uncanny structure is mirrored by *Vertigo*'s emotional content: surprise repetitions lead – as in Freud's theory – to a sense of horror and dread. To cite just some of *Vertigo*'s many striking repetitions: the narrator's companion, Clara, returns to her former elementary school 30 years later, only to break into tears when she sees her same teacher, 'voice quite unchanged – still warning the children to keep at their work, as she had done then'; Grillparzer, preceding the narrator in Venice by over 150 years, sees Venice's long-dead 'murderers and victims' rising up 'uncann[ily]' before him; the narrator himself discovers to his 'considerable alarm' that he was reading Grillparzer's description of Casanova's escape from a Venetian prison on the very date (31 October) of Casanova's escape; later, the narrator is frightened when he sees two strange men at two different spots in Venice; on a bus to Riva, twin boys bear an 'uncanny' resemblance to Kafka, which gives the narrator a fright that freezes his limbs; Kafka himself senses with terror that he has inadvertently wandered twice into the selfsame Veronese church; the narrator, in an attic in his hometown, comes across the 'uncanny', horrifying mannequin of a hunter whose spectre had tantalised him as a child.[10] Over and over again, then, uncanny experience leads to dismay and fear.

In the aforementioned scenes from *The Trial*, *Death in Venice* and 'The Uncanny', however, uncanniness signals more than just this: it also has an erotic component. Josef K. sits on Titorelli's bed, pursued hysterically by half-dressed girls; Aschenbach wanders Venice in search of his beloved Tadzio; Freud keeps returning, against his will, to the same red-light district.[11] Where is this erotic uncanny in *Vertigo*, and what might it have to do with the narrator's inability to get lost? Helpful here is Freud's theory of uncanny neurotic male heterosexuality, upon which Sebald could well have drawn.[12] Freud claims, in 'The Uncanny', that neurotic heterosexuals perceive intercourse to be uncanny because it reminds them of an internal 'compulsion to repeat' (*Wiederholungszwang*; 1919: 238). 'Love', he continues, is a kind of 'home-sickness' in which a young man figuratively travels to a far-flung 'place or country' only to notice that 'this place is familiar to me, I've been here before': this 'place', Freud continues, is 'his mother's genitals or her body' (1919: 245). Although not referring directly to the female genitalia, Sebald borrows Freud's diction and his notion that neurotic heterosexuality is an experience of *not* getting lost: as Sebald's 'Kafka' tells his female companion, sexuality is a *Wiederholungszwang* that blurs the image of one's lover until she eventually exists as nothing but a phantasmagorical repetition (*V*: 158/173).

Moreover, Sebald makes use of Freud's further, widely disputed claim that men also experience events as uncanny because these events recall fears of castration.[13] After Sebald's young narrator first views the *Wiederholungszwang* of heterosexuality in action (with Romana and the huntsman), he begins fearing barbers' knives and imagining Salome holding John the Baptist's severed head.[14] His reaction to this sex scene culminates in a 'grave illness', which leads to a delirium reminiscent of the scene of castration/blindness that Freud observed at the end of E. T. A. Hoffmann's 'The Sandman' ('Fine eyes – fine eyes!') (V: 249/272; Freud 1919: 230). The young 'Sebald' imagines pushing his hand through the chalky surface of a liquid filled with his landlady's 'eggs', only to find not eggs but rather, to his 'horror', 'something soft, something that slipped through my fingers and which I instantly knew could only be eyeballs gouged from their sockets' (V: 250–1/273–4). This hallucination presages a correspondence between vision and sexuality that haunts the narrator throughout his life: whenever he is touched by an unknown woman, he senses something 'disembodied and ghoulish' that makes 'everything out of focus, as if through lenses not made for my eyes' (V: 97–8/111–12).

Sebald thus borrows from Freudian sexual theory, but he also pushes Freud's model beyond its borders. Specifically, Sebald suggests that homosexuality might offer a way out of a system of eternal heterosexual return – not least because homosexuality implies, in both biblical and psychoanalytical jargon, losing one's way. Luther's translation of Paul's Epistle to the Romans describes homosexuality pejoratively as a *Verirrung* (an 'aberration' but also a 'going astray'), and Freud considers homosexuality to be a 'perversion' in the etymological sense of 'digressing' from vaginal intercourse (as in the Latin root *vertere* ['to turn'] + *per-* ['utterly'] = to 'overturn' or 'turn the wrong way') (Rom. 1:27). But whereas such disorientations in Paul and (however ambiguously) in Freud become tragic,[15] Sebald depicts sexual straying as a desired goal: in Venice, the narrator meets a man in a (gay?) bar and joins him for a pleasurable boat ride along the canals (V: 228/249); later, he repeatedly dreams of a strange man reaching out his hand toward him until they can at long last 'touch'; 'Kafka', whom the narrator considers to be secretly gay, follows a man down a Prague alleyway 'with a feeling of unbounded pleasure', 'veritably lusting' (V: 167/182; see McCulloh 2003: 94). This last image of following one's desire down an alley condenses Sebald's figures of topographical and sexual drifting in the metaphor of wandering desire.

But neither the narrator nor Kafka ever makes the decisive step toward this (dis)orientation. Instead, each returns to the beaten path of his heterosexuality and, what is more, to the equally uncanny track of historical repetition (V: 167, 252/182, 275). In *Vertigo*'s final pages, the narrator – his Venetian flirting now behind him – pleasurably loses his sense of direction in London's underground 'catacombs' only suddenly to see disturbing visions of recurrence: he dreams of words 'return[ing]' to him as if in an 'echo', recounting the Great Fire of London (V: 262/287). The date written beneath the text's final lines – '2013' (deleted from the English translation) – further draws our attention to the repeatability of historical disaster: 2013 echoes 1813 and 1913, the dates of *Vertigo*'s first and third sections respectively and, more importantly, of the end of Napoleon's disastrous retreat from Russia[16] and the final preparations ʀ.ɪ the First World War.[17] What is more, this unexplained 2013 suggests an imagined future (in which the narrator is now apparently writing), which will likewise suffer from a 'silent rain of ashes' that spreads 'as far as Windsor Park' (*V*: 263/287). The narrator has thus returned 'home' in literary, biographical and historical terms: he has gone to Italy, Allgäu and England and, what is more, revisited the sites of past catastrophes.

THE RINGS OF SATURN: UNHEIMLICHKEIT AND DEATH

Such uncanny returns likewise run through *The Rings of Saturn*. Here, the melancholic repetitions of the Saturnal rings serve as a model for the circular mental and geographical paths of the narrator (again, 'Sebald') – who, try as he might, cannot escape these orbits. *The Rings of Saturn*'s opening lines, like those of *Vertigo*, describe how the narrator has invested great hopes in random wandering: 'In August 1992 . . . I set off to walk the county of Suffolk, in the hope of dispelling the emptiness that takes hold of me whenever I have completed a long stint of work'. But this typically Romantic plan of reinvigoration through wandering falters when the narrator ends up not seeing the thrillingly strange but rather only familiar visions from a history he has tried to repress. He is 'confronted with the traces of destruction, reaching far back into the past'; because of this confrontation, a near total paralysis overtakes him and leads to his hospitalisation (*RS*: 3/11). The stakes of *The Rings of Saturn* are thus, like *Vertigo*, structured around the master trope of mobility: random wandering, the narrator hopes, will allow for a salutary Romantic self-reinvention; instead, it leads to unwanted repetitions and, finally, to a near-total mental and physical 'immobility' similar to that felt by the narrator of *Vertigo* (*RS*: 3/12; *V*: 36/42).

Temporary disorientations recur throughout *The Rings of Saturn*: the narrator gets 'completely lost' in the Somerleyton yew maze; senses that he has gone the 'wrong way' in Scheveningen; 'lose[s]' his 'bearings' in a labyrinthine system of rural Suffolk footpaths; and reports on a gigantic manor house in which an entire army might 'lose' its way (*RS*: 38, 84, 249, 257/51, 105, 296, 306). But most notable is the narrator's description, in chapter 7, of the ephemeral nature of such disorientations. Here, he outlines his *inability* finally to get lost. After walking through an especially thick patch of overgrown scrubland around Dunwich, he emerges onto a heath, where he begins to wander: the heath's lilac beauty, he claims, seduces him to keep moving along its gently curving path. Spurred on by the heath's fairy-tale beauty, 'numbed by this crazed flowering', the narrator relinquishes his self-discipline and loses himself in his thoughts. But this moment of free-spirited topographic and mental peregrination – the goal of the entire novel – is cut short by a return. Inadvertently and distressingly, the narrator finds himself back where he began:

> I stuck to the sandy path until to my astonishment, not to say horror, I
> found myself back again at the same tangled thicket from which I had
> emerged about an hour before, or, as it now seemed to me, in some distant
> past. (*RS*: 171/204)

Why 'horror'? Why is the narrator terrified? Several pages later, he offers us
a clue: after meeting with the poet Michael Hamburger and discovering how
much the 'paths' of their two lives had in common, the narrator is overcome by
his fear of the 'ghosts of repetition [*Wiederholung*] that haunt me with every
greater frequency'. The return to the tangled thicket near Dunwich heath top-
ographically literalised this horrible repetition, which eventually signals a
malevolent stasis in the narrator's body: 'The physical sensation closest to this
feeling of repetition . . . is that of a peculiar numbness brought on by a heavy
loss of blood', often resulting in a temporary paralysis of the mind, the mouth,
and the limbs, 'as though, without being aware of it, one had suffered a stroke'
(*RS*: 187/223–4). The narrator's fear of repetition again recalls – as Sebald certainly knew – Freud's model of the *Wiederholungszwang* from *Beyond the
Pleasure Principle*,[18] which signals the body's desire to be still: to 'return',
through a final paralysis, to an original state of lifelessness (*Leblosen*, Freud
1920: 38).[19] For Freud, the *Wiederholungszwang* reveals the death drive's
attempt to delimit life's instinctual wandering and straighten the path to death.
As in the case of neurotic heterosexuality, Freud stages this battle between life
and death as a narrative of disorientation and return: life attempts to lengthen
the 'road to death' through 'detours' ('jerks' and 'fresh start[s]'), but the death
drive finally 'rushes forward' towards its 'final aim' of returning to an 'earlier
state' (Freud 1920: 40, 39, 41). The stakes of getting lost are thus even higher
in *The Rings of Saturn* than in *Vertigo*: in the latter, the inability to get lost corresponds to sexual repression and neurosis; in the former, this incapacity leads
to the final paralysis of death.

This story of unwanted return presents the entire *The Rings of Saturn* in
microcosm: the narrator wants to get lost through walking in the hope of reju-
venation, but he is greeted only by the horribly familiar and, in turn, by a physical paralysis that resembles death. In contrast to Freud, however, Sebald seems
to offer a possible way out of this biologically determined circularity. Complex
systems, Sebald suggests in the final pages of *The Rings of Saturn*, offer a possibility of a lostness not always short-circuited by preordained returns.
Comparing silk weavers with writers, Sebald suggests that weaving and writing
both offer possibilities of successfully getting lost – in a way that is at once terrifying and passionate: weavers and writers, he claims, are people who 'even
after the end of the working day, are engrossed in their intricate designs and
who are pursued, into their dreams, by the feeling that they have got hold of
the wrong thread'. This metaphor of the wrong thread signifies the possibility

of madness (feeling 'despair' in lostness) but also the freedom born of a bewildering, intricate design (experiencing 'iridescent, quite indescribable beauty') (*RS*: 283/335). Sebald's fascination with the labyrinth – already present in *Vertigo* (*V*: 107/122) – explains his ongoing obsession with silk weavers and cultivators, which carries through to the book's final photograph of three East Indians standing next to their silk cultivations (Fig. 9.1). This image, barely commented on by Sebald, can be seen as a symbol of the entire text: an intricate model of getting lost which, nonetheless, has the tendency to circle back to its own familiar centre.

Although *The Rings of Saturn* never finally resolves this tension between disorientation and return, it is worth noting that the opening image (of the narrator 'paralysed' after his wanderings, lying in a hospital bed) is directly countered by the final one: citing Thomas Browne (a writer and son of a silk merchant) Sebald suggests that there might be a journey toward death that transcends the restrictive Freudian model of biological return. Such a journey is not a homecoming to the hauntingly familiar objects of one's *Heimat* but rather a trip far away from it, until this *Heimat* becomes salutarily and irretrievably lost: 'The soul, as it left the body', Browne writes, is not 'distracted on its final journey, either by a reflection of itself or by a glimpse of the land now being lost forever' (*RS*: 296/350).[20]

THE EMIGRANTS: UNHEIMLICHKEIT AND HISTORY

If *The Rings of Saturn* hints at disrupting the 'ghosts of repetition' through writing and the blind lostness of death and *Vertigo* offers the possibility of redemptive sexual (dis)orientation, then *The Emigrants* – the middle section of Sebald's travel-writing 'triptych'[21] – presents neither sort of escape from repetition. Instead of recounting the journeys of travelling writers (Stendhal, Kafka, Conrad, 'Sebald'), *The Emigrants* reports on exiles and émigrés who flee from economic or political crises. Thus *The Emigrants*, like *Vertigo* and *The Rings of Saturn*, presents lostness as its master trope, but its resolutely *unheimlich* returns preclude a final flight of the soul. In the first of *The Emigrants'* 'four long stories', Dr Henry Selwyn, a Lithuanian Jew, tells a paradigmatic tale of disorientation and return: he accidentally emigrated in 1899 to London having embarked on a ship he thought was destined for the United States, and then began an exemplary career as a scholar and a doctor. But in old age he is overcome by melancholic orbits that pull him back toward childhood memories, and he eventually commits suicide. Years later, Selwyn's memory abruptly revisits the narrator, who reflects on how stories have a habit of 'returning' to us 'unexpectedly': 'And so they are ever returning to us, the dead' (*E*: 23/36). This sense of ghostly *Wiederholung* runs through the second story, 'Paul Bereyter', as well: forced out of his post as a schoolteacher in 1935 because he had a Jewish grandfather, Bereyter moves to France but then returns home to 'S.' in

Fig. 9.1

the Allgäu to serve in the Wehrmacht and again returns after the war to assume his former position. Even after retiring and moving to Yverdon, Bereyter continues to come back to S. On his final, explicitly uncanny visit in 1983, Bereyter throws himself in front of a train. This train evokes three forms of return: lexical, psychoanalytical, historical. Paul literalises the pun from his childhood fantasy to 'end up on the railways'; he feels, like Freud, that trains symbolise a return to the dead (they are 'headed for death'); and the railway's emblematic relation to Auschwitz revisits German-Jewish history – it becomes the 'very image and symbol of Paul's German tragedy' (E: 60–3/89–92).

The third section, 'Ambros Adelwarth', likewise tells of emigration and return, but it departs from the genre of émigré literature by describing also the playful 1913 literary tours of Ambros (an émigré to the United States) and his companion, Cosmo Solomon. Like the narrators of *Vertigo* and *The Rings of Saturn*, the two travellers gain pleasure from losing their way. Istanbul becomes their equivalent of Goethe's Venice:

> Every walk full of surprises . . . You go to a theatre and a door in the foyer opens into a copse; another time, you turn down a gloomy back street that narrows and narrows till you think you are trapped, whereupon you take one last desperate turn round a corner and find yourself suddenly gazing from a vantage point across the vastest of panoramas. (E: 130–1/192–3)

Unlike Goethe, however, Sebald encloses such lively disorientations within a larger narrative emphasising, as before, uncanny relocation, sexual suppression and death. In the very next sentence, for example, the travellers' lost-and-found game leads to a cemetery instead of a sparkling panorama: 'You . . . enter a house gate and are in the street, drift with the bustle in the bazaar and are suddenly amidst gravestones'. And, at the end of this series of urban twists and turns, Ambros and Cosmo round a corner in a densely populated quarter only to catch unexpectedly a glimpse of 'a blue line of mountains and the snowy summit of Olympus' that 'for one awful heartbeat' resembles Switzerland or, even worse, 'home' (E: 131/193). This terrifying homecoming recurs later when the travellers move on to Jerusalem, where, in a dream, Ambros visits a poor village in the Jordan valley filled with gouty beggars and lepers only to discover that all of these people are actually 'from Gopprechts' (his hometown in Allgäu) (E: 142/210).

This uncanny return during a tourist lark outlines the larger structure of the entire narrative. Ambros and Cosmo travel, in the end, to the site of mythical homecomings, but their 'Ithaca' is in upstate New York and proffers a homecoming only in the sense of returning to a state of inanimate stillness. This motionlessness marks the end of Ambros's and Cosmo's disorientations (including their enigmatic erotic bond): Cosmo does not 'mov[e] a muscle' on his deathbed and Ambros dies after a 'progressive paralysis of the joints and limbs' (E: 98, 115/143, 169).

Like these earlier stories from *The Emigrants*, the fourth and final one, 'Max Aurach', presents uncanny return as its governing metaphor. It begins with a typically optimistic, Bildungsromanesque description of a young man needing figuratively to lose his way in order, later, to find his identity as a man: attempting to escape his German *Heimat*, he flies over London on his way to Manchester and gazes down 'lost in wonder' at the endlessly bewildering network of lights. This labyrinthine, illuminated cityscape signals to him that he has finally sufficiently confused himself, is finally really travelling, will finally 'be living in a different world' (*E*: 149/220). The story continues according to this developmental model requiring initial disorientation: our naïve narrator gets lost in his old-fashioned hotel's 'maze of dead-end corridors, emergency exits, doors to rooms, toilets and fire escapes, landings and staircases' (*E*: 153/225).

But this lostness does not lead to the narrator's finding a 'new' and better life. Rather, we discover, as in the other Sebald travel texts, that the narrator is unable to lose his way at all. Like Goethe in Venice, the narrator leaves his hotel with the intention of aimless 'wandering', and, like Goethe, this goal takes him to the unfamiliar, outlying regions of the city: to the old Jewish quarter, behind Victoria station. But what he discovers is not the imagined maze of tangled old streets in which he might lose his way. Rather, the city authorities have razed and newly rebuilt this old quarter such that 'all that was left . . . was the grid-like layout of the streets' (Fig. 9.2; *E*: 157/233). This grid symbolises the subversion of the narrator's typical lost-and-found story: he cannot lose his way and, thus, cannot find it either. On a more conceptual level, these same wanderings finally lead him to the studio of Max Aurach, whose story of a childhood torn apart by the Holocaust abruptly returns the narrator – who has not even yet managed sufficiently to lose his *Heimat* – to the Germany that he had been trying 'for various reasons' to escape (*E*: 149/219).

Aurach's story, which the narrator now begins to recall, constructs a similar tension between desired disorientation and unwanted return. Since escaping Germany alone as a child, Aurach identifies himself as a nomad, most notably in his favorite African restaurant in Manchester, where he regularly sits beneath the image of a 'caravan moving forward . . . across a wavy ridge of dunes'. When Aurach sits in this seat, the narrator claims, he seems to 'have just emerged from the desert scene, or to belong in it'. And Aurach concurs with this characterisation of himself as a nomad: looking at his hands, which are blackened from his drawing charcoal, he claims that 'in his dreams, both waking and by night, he had already crossed all the earth's deserts of sand and stone' (*E*: 164/244). But this self-identification as a wanderer does not, finally, hold true. As Aurach remarks at the end of his story, he, like the narrator, had always 'intended to move in the opposite direction', away from his German-Jewish *Heimat*, but that he had returned against his will: in Manchester, his new home, 'the German and Jewish influence was stronger' than in 'any other

Fig. 9.2

European city'. Thus, Aurach 'had come home' uncannily. With every further year that Aurach spends in this black, industrial city, he realises with increasing clarity that he has returned: 'I am here, as they used to say, to serve under the chimney' (*E*: 192/287). By recalling the smokestacks of the Nazi crematoria, Aurach's chimney duty reconnects him to a German-Jewish *Heimat* that is already in ruins. This return to a past he had tried to lose is, to his mind, a compulsion (*Zwangsvorstellung*) – not unlike the *Wiederholungszwänge* that contain the narrators' attempts to get lost in *Vertigo* and *The Rings of Saturn* (*E*: 181/270).[22]

Aurach's compulsive homecoming to the site of the ruins of German-Jewish history reverberates, finally, in *The Emigrants'* frame story: the young narrator had wanted to travel away from the same constellation – to get lost as an exchange student in England – but instead only returns to imagery of the Holocaust. In the book's last pages, the narrator enters a Manchester hotel that suddenly makes him feel as if he were 'somewhere in Poland'. And more than just Poland, this hotel's ambience calls up scenes from the 1940s Lodz ghetto. Fitting for a story of unwanted returns, Lodz, he discovers, used to be called *polski Manczester* (*E*: 233–6/350–2). This involuntary homecoming brings to mind *The Emigrants'* second frame story: the biographical returns of W. G. Sebald himself. Although Sebald insists that his narratives are fictional (thus my use of quotation marks when referring to the narrator, 'Sebald'), he deliberately plays with the connection between 'Sebald' and Sebald, and, in this section of *The Emigrants*, clearly overlays the fiction with his biography. Sebald, like the narrator, moved to England as a young man but continued to write in German and about German topics: most recently and controversially, about the Holocaust (*Austerlitz*) and the Anglo-American air-war on German cities in the Second World War (*On the Natural History of Destruction*). Sebald, it appears, could never escape his *unheimliche Heimat*. In a symbolic move befitting one of his characters, Sebald retained his German passport despite over 30 years of voluntary exile (Angier 1996: 13–14).

CODA: THE LOST READER?

If Sebald's texts compulsively retell stories of disorientation and *unheimlich* return, then what about our own experiences as readers? Do we get lost in Sebald's oft-cited labyrinthine narrative structures? If so, is this lostness enduring? Or do we eventually – by coming up with an interpretative map (such as my own) – imagine that we have found our way out of Sebald's textual maze? As Geoff Dyer notes, Sebald's digressive narrations lead us to lose our way because of long parenthetical discourses tempting us to 'skim' (2002: 18). But does such an unorthodox, apparently careless reading practice – which Sebald's digressions undoubtedly encourage – really disorient us? Or does skimming itself lead to more patterns, whether we want it to or not?

Fig. 9.3

Let us consider the readers who appear in Sebald's text, who engage in similarly casual, random reading practices: they pick up a book they have neglected for years and begin reading it in the middle; they haphazardly select volumes at a library; they skim newspaper articles out of the corner of one eye. I think, here, of the end of the first section of *The Emigrants*, when the narrator rediscovers Selwyn's past because his eye is arbitrarily caught by a report in a discarded newspaper, and of the end of *Austerlitz*, when the eponymous hero arbitrarily picks up an American architecture journal – only to come across a photograph of the file-room at Theresienstadt, where his mother had been murdered (*E*: 23/36; *A*: 395/401). These unexpected returns to familiar memories characterise the reading experiences both inside and outside Sebald's texts. If we seem to find our way out of them and, like Goethe in Venice, climb the figurative San Marco campanile, then our overview will not likely please us. When 'Sebald', following in Kafka's footsteps, climbs the Milan cathedral because he 'no longer had any knowledge of where' he was, he, like Kafka, gains no orienting vision, only a frightening image of death (*V*: 115/130). Similarly, when 'Sebald' dreams of gaining the high ground above a maze that disorients him, he discovers only a sense of 'how fearful it is to cast one's eye so low' and more impressions of devastation (Fig. 9.3). Such vistas do not imply the triumph of finding one's way, rather only an apparition of repetition and death. In this sense, reading Sebald is like 'Sebald' reading: we escape disorientation and gain the high ground only 'fortuitously', when things 'return unexpectedly' (*RS*: 174–5/207–8; *E*: 23/36). And because it is always 'the dead' that eventually come into focus, we gain only momentary pleasure from our overviews: our anatomies, diagrams, and triptychs. Like Sebald's characters, we end up longing – vainly, self-consciously – for a distant city where we might lose ourselves, where we might transcend the uncanny presence of home.

The author wishes to thank Brad Prager for his careful reading of this chapter.

NOTES

1. I think of Albes (2002) and Bauer (forthcoming). Although I agree with Albes's naming of 'disorientation' as a master Sebaldian trope (2002: 289), I ultimately argue the exact opposite: that Sebald depicts disorientation's structural *impossibility*.
2. Although I do not have the space to discuss *Unheimliche Heimat* here, suffice it to say that the writers Sebald discusses (notably Kafka, Jean Améry, Gerhard Roth and Peter Handke) all find it impossible to escape their Austrian *Heimat*. See, for example, Sebald's remarks on Améry, who even changed his name (from Hanns Mayer) in a vain attempt to get away from his Austrian past (*UH*: 141).
3. For a more detailed account of Goethe's economy of return in Italy, see Zilcosky (2003: 45–9).
4. For a critique of Deleuze and Guattari's championing of nomadism's liberatory force, see Zilcosky (2004) and Noyes (2004).

5. For more on Sebald's awareness of poststructuralist theory, see Albes (2002: 295–6).
6. This dangerous aspect of disorientation – its proximity to madness – is the one most present in *Austerlitz*, as in the story of the moths, who 'los[e] their way' and then cling motionlessly to the wall until they die (*A*: 132–3/136–7).
7. Goethe (1994: 120). I am thus defining lostness not cosmologically (as in Samuel Beckett's sense that, because of the earth's rotation, we can never possibly even walk in a straight line) but rather in the specific historical terms of modern tourism. For the tourist's desire to get off the beaten track, see Dean MacCannell's ground-breaking sociological study, *The Tourist* (1976) and Buzard (1993: 1–79). For the tourist's desire to lose his way, see Percy (1975: 52).
8. Barthes (1982: 30). I thus disagree with Albes's depiction of Sebald as a postmodernist who typically privileges 'peripheries' over 'centres' (2002: 280, 281n6). Here, Sebald deliberately overturns this postmodern truism.
9. This attack on subjectivity and originality – in favour of repetition and iteration – is itself generally understood as 'postmodern'. But this allows for an extremely broad and historically vague definition of 'postmodernism': it excludes, I maintain, *Empire of Signs* but includes 'modernist' works such as *Death in Venice*, *The Trial* and Freud's essay 'The Uncanny', as well as eighteenth-century texts (*Tristram Shandy*). For an overview of various attempts to define and redefine postmodernism, see Hutcheon (1988).
10. *V*: 44–5, 54, 59, 68–9, 88, 149, 227/52, 63, 68, 79, 101, 165, 248. The hunter/mannequin is a doubled repetition: it reproduces both the boy's childhood fantasy and the intertextual reference to Kafka's hunter 'Gracchus', whose story haunts all of *Vertigo*. For more on the connections between 'Der Jäger Gracchus' and *Vertigo*, see Sill (1997), Ceuppens (2002), McCulloh (2003: 95–7, 99–100, 103), and Martin Klebes's chapter in this volume.
11. Considering Freud's insistence on the sexual sources of uncanny experience, it is surprising that Mark McCulloh explicitly separates the uncanny (and Sebald's interest in it) from sexuality (2003: 57).
12. For other examples of what appears to be Sebald's deliberate use of Freud, see Long (2003: 125–6) and McCulloh (2003: 57–8).
13. For critical readings of Freud's castration theory, see, among others, Bernheimer (1993: esp. 83) and Felman (2003: esp. 239).
14. Here, Sebald is citing, perhaps unconsciously, Freud's *Interpretation of Dreams*, where the only two examples of 'Dreams of Castration in Children' are Salome-like stories of a man's head on a plate. The latter combines the fear of Salome with a trip to the barber (Freud 1900: 366–7). Again, *Vertigo*'s uncanniness extends to the intertextual level: the huntsman's name is 'Hans Schlag', the same as Kafka's proto-Gracchus figure, who (like the hunter-mannequin in *Vertigo*) is discovered in a forgotten corner of an attic (Kafka 1993: 273).
15. Freud's ambiguous stance on homosexuality (and perversities in general) in his *Three Essays on the Theory of Sexuality* begins with the radical supposition that all human beings have an 'originally bisexual physical disposition' and are all 'capable of making a homosexual object-choice and have in fact made one in their unconscious' (1905: 141, 145n1). By the end of the *Three Essays*, however, Freud stops putting the words 'normal' and 'pathological' in scare quotes and starts to suggest that there is something like a 'normal' heterosexuality. According to Arnold Davidson's Foucauldian reading, Freud tempers his own radical theory because his *mentalité* – his ingrained mental habits – could not keep up with his 'conceptual articulations', with his 'genius' (1987: 276).
16. The *Grande Armée*'s retreat concluded in the winter of 1812–13, reaching

Königsberg in December 1812 and Posen in January 1813. In the first section of *Vertigo*, we read of Stendhal (in autumn 1813) thinking back melancholically on that winter's 'terrible retreat from Russia' (*V*: 22/27).

17. As the narrator's friend, Salvatore, claims: 'In that year [1913] everything was moving towards a single point, at which something would have to happen, whatever the cost' (*V*: 129/145).

18. Freud first develops his theory of *Wiederholungszwang* thoroughly in *Beyond the Pleasure Principle* (1920), but he also mentions it in 'The Uncanny' (1919) and 'Remembering, Repeating, and Working-Through' (1914).

19. Strokes are thus a favorite cause of death in Sebald: they emphasise death's assault on our instinctual propensity for motion (see *V*: 200/218; *RS*: 187, 259/224, 307; *E*: 68, 108/99, 158).

20. This final liberatory flight into death directly opposes that of Gracchus, who cannot make it to the land of the dead because his helmsman is 'distracted' by the beauty of Gracchus's *Heimat* (Kafka 1991: 49–50; 1993: 309). More akin to Sebald's undistracted soul is Kafka's 'Coal-Scuttle Rider', who flies away in the final sentence and is 'lost forever' (Kafka 2000: 198).

21. Hermann Wallmann refers to *Vertigo*, *The Rings of Saturn* and *The Emigrants* as a triptych, with *The Emigrants* forming the middle 'panel' in Braun and Wallmann (1995: 8).

22. J. J. Long reads this passage more optimistically. He sees Aurach's and others' retellings of their stories as attempts, in line with some contemporary trauma theory, 'to take possession of memories that would otherwise take possession of them'. But Long fails to demonstrate how this passage might offer the possibility of some kind of 'working through', considering that, when Aurach finishes confessing, he only becomes rigid and silent: '[He] said nothing more. For a long time he stared into space, before sending me on my way with a barely perceptible wave of his left hand' (Long 2003: 125; *E*: 192/287–8). The examples cited here as well as in *Vertigo* and *The Rings of Saturn* suggest that Sebald might be writing *against* the psychoanalytical notion of salutary reiteration; instead, expressions of repetition serve to heighten (without relieving) our sense of sexual stultification, coming death and recurring historical disaster.

PART IV
INTERTEXTUALITY AND
INTERMEDIALITY

10

INFINITE JOURNEY: FROM KAFKA TO SEBALD

Martin Klebes

1

Manfred Frank's interpretation of Franz Kafka's 'The Hunter Gracchus' in his book *Die unendliche Fahrt* ([The Neverending Journey], 1995) proposes to inscribe Kafka's story fragments into a 'history of the motif' (*Motivgeschichte*) of the infinite journey. That history, Frank claims, affirms the notion of 'transcendental homelessness' in modernity, a term coined by Georg Lukács (1971) to describe the incommensurability of a secularised conception of progress on the one hand and submerged metaphysical desires on the other. Frank's interpretation also entails a more general thesis about literature and literary history to the effect that it is through such a history of a motif that a positive 'moral' may be derived even from such an ambiguous story as Kafka's. According to this view, literature would remind us of what has ostensibly been forgotten in forms of life that have cut themselves off from history by regarding scientific, technological and economic 'advances' as bare facts rather than phenomena whose emergence is conditioned by a complex set of factors. The infinite journey in particular – one prominent variation on the quintessentially modern, post-Renaissance motif of failure – would expose the limitations of a conception of rationality that has increasingly denied the historical dimension of knowledge (Frank 1989: 85). The story of Gracchus would thus be the provisional end point of a chain of texts that includes the myths of the Flying Dutchman, the Eternal Jew Ahasverus and other restless wanderers at sea and on land, all interlinked by their shared function as markers of historical memory. Frank's diagnosis implies that the absence of meaning of a *navigatio vitae* that no longer has a secure endpoint as it does in the *Odyssey* still *makes sense* insofar as there is a therapeutic value to the recognition of historical processes, or stages of the journey.

Reconstructed chronologically, Kafka's story of Gracchus runs roughly as follows: the hunter, whose job is to hunt wolves in the Black Forest, decides to pursue a chamois instead. While doing so he falls to his death and subsequently prepares for his journey aboard the ship that is to take him to the underworld. For an unknown reason, however, the boatman takes a wrong turn, failing to deliver the hunter to his proper destination. Thus unable to reach the great beyond, Gracchus is condemned forever to sail earthly waters aboard this vessel, periodically landing somewhere, but finding rest nowhere. Kafka's short story and a supplementary fragment describe different scenarios of one such meeting of the undead hunter and the living inhabitants of Riva. In one version, Gracchus is carried ashore and into a house by the harbour on a bier. The mayor of the town, Salvatore, comes to meet Gracchus, having been informed of his arrival the night before. Gracchus relates his story to the mayor, eliciting astonishment but little genuine understanding of his plight. Whatever story it was that the mayor expected, Gracchus's narrative does not seem to fit the bill.

The verbal exchange in the supplementary fragment is hardly more promising; in this version Gracchus remains on the barque that brought him, and an unnamed interlocutor comes aboard to question Gracchus about his fate. Gracchus, angered by what seems to him to be excessive self-consciousness on the part of the visitor, here actually plays *host*, consistently encouraging his guest to drink the wine the ship is carrying. Even this intoxication, however, does not help in making communication between the two any smoother. Gracchus is unwilling to tell his story, believing that everyone is already aware of it, whereas the guest points out that in fact no one in Riva is talking about the hunter at all, or is affected in any way by his fate. This fragment, too, breaks off before the demand for narrative closure has been satisfied. The visitor makes this demand explicit when he pleads: 'Gracchus, let me ask one favour. Tell me first how things are with you – briefly, but coherently' (Kafka 1983a: 249). The hunter will not answer this plea. The fragment may be brief, but it is hardly coherent, if by coherence we understand something that follows a clear path, a narrative with a beginning, a middle and an end.

In the context of Frank's thesis about the poetic critique of modern rationality, Gracchus's refusal to accept responsibility for his drifting – he puts the blame for the detour of his vessel on the boatman (Kafka 1983c: 77) – carries with it a message about the power of denial. Gracchus does not face up to the fact that the Christian schema of guilt and deliverance to which he readily subscribes is no longer possible. But *ex negativo* he communicates, according to Frank, the memory of that denial of infinite drift (1995: 48). Casting himself as a writer when he remarks to the mayor that 'no one will read what I am writing down here' (Kafka 1983c: 79), Gracchus assumes that his words will fall on deaf ears – an assumption that a hermeneutic reading would attempt to correct by assigning a meaning to the hunter's *action* of drifting that speaks louder than these words. To maintain, then, that Gracchus is thus both in denial of his own guilt and in error about writing entails the claim that the latter is at least no longer true of us as readers. In assigning a clear historical context to Kafka's story, we would no longer be part of the history of an error made by those subject to the infinite journey. By identifying the significance of the motif of the infinite journey itself, we would be able to arrest the movement of literature described by Jacques Derrida (1978) that ceaselessly displaces the absence detailed on the level of content (the drifting ship as metaphor) onto the level of form (the concept of metaphor itself as a drifting ship, or vehicle).

To assess whether such hope of containing semiotic drift is justified, we should begin by noting Frank's error – either one of reading or of calculation – in identifying the arrival time of Gracchus in Riva as the beginning of the modern age: 'the fragment even mentions the year "fifteen hundred," that is, the time immediately following the discovery of the New World' (Frank 1995: 32). This makes for a good story, but it does not follow Kafka's text, in which Gracchus actually claims that his barque has been adrift *for fifteen hundred years* (Kafka 1983a: 248), casting the meaning of the number 1,500 in a distinctly different light. Likewise, Gracchus's evasive reply at the end of the supplementary fragment to the interlocutor's request for a more precise dating of the hunter's fateful wrong turning suggests that there may *be* no clear answer to a simple calculation of the sort undertaken by the interlocutor. Attempting to delay the narration of his story in this fragment, and thus the determination of his identity, Gracchus points his visitor to the authority of the historians. After the visitor claims that the story, which Gracchus says is 'described as being without end' by historians sitting open-mouthed in their studies, is in fact not generally known at all, Gracchus replies:

> These are your observations, my dear man, other people have made different ones. There are only two possibilities here. Either you are denying what you know of me and do so for some particular reason. If that is the case I'll tell you straight out: you're barking up the wrong tree. Or else you really do believe that you cannot remember me because you are confusing my story with some other one. In that case, I'll just say: I am— no, I can't, everyone knows it and I of all people am supposed to tell you! It's been so long. Ask the historians! Go and see them and then come back. It's been so long. How am I supposed to keep all that in this brain, overflowing as it is. (Kafka 1983a: 251)

The historians, keepers of the archive and experts on dates, are supposed to supply the story, not the hunter himself who claims to be a writer. It is historiography that is in the business of preserving memory and reminding those who, like both the visitor *and* Gracchus, are either plagued by amnesia or feigning it. We could, then, go to the historians, as Gracchus suggests, and afterwards come back to the story. Frank does exactly this, assigning Kafka's story a place in the history of a motif. But Gracchus's suggestion is plainly a ruse: by the time we come back from wherever it is that the historians are, the hunter will already be gone, off on another leg of his never-ending journey, taking with him the secret of who he *really* is. If we were to go to the historians, we would find that they are indeed describing 'that which has long since happened without end' – that which will keep happening before description can give a complete account of it. The historians will never catch the hunter, which means that Gracchus, and Kafka with him, will always be one step ahead of Frank's interpretation.

One of the indications of the instability of Gracchus's identity is his indeterminate status as he hovers between the roles of guest, visitor and host. When the visitor claims: 'never will I forget whose guest I am' (Kafka 1983a: 248) after he has boarded Gracchus's barque docked at the harbour, he is aiming for a preservation of memory that the hunter's own story clearly exposes as problematic. Gracchus's troubles in recalling both to himself and to others who he is are serious enough to drive the whole conversation with the visitor to the edge of failure. In Kafka's other version of the story, Gracchus likewise oscillates between the roles of guest and host. Unconscious or asleep as two men in dark coats carry him ashore, Gracchus is welcomed to Riva not upon coming down from the ship but in a house designated by the boatman. Just arrived in Riva, Gracchus finds himself in a place where 'he has lived for centuries' (Kafka 1983c: 79). In other words, since he can never really go home, any place he visits is as good a home as any other. But a paradox like that is not easy to swallow, and it can make that which one has long known seem quite unfamiliar. Thus, Gracchus himself has as much of a problem identifying the mayor Salvatore in this version as the interlocutor has in coming to terms with Gracchus's identity in the supplementary fragment. When Salvatore comes to wake up Gracchus to talk to him, the hunter starts up with a question: 'Who are you?' When Salvatore identifies himself, Gracchus is quick to reply: 'I knew that, of course, Mr. Mayor, but in the first moment I always forget everything, everything spins around [*geht mir in der Runde*], and it is better for me to ask, even though I know everything' (Kafka 1983c: 76–7). This claim to knowledge remains as unsupported and ultimately untenable as Gracchus's own suspicion in the supplementary fragment that his interlocutor may be feigning forgetfulness of Gracchus's story and his identity. The hunter clearly does not consider himself the best of all possible mnemonic carriers, but neither can we conveniently conclude that what Frank describes as his denial of guilt is based in a determinate lack of memory. Rather, Gracchus's memory seems to be affected by the very condition of his travelling, his circling around the earth without a centre, a disorienting vertigo, *ein Gehen in der Runde*.

After Gracchus has disclosed to the mayor the paradox of being at home nowhere, and therefore everywhere, Salvatore is clearly at a loss.

> 'Extraordinary,' said the mayor, 'extraordinary. And now you propose to stay [*gedenken Sie zu bleiben*] here with us in Riva?'
>
> 'I do not propose to [*Ich gedenke nicht*],' the hunter said with a smile, and, to make up for the mockery, he laid his hand on the mayor's knee. 'I am here, more than that I do not know, that is all I can do. My ship has no rudder, it is driven by the wind that blows in the nethermost regions of death.' (Kafka 1983c: 79)

The mockery with which the guest, at his home away from home, showers his host is reserved for someone who simply fails to grasp the point. Just like the interlocutor of the other fragment, who is forced to admit that he does not know anything about the shipping trade (Kafka 1983a: 248), Salvatore is evidently in no position to learn anything from what Gracchus has just told him. An emblem of a person tied by civic duty to a particular place, the mayor cannot conceive of Gracchus's extraordinary (hi)story (*Geschichte*), one that is not about to end, either here in Riva or elsewhere. Understanding the extraordinary nature of the *Geschichte* would have entailed the realisation that the reversal of the existing order not only prohibits Gracchus from staying permanently in Riva, but that the very distinction of 'you versus us' cannot apply as long as one does not grasp that the hunter is both host and guest, native earthling and eternity-bound stranger at the same time. Gracchus does not 'propose to stay' (*gedenken zu bleiben*) in Riva because it is not for him to propose *anything at all*. But even more importantly, and likewise true to his words, he 'does not commemorate/remember' (*gedenken*). As suggested by the interlocutor's lack of understanding in the supplementary fragment, and by Gracchus's own earlier lapse of memory upon seeing the mayor, here in Riva one cannot count on either remembering or being remembered. In the end, the hunter cancels his own earlier claim to knowledge of the other ('I knew it'), replacing it with nothing but an assertion of his own present identity ('I am here, more than that I do not know'). But we should know better than to take his word for it on either count. Gracchus's presence is not something to be counted on with confidence, for he needs to be absent before he can return again, forever.

2

Gracchus's travel story thus clearly does not make sense in terms of Frank's historical narrative. The historical indeterminacy of the moment of his arrival and departure, it seems, must be because of the nature of writing, the inability of language to fix the meaning of the hunter's peregrinations. Perhaps everything would have been easier if Gracchus had brought along a photograph album. The nineteenth century, after all, had witnessed both the establishment of modern academic historiography and the invention of photography. Conceived as external tokens of an enhanced access to the past, photographs were recognised early on to be essential components of the historical archive that the historians were intent on filling to the rafters. Jacob Burckhardt noted to this effect:

> Surely our time is better equipped for an understanding of the past than any earlier time. In terms of external aids it can draw on the accessibility of all writings (*Literaturen*) provided by extended travel and language-learning in recent times, as well as the greatly increased scope of philology; furthermore, the accessibility of archives, the accessibility of monuments [*Denkmäler*] thanks to travel and the resultant images, photographs in particular. (1956: 10)

Travel thus became first and foremost a means of accumulating images, in a quest for an improved retrieval of historical memory. By the time of the late twentieth century, any family on vacation was able attest to this (Sontag 1979: 9), and the reason had essentially remained the same. Even though photographs present that which they picture in a fundamentally discontinuous manner, they still function as isolated 'pieces of evidence in an ongoing biography or history' (166). Whether it be a matter of establishing the historical record or of validating personal experience, photographs thus attain the status of seemingly incontrovertible links to the past.

As travel narratives of one kind or another, Sebald's works raise the question of whether literature may be said to serve a function comparable to these proverbial 'Kodak Memories' – that is, whether verbal narratives that include images are to be read in terms of their evidentiary quality. Sebald's narrators are all taken by the desire to collect evidence of their travels – whether these are undertaken as an outright escape from self, society or persecution, or in pursuit of particular scholarly projects – and one might quickly surmise that it is these memorabilia (photographs, maps, tickets, postcards) that provide the text with its mnemonic function. By invoking the evidentiary quality of the image, the literary text might thus finally be able to arrest the wandering of its meaning, and become part of the history of the motif, once and for all. However, rather than continuing the hermeneutic lineage sketched by Manfred Frank, Sebald's integration of references to 'The Hunter Gracchus' in his first prose book *Vertigo* undermines the notion that a definite historical meaning may be attached to the infinite journey.

In the summer of 1987, the narrator of the second part of the book, 'All'estero', travels from Vienna via Venice to Verona, in part to probe his rather hazy memories of an earlier trip to Verona seven years previously, and perhaps to record some of them (*V*: 81/97). Part of this process of verification consists in the ongoing collection of photographic mementos. Sometimes these are hard to come by. In Verona, the narrator apparently forgets his camera when he returns to a pizzeria, now closed and boarded up, in which he had had a memorably miserable dining experience on his previous visit. Next door, as fate would have it, there is a photographic shop. For unexplained reasons, the owner of the shop refuses to take a picture of the establishment next door, and the narrator is forced to convince a German tourist to do him the favour. Hesitantly, the German agrees to send the picture to the narrator's home in England once it has been developed, but only after being provided with a ten-mark note. However, for reasons equally unknown, he refuses to take a second photograph of a flock of pigeons sitting on the roof of the building. The presence of the corresponding photograph in Sebald's book suggests that the tourist kept his word and sent the picture, if indeed we choose to believe the narrator's account of the picture's origin (Fig. 10.1). The photograph, it seems, will handily serve as a token of memory of the Verona visit. Not only does the image preserve the memory of this day in August 1987 but also the motivation for taking it ultimately stems, or so the narrator claims, from its connection to an earlier *memory image* dating from October 1980, the time of his previous visit:

> The image that had lodged in my mind when I fled Verona, and which had recurred time after time, with extreme clarity, before I was at last able to forget it (*ehe ich es vergessen konnte*), now presented itself to me again, strangely distorted – two men in black silver-buttoned tunics, who were carrying out from a rear courtyard a bier on which lay, under a floral-patterned drape, what was plainly the body of a human being. (*V*: 125/147)

This 'mental image', of course, has a textual basis: it is taken straight from the opening paragraph of 'The Hunter Gracchus'. The relation between the supposed mental image and the photograph is established by something that is itself absent: the pigeons. The mayor Salvatore learned of Gracchus's impending arrival through a pigeon's waking him and his wife on the night before to let him know – not by delivering a written message but by speaking into his ear – that Gracchus was coming and ought to be welcomed. Not only was this pigeon capable of speech, it was also 'as big as a rooster' – a bird as extraordinary, in other words, as Salvatore will find Gracchus's whole story to be. Also, Salvatore eventually learns from Gracchus that a flock of pigeons flies ahead of his barque wherever it goes, and indeed pigeons are just outside the window of the house into which Gracchus has been carried upon his arrival.

The attempt on the part of Sebald's narrator to have the German tourist take a photograph of the pigeons on the roof of the Pizzeria Verona was apparently motivated, or so we may assume, by a desire to document the coincidence of an involuntary memory image (Gracchus on the bier) and a physical object (pigeons). That photograph, however, is physically absent from the book, and there is nothing about the Pizzeria Verona that would indicate any verifiable

Fig. 10.1

connection between the reported situation and Kafka's story. Rather than confirming the supposedly evidentiary essence of photography, then, this image is marked by an essential lack. We have every reason to be skeptical about the internal memory image Sebald's narrator cites as the trigger for having the photograph taken, the image supposedly providing the plain façade of the building with a deeper meaning. In the picture, the pigeons, trusted carriers of messages for centuries, are nowhere to be seen. They do not speak to us in the way that the mutant pigeon spoke to Salvatore. There is no message, not even one of a successful displacement of the memory image by the photograph, which may – or may not – be what the narrator had in mind when asking the tourist to take it for him. Sebald's story, in other words, is incapable of proving the *truth* of Kafka's own statement: 'The reason one photographs things is to chase them from one's mind. My stories are something like a closing of the eyes' (cit. Barthes 1984: 65). The possibility always remains that, unable to obliterate unwanted memories, one will, like Gracchus, be forced to open one's eyes once again, staring a person in the face who will appear utterly familiar and unfamiliar at the same time, like the mayor Salvatore. And sure enough, a person named 'Salvatore' will meet Sebald's narrator in a bar immediately following the photograph episode, reading a book by Leonardo Sciascia (*V*: 127/149–50).

The absence of a determinate meaning of the pizzeria photograph for a reconstruction of both the psychical economy and the identity of the narrator parallels Gracchus's refusal to come clean about his story. Sebald's text, in its citation of Kafka's, resists its own inscription into a (hi)story of a motif and of motivation. The explicit photographic image and that which cannot be seen in it fail to meet the expectation that the narrative will tell a story 'briefly, but coherently, about how things are' with the narrator – or with the author, for that matter, whose identification papers are presented earlier in Sebald's travel narrative for inspection by the reader (Fig. 10.2). The vertigo overcoming the eternal traveller whenever he tries to pin down his spatial position and his identity remains ineluctably separated from a personal, psychological constitution. The status of such a constitution would make it necessary to ascertain the existence of memory images, either as causes or as effects of certain feelings. Sebald indicates the impossibility of a diagnosis of this sort from the very beginning, in the title itself: *Schwindel. Gefühle.* The full stops separating vertigo from feelings, and feelings from the body of the text, indicate that personal, biographical inferences would be hazardous here. The passport picture presented as part of the text has been voided, its validity as a lawful means of identification struck out. This vertigo, then, is not a personal weakness, nothing for which anyone could be held responsible. By bringing about vertigo, the photograph does not grant us access to the narrator's emotions.

Sebald makes this very clear in the third part of the book, 'Dr. K. Takes the Waters at Riva', a fictional reconstruction of Kafka's journey from Vienna to

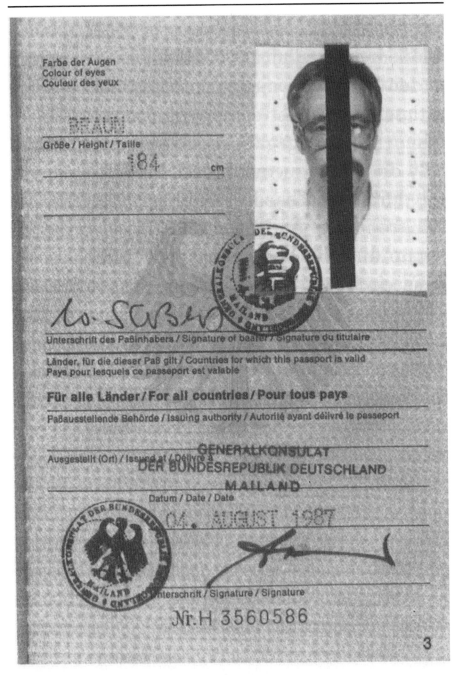

Fig. 10.2

Riva via Venice, Trieste, Verona and Desenzano in September and October of 1913. I say 'fictional' because the object of the narrative is not 'Kafka' but 'Dr. K.' – who may just as well be a certain Dr. Katzenberger, or some other travel-ler.[1] Sebald's reconstruction of Dr. K.'s experiences during this journey draws on remarks in Kafka's letters and diaries, but also ventures into purely specu-lative descriptions of Dr. K.'s emotional state. The narrator speaks, for example, of K.'s 'dejectedness' (*V*: 142/164), his 'violent aversion' (*V*: 143/165), a 'surge of a sociable feeling' (*V*: 144/165), 'feelings of both gratitude and dis-taste' (*V*: 149/171), a 'slight surge of confidence and a species of tacit solidar-ity' (*V*: 157/179) and a 'sense of peaceable quiescence' (*V*: 158/180). To trace these internal states back to Kafka's letters to Felice or to his diary is either to fall into a trap or to set a trap oneself. After all, Kafka himself noted shortly after his return from Riva: 'I am unable to note down anything of importance for the purposes of remembering' (Kafka 1983e: 235). The narrator thus feigns more emotional insight and memory capacity concerning the days in Riva than his ostensible subject, 'Kafka'. The writings by Kafka that do exist from this period and that one might expect to secure the reference of reports concerning 'Dr. K.', in turn, do not necessarily provide a safer ground for biographical spec-ulation. Little over a month after returning from his trip, Kafka notes in his diary: 'I am gripped by reading the diary. Is that because I am now no longer even the least bit secure in the present? Everything seems to me to be a construc-tion. Every remark by someone else, every random gaze turns everything inside me around, even that which has been forgotten' (Kafka 1983e: 241). Everything can be inverted, even as regards what we might consider self-perception, if descriptions are constructions, and if they can affect not only that which was noted down as memory, but also that which has been forgotten. Hence, there is nothing inherently *wrong* with the construction attempted by Sebald's narrator, as long as we recognise it for what it is: a *Schwindel* (decep-tion), or, more precisely yet, a *Gefühlsschwindel* (a deception of the emotions, an emotional deception).

Part of the deceptive story is the supposition that a determinate cause may be found for Dr. K.'s emotional state on his journey, namely, his relation to F. It is this supposition that guides the narrator in a reading of 'The Hunter Gracchus' that maps Gracchus's story onto that of Dr. K.:

> Over the years that followed, lengthy shadows fell upon those autumn days at Riva, which, as Dr. K. on occasion said to himself, had been so beautiful and so appalling, and from these shadows there gradually emerged the silhouette of a barque with masts of an inconceivable height and sails dark and hanging in folds. Three whole years it takes until the vessel, as if it were being borne across the waters, gently drifts into the little port of Riva. (*V*: 163–4/185–6)

Three years, that is, before Dr. K. will write the fragments relating the story of Gracchus, the hunter who is bearing a version of Kafka's name: 'graculus' (Latin) and 'kavka' (Czech) both mean 'jackdaw'. Consistent with his speculative spirit, the narrator offers his interpretation of the story in the light of his descriptions of Dr. K.'s changing emotional seascape: 'it seems to me that the meaning of Gracchus the huntsman's ceaseless journey lies in a penitence for a longing for love, such as invariably besets Dr. K., as he explains in one of his countless *Fledermaus*-letters to Felice' (V: 164/188). This interpretation of Gracchus's infinite journey by Sebald's narrator has next to nothing to do with the history of a motif suggested by Frank, and it is one against which Kafka was unable to guard himself with his written exclamation: 'For the last time, psychology!' (Kafka 1983e: 79). For better or worse, the drift of meaning, for which a 'last time' does not exist, makes possible a reading of the hunter's journey in terms of the personal emotional states of Kafka's doppelgänger 'Dr. K.' By no means, however, does Sebald's narrator therefore have the last word, the one that would fix the meaning of this extraordinary story. After all, he himself even remarks that the suggestion that Gracchus would have shot a chamois in the Black Forest, where these animals have never been at home, must be 'one of the strangest pieces of misinformation in all the tales that have ever been told' (V: 165/188).[2] In other words, Gracchus himself was a swindler (*Schwindler*) all along. Sebald's narrator and his readers are forced to keep hunting the hunter, chasing a ghost.

3

The animal kingdom in 'The Hunter Gracchus' is indicative of anything but a *natural* order. Clearly, we are dealing with artificial constructions: Gracchus, in violation of his job as a wolf hunter, boasts about shooting a chamois in a place where, as far as anyone knows, there could not have been one; Gracchus's arrival is announced by a 'real' pigeon that is as big as a rooster and able to speak; finally, the hunter himself, who bears the name of a bird, locates himself in a different taxonomical class and reveals that he has turned into an insect of the order *lepidoptera*, the one probably most desired by hunters – a butterfly: 'On this infinitely wide staircase I spend my time, sometimes at the top, sometimes below, sometimes to the right, sometimes to the left, always in motion. The hunter has become a butterfly. Do not laugh' (Kafka 1983c: 77). Clearly, Gracchus is not joking. He really *has* undergone a metamorphosis, at least metaphorically, turning himself into that animal which figures in Nabokov (1967: 12) as the master metaphor for translation that, much coveted, remains forever elusive and in continual metamorphosis, or, if caught, turns out to be only an empty shell without content, pinned up in a display case.

Embarking on one more journey, we should thus explore the possibility that Gracchus, butterfly that he turns out to be, eventually does find a home within the confines of Sebald's intertextual cosmos after all. One candidate for catching up with the meaning of the figure of Gracchus would be the man with the butterfly net roaming through the four stories in Sebald's subsequent book *The Emigrants*. One of the places in which this other hunter turns up would seem to articulate the promise of finally coming home: *Ithaca*.[3] It is the place where the narrator's great-uncle Ambros Adelwarth has committed himself to a 'private mental home' after travelling the world for many years as valet and travel companion of the rich New York eccentric Cosmo Solomon. In apparent contrast to Gracchus, those two eventually do return from their travels, but Cosmo, suffering from depression and failed attempts to 'regain the past' (*E*: 96–7/140) eventually perishes in the Samaria Sanatorium in Ithaca, NY. His erstwhile companion remains in the services of the Solomon family for many years to come, but eventually he, too, falls prey to both depression and what appear to his niece Fini to be symptoms of Korsakoff's syndrome, namely, the compensation of amnesia by means of fantastic inventions of what he claims are experiences from his travels. In 1952, he suddenly disappears from his home in Mamaroneck, leaving behind a visiting card on which he has scribbled: 'Have gone to Ithaca. Yours ever, Ambros'. Adelwarth's niece Fini remarks to the narrator that it took her a while to understand what he meant by Ithaca (*E*: 103/150). Indeed, as Sebald's readers we share the difficulty of ascertaining what this message means. The metaphorical reading would suggest more closure than seems warranted, given that both Cosmo and Ambros hardly find a home in any meaningful sense in upstate New York. One time, after Fini has found out about her uncle's whereabouts and visits him at the sanatorium, they both happen upon a strange sight as they are looking out of the window of Ambros's room where

> a middle-aged man appeared, holding a white net on a pole in front of him and occasionally taking curious jumps. Uncle Adelwarth stared straight ahead, but he registered my bewilderment all the same, and said: It's the butterfly man, you know. He comes round here quite often. (*E*: 104/151)

He comes round here quite often. The butterfly hunter, that is, like the butterfly Gracchus, who periodically reappears in places like Riva, taking leave only to reappear at some unspecified later date. There is something extraordinary in this. Vladimir Nabokov, the referent of Sebald's allusion as a lifelong 'butterfly man' and resident of Ithaca, NY, around the time of Adelwarth's stay at the Samaria Sanatorium, would not have disagreed:

> America has shown even more of this morbid interest in my retiary activities than other countries have – perhaps because I was in my forties when I came there to live, and the older the man, the queerer he looks with a butterfly net in his hand. (Nabokov 1967: 131)

Hardly has he arrived in Ithaca than Sebald thus sends us on our way again by means of his text. The town of Ithaca is ultimately no more than a place one passes through on the way to somewhere else, and it seems fitting that its one-time resident Nabokov, who performed his 'retiary activities' wherever he went, should likewise pass through the tales of all four narrators in *The Emigrants*. He appears in a photograph (Fig. 10.3), a bibliographical reference (*E*: 43/65), and an uncertain memory image that Max Ferber tries but fails to capture in a painting (*E*: 174/259–60). Ithaca, it appears, is not as homely a place as one might have hoped.

As far as Ambros Adelwarth is concerned, he does come to his physical end in the Samaria clinic, where the electric shock treatments devastate him at least as much as his illness itself. Still, the excuse he provides for showing up late to the appointment that will prove to be his last only underlines that unfinished business, signified by a reappearance of the Nabokov figure, is bound to come around even in the face of death: 'It must have slipped my mind whilst I was waiting for the butterfly man' (*E*: 115/170). Dr. Abramsky, assistant at the time and eventual successor to Prof. Fahnstock, who had ordered Adelwarth's treatments, relays these words verbatim to the narrator, who has travelled to Ithaca in hope of finding out more about his great-uncle. Fahnstock has long since died when the narrator comes to Ithaca in 1984; the sanatorium is now closed, and Abramsky lives on the estate with a butler as his only companion. He has come to realise and reject the 'scientific furor' with which his erstwhile superior Fahnstock had applied excessively high doses of electric shocks, propelled by the belief that he had discovered a 'psychiatric miracle cure'. It was Adelwarth's case, Abramsky reports, that initiated a complete change (*E*: 110/161) in his own thinking, culminating in his eventual abandonment of all professional activities in 1969. Living at Samaria, he now keeps bees and listens to the mice who are chewing away at Fahnstock's archive where the records of his patients are stored:

> at all events, on nights when there is no wind blowing I can hear a con-
> stant scurrying and rustling in the dried-out shell of the building, and at
> times, when a full moon rises beyond the trees, I imagine I can hear the
> pathetic song of a thousand tiny upraised throats. Nowadays I place all
> my hope in the mice. (*E*: 112/165)

Yet another Linnean class: not birds or insects this time, but quadrupeds. The mice, destroying the archival memory of a psychiatric approach that failed to cure Adelwarth or to tell us what the real reasons were for his breakdown and what its relation was to his life of travel, point us back from Ithaca to where we came from: to Kafka and the question of hope. Abramsky intimates that only the ongoing destruction of the historical record would be an occasion for hope, not its further production or the deciphering of what has already been

Fig. 10.3

written. In Kafka's story 'Josefine the Singer, or the Mouse People' (Kafka 1983d), the mouse people, 'a people strong in hope' and at the same time threatened by 'a certain exhaustion and hopelessness' (Kafka 1983d: 209), ambiguously articulate that very same hope. Separated by an ineradicable difference from the artist Josephine both in their admiration for, and their misunderstanding of, her, they are in much the same position as the mayor Salvatore is to Gracchus, or – as indicated by the comma in Kafka's story title – like the narrator of 'All'estero' from the subject of his account, 'Dr. K.'. Sebald's typographical manipulation in the title of his book points to the vertiginous dissociation of literature from any emotional 'truth', and this functions analogously to the separation of Josephine's 'artistry' from the hermeneutic horizon articulated by what reappears in Sebald as the 'pathetic song' of her audience. The very fact that the song of the singular artist Josephine is ultimately 'nothing special in and of itself' from the perspective of those who listen to it prevents any 'true' mutual understanding, rather than facilitating a common bond. Ultimately, the vertigo induced by such lack of understanding is owing not to the kind of feelings transmitted in writing but rather to the radical uncertainty concerning the very act of transmission itself. Secure transmission would be crucial to any kind of reliable historical memory – a notion which the mouse people in Kafka's story emphatically oppose, 'since we do not do history' (Kafka 1983d: 216). Instead, they interpret Josefine's eventual disappearance – the last sign of her struggle for identity – as a miscalculation in terms of mnemonic economy:

> Strange, how wrongly she calculates, smart as she is, so wrongly that one would almost think that she is not calculating at all but is only being pushed on [*weitergetrieben*] by her fate that in our world can only be a very sad one. (Kafka 1983d: 215–16)

Like Gracchus, Josefine may or may not be counting (on) something, driven to the limit of calculation by the driving wind. In the end, the narrator concludes, she will be 'nothing but a small episode in the history of our people' (Kafka 1983d: 216) – so small, indeed, that its size is forever approaching zero. The mouse people will forget Josefine. After all, how could they so much as measure – much less retain – the significance of a 'historical episode' if they don't subscribe to the tenets of the historians? Josefine's singing, produced by means of 'this nothing of a voice' (Kafka 1983d: 207), did not convey a message to them that would keep her in their memory. Sebald's integration of references to Kafka's travellers Gracchus and Josefine thus articulates a perspective thoroughly sceptical of the reliability and permanence of biographical and historical forms of memory that would fix the meaning of the stories told by Kafka's and Sebald's narrators.

NOTES

1. With the title (in its original German) of this part of the book, 'Dr. K.s Badereise nach Riva', Sebald is alluding to Jean Paul's novella *Dr. Katzenbergers Badereise* (1809), in addition to the more obvious point of reference, the protagonists named 'K.' in Kafka's *The Trial* and *The Castle*.
2. Manfred Frank, too, notes that the chamois, puzzlingly enough, is not native to the region (Frank 1989: 58), but he still seems inclined to take Gracchus and his alleged motivations at face value.
3. The city of Ithaca in ancient Greece is, of course, Odysseus's hometown to which the mythical hero finally returns after his lengthy seafaring adventures.

11

ARCHITECTURE AND CINEMA:
THE REPRESENTATION OF MEMORY IN
W. G. SEBALD'S *AUSTERLITZ*

Russell J. A. Kilbourn

Sebald's universally lauded novels – *Vertigo, The Emigrants, The Rings of Saturn* and *Austerlitz* – pay little or no overt attention to contemporary mass culture in their unrelenting obsession with modern European history, focused in the individual's relation to a past that is ultimately as irrecoverable as it is inescapable. Sebald's implied rejection of a potentially ephemeral, technologically mediated mass culture, in favour of a scholar's mining of literary, historical, architectural and other sources has resulted in a comparable disregard by critics of his engagement with such paradigmatic twentieth-century cultural forms as cinema. With respect to *Austerlitz*, at least, this critical oversight must be addressed in the context of Sebald's abiding, if obliquely presented, preoccupation with the Holocaust, as not merely the central, signal historical event of the last century, but in terms of its endurance, in however repressed a form, for individual memory.

In what follows I compare Sebald's use in *Austerlitz* of architecture and cinema – the latter following historically and conceptually upon the former – as successive metaphors for memory as an exteriorised, visually constituted phenomenon. Sebald's emphasis on memory as culturally constructed through historically determined modes of representation does not so much override an overtly psychoanalytical model as demonstrate implicitly the irreducibly metaphorical or tropological nature of the psychoanalytical account of memory. This is particularly true for a Freudian topographical model (the conscious/unconscious binary) whose mechanism or trope of repression can be seen as a kind of modern variation of the conscious forgetting required by premodern, self-consciously text-based, apophatic theology. Psychoanalysts might argue that the centrality of trauma to this negative model of memory is the feature that in *Austerlitz* defines the difference between the premodern and the modern (or postmodern) subject of memory. In short: it is only through recourse to highly visual and spatial tropological systems that memory in *Austerlitz* becomes conceivable, let alone representable in textual form. That Sebald favours the cinematic and architectural over the doctrinaire psychoanalytical becomes clear in the novel's unflagging interrogation of the mediation of language and text in the construction of collective and individual identity alike.

The textual surface of Sebald's pseudo-documentarist narratives is regularly interrupted by uncaptioned black-and-white photographs. With this simple technique Sebald has succeeded either in inventing a new genre or in furthering an existing sub-genre and making it his own. He also establishes a visual-verbal dialectic, shoring up the alleged veracity of his narrative by exploiting the reader's faith in the authenticity of *visual* evidence, while simultaneously calling into question the limits of representation in general. *Austerlitz* in particular is concerned at its heart with the twin questions of the unimaginable and the forgotten. By the end of the book the reader is left wondering whether the plethora of concrete images has clarified or complicated the process of interpreting Sebald's protracted meditation on memory within a highly sophisticated fictional narrative.

While extending the writer's habitual use of photographic images, *Austerlitz* goes further than the earlier novels in forging a subtle but powerful relationship with cinema. First, references to such actual works as Fritz Lang's 1924 *Nibelungen* films (*A*: 6/10) are integrated into the novel's quasi-fictional world.[1] More significantly, specific films in the European 'art cinema' tradition by Jean Cocteau, Alain Resnais[2] and others are quietly referenced in the course of the story, scenes and images woven into the novelistic text in an allusively dream-like manner reminiscent of Nabokov who, with Kafka, is one of Sebald's primary literary antecedents.[3] Cocteau's resetting of the Orpheus myth (*Orphée*, 1949) and Resnais's *Last Year at Marienbad* (1961) are seminal cinematic meditations on memory, longing and death, engaging in very different types of formal experimentation. Each of these films contributes in its own way to Western culture's long-standing association between memory and death, a relation often figured in spatial terms as a realm of enigmatic forms and meanings. This association finds its *locus classicus* in epic, from Homer through Virgil to Dante, after which it persists in the modern period in the novel's extension of certain epic tropes within a radically different epistemology. More generally, the conflation of different architectural metaphors for memory – memory as both labyrinth and city of the dead, through which the protagonist must journey as in the *katabases* of classical epic and the ironic, metaphorical underworld journeys of novelistic heroes – acquires renewed and increasingly specific significance in the post-Holocaust context in which Sebald writes.[4] Thus the intertextual relation between *Austerlitz* and the aforementioned films conditions and amplifies the novel's preoccupation with an analogous set of themes, justifying a comparison of otherwise disparate forms of narrative.

Of *Austerlitz*'s cinematic intertexts, however, the most significant is a 1944 pseudo-documentary produced by the Nazis in the Theresienstadt ghetto outside Prague. This film (originally titled *Der Führer schenkt den Juden eine Stadt* [The Führer Gives a City to the Jews])[5] represents the successful effort to present as real to visiting Red Cross officials a simulated 'Jewish utopia', constructed ostensibly for the 'security' of its inhabitants and the 'preservation' of their culture. Jacques Austerlitz, the novel's eponymous protagonist, learns that his Czech-Jewish mother perished in the eastern camps after deportation to Theresienstadt. He becomes obsessed with obtaining, viewing and re-viewing a copy of this 'documentary', in a vain effort to glimpse her still-young face, all memory of which, in the intervening fifty years, he has unwittingly obliterated.

Sebald uses the Theresienstadt film to represent Austerlitz's sudden and traumatic recovery of his childhood memories, after a life-long, self-imposed amnesia: a response, governed by the need for self-preservation, to the primal trauma of being sent in 1939 on a *Kindertransport* from Prague to a new life with a new name and new parents in an entirely alien place – an experience which deprives him in one stroke of language, country, family and identity (Jaggi 2001b: 2). Austerlitz grows up in a remote part of Wales, raised by a Methodist minister and his sickly wife.

The novel's nameless narrator meets Austerlitz (an architectural historian) for the first time in 1967 in the Antwerp Central Train Station waiting room. In keeping with this opening context, the novel's presiding spirit is quite literally Time, the reigning deity of both narrative and of the capitalist age – of which Europe's great train stations are emblematic (*A*: 12/17–18). Their first colloquy takes place under the bored gaze of the 'goddess of time past', in the person of a peroxided barmaid ensconced beneath an enormous clock, the six-foot-long hand of which jerks forward like a 'sword of justice . . . slicing off the next one-sixtieth of an hour from the future and coming to a halt with such a menacing quiver that one's heart almost stopped' (*A*: 9/12–13). Austerlitz describes clock time as one of modernity's greatest inventions. After all, it was only by standardising time in the mid-nineteenth century – by synchronising clocks and dividing the world up into time zones and thus imposing a new kind of order, says Austerlitz – that we could then 'hasten through the gigantic spaces separating us from each other' (*A*: 14/18). But Austerlitz is critical of prevailing conceptions of time. Time, for him, is inherently artificial, and the view of time he advocates is one that recognises the conceptual interpenetration of time and space. Time in his view is inherently subjective, predicated on the individual's experience of duration and change. In effect, Austerlitz represents a phenomenology of time that owes as much to theories of visual perspective (and other technologies of seeing) as it does to Nabokov, Proust, Bergson, St Augustine or classical thought. In fact, it gradually becomes clear that what interests Austerlitz is not time per se – however we may define it – but memory, which, instantiated through specific spatial-visual metaphors, can be seen to determine a particular phenomenology of time. It is in this respect that cinema more fundamentally enters the novel's fictional world, providing Sebald with yet another frame of reference that is at once necessarily time bound (as a narrative medium) and yet inescapably spatial in its visual realism. It is also this concrete, spatial, exteriorised characteristic of cinema as a predominantly visual medium that will be revealed, much later in the novel, as a paradoxical obstacle in Austerlitz's quest to uncover the 'truth' of his past via the technologies of a century biased toward visual modes of representation, within a culture increasingly determined by the logic of mass production.

What neither interlocutor knows is that their conversations about pre-twentieth-century architectural history are only the beginning of the long and difficult process of Austerlitz's quest to discover the history of which he does not speak: his forgotten early childhood and his memories of his real parents in 1930s Prague. In a later conversation Austerlitz tells the narrator how he is haunted by hallucinatory faces and figures, eidetic images from the faded world of his own childhood manifesting themselves in 1980s London as if from the past or from an afterlife (A: 180/184). These visions come to a head in Liverpool Street Station, which Austerlitz visits by chance a few weeks before the completion of major renovations which would completely change the station's internal layout (A: 195/199). At this point the station is its 'dark' and 'sinister' nineteenth-century self, which Austerlitz describes as 'a kind of entrance to the underworld' (A: 180/184) – a place through which 'innumerable people passed in great tides', like the untold numbers 'undone by death' of which Eliot speaks in The Wasteland.[6] For reasons he cannot explain, when Austerlitz sees a turbaned porter disappear through a low portal in a construction hoarding, he follows the man through the door, parts a heavy curtain and steps into the past, in a sense that is neither exclusively figurative nor exclusively literal. He felt, he says, 'like an actor who, upon making his entrance, has completely and irrevocably forgotten not only the lines he knew by heart but the very part he has so often played' (A: 189/193). The cavernous disused Ladies' Waiting Room opens up before him in a vision of a vast, infinitely involuted universe of architectural impossibility, a 'vision of imprisonment and liberation' (A: 189/195; cf. Annan 2001: 1), which he cannot resolve into either 'a ruin or a building in the process of construction' (A: 191/195). Austerlitz remarks that both ideas are right in a way, since he has entered a part of the station undergoing renovation right on top of its original structure, but also because he has entered, seemingly entirely by chance, the labyrinth of his own lost memories. 'Scraps of memory [began] to drift through the outlying regions of [his] mind: images . . . memories behind and within which many things much further back in the past seemed to lie' (*A*: 192–3/196). 'I felt, said Austerlitz, that the waiting room where I stood as if dazzled contained all the hours of my past life, all the suppressed and extinguished fears and wishes I had ever entertained' (*A*: 192–3/196).

Both the tone and the setting here invoke St Augustine, who, in Book 10 of the *Confessions* lays the foundations for a conceptual bridge between a mnemonic topology of classical rhetoric and a 'postmodern' phenomenology of memory predicated on a premodern approach to the representability and 'exteriority' of this aspect of individual subjectivity.[7] Behind Augustine's theory of memory lies the classical art or 'technique' of memory, in which a public speaker or narrator constructs a mental *topos* (often in the form of a sizeable architectural structure), a series of *loci* or positions and the mnemonic images specific to these *loci*. The speaker, as subject of memory, then associates specific words, phrases or concepts with each image. By moving through this imaginative space, the subject can pick and chose from among the images with their corresponding discursive 'labels'. In this manner (after much conscious training) long and complex speeches or narratives can be recalled with relative ease (Yates 1966: 1–26). This amounts to an artificial model of memory as a set of practices carried out within a purely imaginative space.

Heir to this habit of thought, Augustine finds the architectural metaphor inadequate, particularly when it comes to a rationalisation of the 'presence' of a certain kind of radically *negative* mnemonic content – in other words, the presence in the memory of something or someone never before encountered – God, for example. As Augustine says: 'there are some things in man which even his own spirit within him does not know' (*Confessions* 10. Cf. Gasché 1994: 12). The crucial difference between Austerlitz and Augustine as subjects of their respective narratives is that Austerlitz's experience is predicated on the transformation of concrete built space, through narrative description, into the exteriorised space in which memory operates. This transformation temporarily effaces the gap between Austerlitz's past and present, as he is suddenly granted entry to a space of whose historical existence he had long since ceased to be aware. According to Brian Stock, for Augustine the written and read text itself inevitably replaces architecture as the metaphor for memory (1996: 216). For Austerlitz, however, architecture becomes the *literal* mnemonic space, the operation of which is recounted in a narrative whose meaning cannot be divorced from its textual status.[8]

Austerlitz's encounter with his forgotten past in Liverpool Street Station harks back to Augustine's discussion in *Confessions* of the *anamnesic* aspect of his memory: his capacity to recall certain things that he was not aware he already knew, and only had, as it were, to produce from their 'place of storage' (Augustine 1988: 218). While Austerlitz's memory of himself and his foster parents is clearly not something he always already held in 'storage', the effect of his sudden and traumatic recovery of this memory is nevertheless an *anamnesis*, not in the Platonic sense but in the literal sense of an 'unforgetting' that is brought about in the first place through an involuntary act of unremembering, or *apomnesis* (literally 'to remember away').

According to Stock's persuasive reading of the *Confessions*, Augustine's meditative analysis of memory moves in a direction opposite to that of the specific concerns of this study, as he comes to abandon the 'hopeless quest' to make, with memory's aid, 'an inventory of things that he has experienced in the world in an effort to rise above himself' (1996: 208). This *apomnesic* approach – a kind of forgetting-as-divestment – is according to Stock abandoned 'in favour of a pragmatic approach' through a revalued and inverted form of Platonic *anamnesis* (Stock 1996: 213). My argument is that one of the results of the emergence of modernity is the inversion of this sequence from a positive modality (*anamnesis* as 'un-forgetting') to a negative one, a form of initially *wilful* forgetting: memory as the only means of 'measuring' the incommensurable gap between the self and an absolutely absent other (*apomnesis* as 'un-remembering'). (As we will see below, the act of will involved effaces itself in the process, invoking inevitable comparisons with Freudian repression.) This approach to memory partakes of the logic of premodern *apophatic* theologies, even if it does not share their orientation toward a radically negative conception of God, whose operation is inseparable from the text in which it is expressed.[9] This is therefore not truly the opposite of Augustine's complex, nuanced thought so much as an alternative to it, the difference turning on the primary issue of the self's relative autonomy in a world from which God – which is to say an *idea* of God – appears to have withdrawn, or rather *to have been* withdrawn. Similarly, Augustine's theory of memory, predicated on his essentially *positive* relation to God, has an internal orientation one might assume is utterly lacking in the mnemonic dynamics of most modern literature. However, a closer examination of representative literary and critical materials suggests that the notion of a thoroughgoing secularisation of modern subjectivity is inadequate. *Austerlitz* affords one very telling example of a protagonist who is profoundly shaken by the discovery, late in life, that his subjectivity is constituted in a negative dialogic relation with an other, all memory of whom he repressed while still a young boy.[10]

It is tempting to describe the scene in the waiting room as Austerlitz's Proustian moment, where his 'involuntary memory' is engaged through a series of serendipitous events. But the differences are telling: rather than a catalyst for involuntary memory, the station and waiting room operate in a more complex manner as the externalised, concrete representation of the structure (*topos*) of Austerlitz's hitherto suppressed and/or displaced long-term memory, laid bare to him for the first time, in a description that signifies at both individual and socio-historical levels. Within this vast pseudo-metaphorical structure he encounters highly realistic mnemonic images: bodies, but especially *faces*, for it is in the face that identity can be read – or so our predominantly visual culture would have us believe (Yates 1966: 4; Melchior-Bonnet 2001: 101). Sebald engages with this culture not only through photographs, but through extensive thematisation of architecture and cinema. The scene in the Ladies' Waiting Room foregrounds the novel's exploitation of the vast spaces and perspectives of a particular, imaginatively reconstituted, edifice. At this moment Austerlitz sees not just his long-dead Welsh foster parents but also the one they have come to meet, his six-year old self:

> for the first time in as far back as I can remember I recollected myself as a small child, at the moment when I realized that it must have been to this same waiting room I had come on my arrival in England over half a century ago. (*A*: 193/197)

In a sense that cannot be described as simply figurative, this little boy, who is Austerlitz's past self, has been waiting there in the disused waiting room ever since, for his adult self to step through the curtain across the threshold of time and remember his own experience.

What the adult Austerlitz does *not* articulate is that he, too, has spent his entire life waiting for this moment of transcendence. And it is only at this meta-mnemonic moment that the adult Austerlitz begins to experience time no longer as a form of space but as something that constantly passes:

> when I saw the boy sitting on the bench I became aware . . . of the destructive effect on me of my desolation through all those past years, and a terrible weariness overcame me at the idea that I had never really been alive, or was only now being born, almost on the eve of my death. (*A*: 194/198)

This chance encounter across the borders of time and memory triggers the life-changing memory-work that is to follow.

Eventually Austerlitz makes his way to Prague, in the hope of tracing his story back to its beginnings – a process which inevitably and irretrievably complicates the familiar conception of time as an inexorably linear process (*A*: 142–3/147–8). Tracking down the now very elderly woman who had been his childhood nanny, Austerlitz learns from her all about his idyllic childhood in mid-1930s Prague, before the War. Gradually his quest crystallises into the desire to recapture his memory of his mother, specifically her face, of which he has no clear recollection, nor any photographs to prompt his memory (*A*: 226–9/231–3).

To this point Austerlitz's personal and scholarly obsession has been the monumental architecture of the age of bourgeois capitalism: 'outsize buildings

[that] cast the shadow of their own destruction before them, and are designed from the first with an eye to their later existence as ruins' (*A*: 23/28) – a remark made when Austerlitz still lacks any direct knowledge of fascist architecture, with its 'Law of Ruins', that would develop out of the great public buildings of the nineteenth century (cf. Eksteins 2000: 317). Such imposing architectural edifices serve the ironic function of abetting rather than dispelling Austerlitz's repression of this specific aspect of Europe's recent past. He reveals to the narrator that his accumulation of architectural historical knowledge had 'served as a substitute or compensatory memory' (*A*: 198/202):

> As far as I was concerned the world ended in the late nineteenth century. I dared go no further than that, although in fact the whole history of the architecture and civilisation of the bourgeois age, the subject of my research, pointed in the direction of the catastrophic events already casting their shadows before them at the time. (*A*: 197/201)

It is as if late nineteenth-century architecture has the capacity to act as harbinger of future events, even as it provides the literal context for his rediscovered memories. The sheer enormity of the hallucinatory dream-vision Austerlitz experiences in the waiting room becomes highly ironic in light of his admission that, over the course of his life, he had 'maintained [his] existence in a smaller and smaller space, [protecting him] from anything that could be connected in any way, however distant, with [his] own early history' (*A*: 198/201–2).

The stations and other monumental buildings of the bourgeois age are not the only architectural structures or public spaces exploited in the elaboration of both setting and character in *Austerlitz*, however. Famous nineteenth-century European resorts feature in all of Sebald's novels. In *Austerlitz* it is the almost mythical spa at Marienbad, now in the Czech Republic, that plays a central but enigmatic function in this novel's plot. This is obliquely anticipated in Austerlitz's lengthy disquisition on European military architecture, exemplified in the star-shaped fortresses of Antwerp and Theresienstadt (*A*: 20; 264–6; 268–70) – a discourse he commences after admitting to the narrator that, in 'his studies of railway architecture . . . he could never quite shake off thoughts of the agony of leave-taking and the fear of foreign places' (*A*: 16/20–1). 'Yet,' he continued, 'it is often our mightiest projects that most obviously betray the degree of our insecurity' (*A*: 16–17/21). As Austerlitz makes clear, such massively fortified towns became militarily redundant before they were even completed, not least because offensive strategies and technologies evolved at a faster pace than construction, which could span decades (*A*: 20/23–4).

With the twentieth century, however, the age-old offensive/defensive binary of a ground war with relatively clear objectives was superseded by a modern form of war, pursued on two simultaneous fronts: mass-produced propaganda concealing mass-produced destruction and death – a war of *representations* as much as violence. According to Jean Baudrillard (1995), this form of *simulacral* warfare began with the Gulf War as the first 'TV War'. In this paper, however, I use the term 'simulacrum' not in Baudrillard's sense of a copy without an original, but in the older, Platonic, meaning of *dis*-simulation: there is something 'real' that is being covered up, something now absent that had been there before – an authentic form of social life, historical reality, or such like.[11] This 'Platonic' simulacral logic can be applied to the two World Wars as the first global conflicts of the age of cinema. There is no space here to explore the extent to which both sides in these conflicts exploited cinema for the propagandistic construction of alternative realities. Of specific interest here is the role played by the film commissioned by the Nazis at Theresienstadt, after its conversion into first a ghetto and then a simulacral all-Jewish spa-town. At a fatal remove, in a series of fragmentary, disjointed scenes, the restored film records for a stunned posterity the faces and gestures of the town's denizens, the vast majority of whom would either die there or after deportation to the death camps in the East, whose existence Theresienstadt was meant to dissimulate.

Restrictions on clientele were not uncommon in many Central European spa-towns, but Marienbad was frequented by well-to-do Jewish families well into the early decades of the twentieth century. When Austerlitz takes his leave of the elderly Vera, his guide to his Prague childhood, she suddenly recalls how, on the day in 1939 that they put him on the train for England from that same station platform, Austerlitz's mother had turned to Vera and remarked how it had only been last summer that they had all left together for a vacation at Marienbad – last year at Marienbad (*A*: 289/293). While Resnais's 1961 film concerns the endless, circular quest for the truth of the past within a planar model of time, Marienbad becomes in *Austerlitz* a signifier for an irretrievably idyllic interlude of happiness (*A*: 289/294). At the mention of the 'three wonderful, almost blissful weeks' he and his family spent at the resort – of which he has no memory – Austerlitz is suddenly reminded of a subsequent trip to Marienbad he made in the early 1970s with the one woman in the novel with whom he has what might be called a romantic relationship (*A*: 290/294).[12] This second trip, intended by his friend Marie de Verneuil as a means of liberating Austerlitz 'from his self-inflicted isolation', turns out to be a quiet disaster, like a trip to a looking-glass underworld in which the Orphic hero loses his beloved to life while he is drawn uncomprehendingly towards death (*A*: 304–5/308–9).[13] He finds no salvation in Marie's offer of love.

The second trip to Marienbad thus stands as one of the book's several ironic *katabases*; as with the waiting-room scene, Marienbad as a physical place is really a metaphorical city of the dead or underworld in *temporal* terms: Austerlitz is incapable of seeing that the profound unease he experiences while there is caused by the fact that he was there before in a time of happiness that he has lost by virtue of his wilful 'unremembering' of his Prague childhood.

That the act of will involved effaces itself in the process is emblematic of the irony of his entire situation. Austerlitz tries to explain himself: 'I had always believed I must be alone, and in spite of my longing for [Marie] I now felt it more than ever before' (*A*: 304/308). Austerlitz then retraces his own journey by train, made in 1939 when he was just five years old, across Germany to the English Channel and, by boat, to Great Britain, where he has resided ever since. At this point the adult Austerlitz realises that his having discovered the sources of his distress had done him little good; his 'reason was powerless against the sense of rejection and annihilation which [he] had always suppressed, and which was now breaking through the walls of its confinement' (*A*: 322/326).

Upon his return to London, Austerlitz suffers a complete mental and physical breakdown – symptomatic, as it seems, of the returning-to-consciousness of his buried past. As part of his recuperation, he studies a book which, not surprisingly, actually exists: H. G. Adler's exhaustive account of 'the setting up, development, and internal organization of the Theresienstadt ghetto' (Adler 1955) written shortly after the end of the war (*A*: 327/331). Austerlitz finds himself mystified by what he calls the ghetto's 'almost futuristic deformation of social life' in its infernal parody of a nineteenth-century worker's paradise (*A*: 331/335). It is at this point in the narrative, in his recounting of Adler's account, that Austerlitz launches into the longest sentence in the entire book, spanning ten pages in the German text (335–45). In the midst of this sentence (as if unconsciously parodic of the insanely bureaucratic discourse of the regime in question), we learn that a significant portion of the people incarcerated in Theresienstadt were sent there under the impression that they were heading to a 'pleasant resort in Bohemia called *Theresienbad*' (my emphasis) – a terrible play on words propagated by the Nazis themselves – a place 'with beautiful gardens, promenades, boarding houses, and villas' (*A*: 335/339). As if inspired by their own deception, in the summer of 1944 the Nazis instigated

> what was described as a *Verschönerungsaktion* or general improvement campaign . . . with an eye to the imminent visit . . . of a Red Cross commission, an event regarded by [the Reich authorities] as a good opportunity to dissimulate the true nature of their deportation policy. (*A*: 339/343)

The plan was carried out to the letter, and the Red Cross officials were fooled, having seen for themselves 'the friendly, happy folk who had been spared the horrors of war' (*A*: 341/344). During the summer of 1944 the Nazis then produced a film about their 'model' ghetto in order to deceive the rest of the world about the true plight of the Jews in occupied Europe – *The Führer Gives a City to the Jews*. As Austerlitz notes, by the time the soundtrack of so-called Jewish folk music was completed, a considerable number of the people who had appeared in the film were no longer alive (*A*: 342/345). According to statistics provided in the restored film's opening credits, '140,000 Jews were brought to

Terezin; 33,430 died in Terezin; 87,000 were deported to death camps in the East'. That leaves a mere 19,570 survivors. What neither Austerlitz nor Adler mention is that this film was directed not by the Nazis themselves but by one of their most famous prisoners, actor and film director Kurt Gerron, known for originating the role of the Street Singer in the first production of *The Threepenny Opera* in 1928. Not long after completing the film, for which he had been brought to Theresienstadt with the promise of survival, Gerron too was deported to Auschwitz. Nor did the film survive the war, apparently: 'Adler himself, said Austerlitz, never saw [the film], and thought it was lost without a trace' (*A*: 342/345). With these words Austerlitz's ten-page sentence comes to an end.

The complete absence of photographic or other images in Adler's tome leaves Austerlitz 'unable to cast [his] mind back to the ghetto and picture [his] mother . . . there at the time' (*A*: 342/346). He imagines viewing this film and recognising his mother, 'beyond any possibility of doubt, a young woman as she would be by comparison with me today' (*A*: 342/346). He obtains a copy of the film and eventually, after careful and repeated scrutiny in super-slow-motion, like a latter-day Odysseus he finds in a sequence towards the end of the film what he takes to be his dead mother's young face (*A*: 350–1/354). The face Austerlitz discerns is indeed clearly visible in the film in its extant form. This anguished sequence reveals itself as perhaps the central ironic underworld journey in the book, although this one transpires in an entirely metaphorical manner, insofar as Austerlitz has moved from his physical travels to the site of 'Theresienbad', to reading Adler's tome in an attempt to comprehend better what he could not at first hand, to viewing the long-lost film in a final effort simply to find the image of his mother's youthful self – at once very near and yet at an infinite remove, by virtue of cinema's uniquely powerful capacity for verisimilitudinous representation of what is no longer and perhaps never was.

As the camera pans the members of the audience (Fig. 11.1), the young, attractive woman is briefly visible, listening with an almost beatific smile to 'the first performance of a piece of music composed in Theresienstadt, Pavel Haas's study for string orchestra' (*A*: 350/353) (Fig. 11.2).

> She looks, [says Austerlitz] so I tell myself as I watch, just as I imagined [my mother] from my faint memories and the other few clues to her appearance that I now have, and I gaze and gaze again at that face, which seems to me both strange and familiar. (*A*: 351/354–5)[14]

But where Odysseus, at the inception of this *topos*, tries and fails three times to embrace his mother's shade, he does at least meet her and recognise her there, in the Homeric underworld.[15] Austerlitz, by contrast, tries in vain to recognise his dead and unknown mother in the face of a stranger, another young woman interned in the camp and compelled to take part in the charade of 'Theresienbad'. As it turns out, Vera summarily dismisses Austerlitz's discovery as a mistake, but

Fig. 11.1

Fig. 11.2

immediately and unreservedly accepts the veracity of another image he digs up in the Prague archives, a photo of 'an anonymous actress who seemed to resemble [his] dim memory of [his] mother' (*A*: 353/356). Where the woman in the film looks like what Austerlitz *imagines*, this second photograph (also reproduced in the text) resembles his *actual* recovered memory, however dim. But at this stage, the narrative has offered so many examples of the mendacity or mystery or outright unfathomability of visual images, that their worthiness as standards of authenticity on any level is cast irredeemably into doubt. And this is clearly part of Sebald's formal strategy of incorporating so much visual imagery, including stills from a real film documenting an instance of the most egregious deformation of social life, where the film itself constitutes an outrageous and horrifying deception on an even greater scale. Within the narrative, as we have seen, Austerlitz as it were allows the Theresienstadt film to momentarily deceive him, in a far more intimate manner. In the end, then, the archival photo of his mother is just another *possibly* authentic trace of her now absolute absence.

Through his subtle evocation of specific elements from a few key moments in European art cinema, and his explicit invocation of a Nazi propaganda film masquerading as documentary, Sebald weaves a narrative that is concerned in part with the representation of a particular subjectivity coming into a new, more deeply negative and therefore ironic, self-awareness through memory. This is only accomplished, though, after the protagonist has worked through and eventually abandoned a model of time figured subjectively, based in architectural – or generally spatial – metaphors of memory; metaphors whose figurative status is lost, folded into the erstwhile 'virtual reality' of represented space transformed by the enormous pressure exerted by the past upon the present. More directly, Sebald's vivid descriptions of the Theresienstadt propaganda film provide the immediate backdrop for Austerlitz's acting upon his vain but all-too-human desire to embrace the mother he does not remember knowing through the ghostly cinematic images of her last days in a simulacral city of the dead – an elaborate and economical interweaving of literature and film, history and memory, desire and mourning, that is emblematic of Sebald's renovation of the novel form. In *Austerlitz* Sebald's ironic recontextualisation of a hero's underworld journey connects his protagonist to a line of thoroughly modern seekers whose ultimate goal is always knowledge of *self* via an other. The self's recuperation of lost memory-content allegorises his re-emergence into the land of the living; the state of 'unremembering' or mnemonic divestment is shown to be emblematic of the self's sojourn through a living death. In the end, *Austerlitz* presents not the *production* of an individual subjective interiority but its ironic *deconstitution*. This strangely productive dismantling is the result of the *reconstitution* of subjective memory mediated through a novelistic incorporation and manipulation of cinema as itself a kind of uniquely modern substitute or compensatory memory on the level of collective cultural experience.

'And so they are ever returning to us, the dead,' Sebald writes in *The Emigrants* (*E*: 23/36). As Austerlitz's experience eloquently demonstrates, however, we do not because we *can*not ever 'get them back'; for it is not *themselves* that they bring but rather, inevitably perhaps, *ourselves*. What Austerlitz gains from his quest to rediscover his real parents' fate, and thus to reconstitute his own memories of them, is a kind of knowledge of who he really is, or was, or might have been. Whether or not this is a question of the substitution of an inauthentic for an authentic life and identity is left to the reader to decide. What is irrefutable is that, once reconstituted, even in part, these compensatory memories cannot erase the person Austerlitz has been in the five-decade interval – in effect his entire life – the person determined increasingly by a nameless and seemingly implacable longing, emptiness and despair, as he moves through the uncanny spaces of memory, driven by an unnamable desire, until he confronts at last the vain attempt to embrace the loved one he does not remember having known. As Augustine asks of God in his *Confessions*, before abandoning this approach outright: 'How, then, am I to find you, if I have no memory of you?' (Augustine 1988: 224).

NOTES

1. For Sebald's analyses of other Lang/Thea von Harbou films in the context of his critique of the ethical-aesthetic response in Germany to the fire-bombing of German cities, see *On the Natural History of Destruction* 54–6; 97.
2. Besides *Last Year at Marienbad*, *Austerlitz* makes explicit reference to another of Resnais's films, *Toute la mémoire du monde* (1956), in which 'the camera wends through the Bibliothèque Nationale in Paris, past rows and stacks of books, each unique, but which together, we're told, comprise our universal memory. Because man is forgetful, the library is chosen as the place where all is remembered, and where that which was forgotten can happily be found' (University of California, Berkeley Art Museum and Pacific Film Archive, 16 February 2003 http://www.bampfa.berkeley.edu/resources/film_notes/index.html.
3. See the chapters by Ceuppens and Klebes in this volume.
4. *Katabasis*: from the Greek: a going down; used in reference to any underworld journey undertaken by a hero in quest of special knowledge.
5. This film has been restored by and is available from The National Centre for Jewish Film at Brandeis University (www.jewishfilm.org).
6. Eliot is here alluding to a passage from Dante's *Inferno* which, interestingly, is quoted at length by Sebald in *On the Natural History of Destruction* (*NHD*: 166), in connection with Jean Améry's novelistic account of his sojourn in the 'city of the dead' that was Auschwitz.
7. Tellingly, *Confessions*, Book 10, is a significant text for Derrida's work on memory in the 1980s and 1990s.
8. The justification for this comparison between Sebald and the classical notion of an 'art of memory' is the word 'art' or *techne*. This premodern approach elaborates an artificial memory as a 'technology' in a literal, non-metaphorical sense – something that cannot always be said of many of the models of memory that interpose themselves in the transition to the modern. Modern theorists of memory have long recognized that in speaking of memory one is describing not a unitary subjective

phenomenon but a grouping of cognitive functions – or, in terms more amenable to this study, a constellation of interconnected metaphors. These metaphors continue to be both familiar and powerful, most notably in terms of modernity's stubborn insistence on memory's *spatial* nature. This might seem to run counter to Freud's or Proust's 'psychological' memory theories, but in practice the two approaches are more complementary than contradictory. The metaphors do not simply persist; they continue to contribute in an active way to the very shape of thought. Today of course the metaphors may have changed, to the archive or data bank or 'matrix' – or, indeed, may have been displaced altogether into the catachretic computer 'memory', which, like writing in Plato's *Phaedrus*, is a technology that *literally* replaces memory in its naturalised modes.

9. The literature on negative or apophatic theologies is vast. See for example: Derrida 1992; Budick and Iser 1989; and Gasché 1994.

10. I use 'repression' here in the Freudian sense of the mechanism that contributes to the shaping of identity while concealing its own origins from it (see O'Brien and Szeman 2003: 173). While invoking the Freudian model, however, I also want to suggest its limitations in representing structures and functions that are figured in *Austerlitz* according to metaphorical registers at once pre- and post-Freudian.

11. Cf. Eksteins 2000: 317.

12. Cf. Deleuze's discussion of "The Simulacrum and Ancient Philosophy" (1990: 253–79).

13. This is apart from implied homosexual relationships, such as the friendship with Gerald Fitzpatrick.

14. In this invocation of the Orpheus myth Austerlitz is much closer to Cocteau's thoroughly ironic modern version than any of the classical avatars. In fact, my reading of Sebald's version suggests that he goes beyond Cocteau in that here the hero is made to play the roles of *both* seeker and sought.

15. See Homer, Bk 11, ll. 233–43.

12

TRAUMATIC PHOTOGRAPHS: REMEMBRANCE AND THE TECHNICAL MEDIA IN W. G. SEBALD'S *AUSTERLITZ*

Carolin Duttlinger

The association between photography and experiences of trauma, loss and death is a recurrent theme in writings on the medium. While Susan Sontag claims that 'all photographs are *memento mori*' (1979: 15), both Walter Benjamin and Roland Barthes have been particularly drawn to photographs in which they believe they discern the anticipation of an impending misfortune, accident or catastrophe (Benjamin 1999: 510; Barthes 1984: 95–6). Most recently, Ulrich Baer has explored the parallels between the representational technique of photography and the phenomenon of trauma. More often than not, however, such associations remain based on structural, symbolic or meta-phorical analogies between the two phenomena. Indeed, photography has led even supposedly 'critical' or 'theoretical' writers to adopt a more associative, discursive style of argument which problematises the boundaries between 'theory' and 'literature' – Barthes's *Camera Lucida* is a case in point.

In this chapter I explore the discourse on photography, loss and trauma in W. G. Sebald's final novel, *Austerlitz*. Although his treatment of photography echoes some of the arguments developed within the critical tradition discussed above, Sebald's prose works, and *Austerlitz* in particular, take these approaches a step further, demonstrating the implications of this structural analogy when it is transposed into the context of a literary narrative. While Sebald's works contain both documentary material and theoretical reflection in the tradition of critical writings on photography, his novels belong primarily to the field of literature. This is not to say, however, that his literary, poetic mode of writing prevents him from engaging in a theoretically sophisticated discourse on photography. Here I shall examine the ways in which Sebald's narrative exploration of the intersections between photography and trauma illuminates both the complexity of this configuration and the paradoxes inherent within it.

I focus on Sebald's last novel, *Austerlitz*, a work which, while developing many themes from his earlier works, also constitutes something of a new departure in its exploration of photography. Although the integration of photographs in the text is generally one of the most striking features of Sebald's prose, *Austerlitz* is the work where photography is most extensively and systematically thematised within the narrative itself. The novel's eponymous protagonist is himself an amateur photographer, and allegedly takes a large number of the photographs included within the text. At the same time, Jacques Austerlitz is also the principal interpreter of other photographs, especially of those pictures which he discusses in his attempt to trace his origins. The choice of such a protagonist allows Sebald to present a relatively coherent textual account of individual pictures as well as of the medium in general, while also integrating these theoretical reflections into the specific context of the narrative and thereby investigating their psychological implications for the protagonist. In this respect, the discourse on photography in *Austerlitz* cannot be reduced to a theoretical, cultural or aesthetic exploration, since it derives its argumentative complexity as well as its literary potential from the fact that it also figures as a symptom of the protagonist's traumatised psychological disposition.

Because of the novel's division into a framing narrative and the embedded story told by its protagonist, the role and significance of the photographs inserted into *Austerlitz* is dependent on their position within the text. Those images situated within the narrator's framing narrative are rarely referred to directly in the text and thus underpin the narrative in a more implicit, associative manner – as is the case in Sebald's earlier works such as *Vertigo* and *The Rings of Saturn*. The sections recounted by the protagonist, however, are characterised by a much closer relationship between text and image in which individual photographs, the act of recording and the more general characteristics of the medium are all subject to extensive textual commentary. Here, I shall explore the different ways in which photography is incorporated, thematised and analysed within the novel, in order to assess how these different narrative and interpretative contexts interrelate, complement and perhaps contradict each other.

An atypical but highly interesting example of the implicit interaction between text and photography in the narrator's framing narrative is the novel's opening scene, which is set in the Antwerp 'Nocturama'. The narrator is struck by the unusually large eyes of the exhibited animals, whose 'fixed, inquiring gaze' reminds him of 'certain painters and philosophers who seek to penetrate the darkness which surrounds us purely by means of looking and thinking' (*A*: 3/7). The concepts of the gaze, darkness and visual perception are central to the novel as a whole, where the protagonist's reflections on memory, identity, architecture and history are inextricably linked to questions of vision and perception. The photographs reproduced here at first merely seem to complement the narrative, but they also raise some interesting questions about the more general role of photography in *Austerlitz*. Inserted into the text are two pairs of photographs, the top pair showing the eyes of two nocturnal creatures, probably a lemur and an owl, the bottom pair depicting the eyes of the German painter Jan Peter Tripp (born 1945) and the Austrian philosopher Ludwig Wittgenstein (cf. Köhler 2002). All four images are reproduced only in sections, and their referents and origin remain unacknowledged in the text. The interaction between text and photography thus has the effect of a riddle, challenging the reader to track down the pictures of 'certain painters and philosophers' from which the reproduced details are taken. While on one level the inserted photographs seem merely to illustrate the text, they also point to an element which underpins the discourse on photography throughout the novel, and especially the protagonist's own engagement with the medium: the fact that photographs, despite their representational realism and apparent immediacy, do not necessarily provide straightforward access to the scenes or experiences they record. This applies particularly to those photographs with which the protagonist engages in his search for the past and which remain, despite detailed scrutiny and extensive textual commentary, fragmentary, decontextualised and opaque.

In contrast to the implicit text-image relationship in the framing narrative, photography is a recurring theme within the story told by the protagonist. The prominence of photography within Austerlitz's account is due partly to the fact that he is himself a photographer. The textual description of a scene or encounter is thus often accompanied both by the corresponding image and by a textual reference to the act of photographing. This photographic practice is also subject to more abstract, theoretical reflections which bring out the psychological implications of this strategic representational combination of photography and narrative. The act of recording, the subsequent development process, and the viewing of the resulting images are all associated with the questions of memory, recollection and trauma. This notion of a structural similarity between photography and memory, which is here developed in a literary, narrative context, is reminiscent of the theoretical reflections of writers such as Freud and Benjamin as well as more recent trauma theorists.

When the narrator first visits Austerlitz in his London home, he notices dozens of photographs taken by his host which are laid out on the table, 'most of them dating quite a long way back and rather worn at the edges' (*A*: 167/171). As the narrator describes these pictures, it emerges that several of them have already been inserted into the protagonist's narrative without commentary; the photographs of 'a number of heavy doors and gateways' in turn anticipate Austerlitz's subsequent account of his visit to Theresienstadt

(Terezín) (A: 167/171). This technique, whereby photographs refer in a retrospective or anticipatory way to the verbal narrative, reflects a sense of discontinuity between experience and photography which underpins the protagonist's engagement with his pictures. Austerlitz subjects the photographs to repeated scrutiny, using them for a game of 'patience' in which he turns over the images 'always with a new sense of surprise' and rearranges them 'in an order depending on their family resemblances' (A: 168/171–2).[1] The 'effort of thinking and remembering' (A: 168/171–2) which accompanies this process invests it with a psychological dimension. The German formulation 'Denk- und Erinnerungsarbeit' brings out this dimension more clearly, as it is reminiscent of Freud's concept of 'working through' (Durcharbeiten), the patient's therapeutic, recuperative engagement with his or her repressed memories. In a more extensive comparison between photography and memory, however, Austerlitz emphasises the precarious, transient character of both concepts:

> In my photographic work I was always especially entranced, said Austerlitz, by the moment when the shadows of reality, so to speak, emerge out of nothing on the exposed paper, as memories do in the middle of the night, darkening again if you try to cling to them, just like a photographic print left in the developing bath too long. (A: 108–9/112–13)

The development process in the darkroom is here figured not as a straightforward, irreversible transition from the negative image to the developed photograph, but as a precarious process encompassing both the manifestation of the image and its subsequent disappearance. Importantly, then, it is the latency and transience of the photographic image, rather than its permanence and stability, which serve as a model for the process of memory, as the images of neither photography nor memory can be grasped or arrested, and are hence both prone to disappearance. Photography is thus figured as a model not for the permanence of memory but for the phenomenon of forgetting. Interestingly, all three processes – photography, recollection and forgetting – take place in the dark, either in the darkroom or at night, and therefore in the liminal sphere between dreaming and waking, consciousness and the unconscious, echoing the dialectic between darkness and vision developed in the opening scene in the Nocturama.

Sebald is not the first writer to compare the photographic development process to the workings of memory. Freud, for example, repeatedly draws on the metaphor of the darkroom as an explanatory model for psychical process, in particular for the transition of unconscious impressions into consciousness. In the Introductory Lectures, for instance, he states that

> every mental process . . . exists to begin with in an unconscious stage or phase and that it is only from there that the process passes over into the

conscious phase, just as a photographic picture begins as a negative and only becomes a picture after being turned into a positive. Not every negative, however, necessarily becomes a positive; nor is it necessary that every unconscious mental process should turn into a conscious one. (1917: 295)

In contrast to Sebald, Freud describes both the photographic and the psychological paradigm as a straightforward, irreversible transition from 'negative', unconscious impressions to 'developed', conscious experiences, although he also remarks that not all unconscious impressions are subject to such a 'development process'. In *Moses and Monotheism*, Freud returns to this model, arguing that the unconscious, undeveloped state is particularly characteristic of childhood memories which often remain undeveloped because of the insufficient receptivity of the child's psychical apparatus (1939: 126). This conception echoes the theory of trauma developed in *Beyond the Pleasure Principle* where Freud attributes the traumatic effect of certain experiences to the inability of the psychical apparatus to cope with the overwhelming intensity of the encountered stimuli.

Indeed, the concept of trauma, and in particular its relation to childhood, are central to Austerlitz's own disposition, as his inability to remember his Prague childhood is effected by the traumatic separation from his parents and his emigration to Britain with the *Kindertransport*. As a consequence, Austerlitz's traumatised state underpins his engagement with various phenomena such as architecture, art history and especially photography. During his stay in Paris in the late 1950s, Austerlitz takes hundreds of photographs of the Parisian *banlieues*, 'pictures which in their very emptiness, as I realised only later, reflected my orphaned frame of mind' (*A*: 370/372). Again, the photographer's realisation of the pictures' significance is characterised by a notion of belatedness, and involves only a sense of emptiness rather than any positive realisation. This notion of emptiness, however, is intensified when, after a visit to the veterinary museum at Maisons-Alfort, Austerlitz experiences

> the first of the several fainting fits I was to suffer, causing temporary but complete loss of memory [*Auslöschung sämtlicher Gedächtnisspuren*], a condition described in psychiatric textbooks . . . as hysterical epilepsy. Only when I developed the photographs I had taken that Sunday in September at Maisons-Alfort was I able, with their aid and guided by Marie's patient questioning, to reconstruct my buried experiences. (*A*: 374/377)

If the photographic development process had previously been associated with notions of latency and forgetting, then this model is radicalised in this passage, where the act of taking photographs comes to signify a profound dichotomy between the photographically recorded experiences and their assimilation into consciousness. While in the previous passage photography and the process of recollection (and forgetting) were figured in terms of their correlation, they now take on contrasting positions, since the photographs come to stand in for the memories that are lost after the protagonist's hysterical attack. Central to this configuration is the fact that Austerlitz himself records the scenes that he subsequently forgets, a fact which suggests some inherent, structural connection between his amnesia and the very act of photographing.

Interestingly, Sebald in the original uses the term 'Gedächtnisspuren', 'memory-traces', to describe the protagonist's memory loss. This term alludes to Freud's famous formulation in *Beyond the Pleasure Principle*, 'consciousness arises instead [literally: in the place] of a memory-trace [*Erinnerungsspur*]' (1920: 25), a statement which marks the core of Freud's theory about the breach between consciousness and memory in trauma. Austerlitz's memory loss thus bears traumatic characteristics insofar as his strategy of recording the experiences in question is not dependent on their conscious realisation. In this respect, photography serves not to enhance or to supplement the viewer's perceptual and mental capacities but to distance him from the recorded experiences, acting as a protective shield from the stimuli it simultaneously stores, inaccessible to memory. In a variation on Freud's phrase, then, consciousness here 'arises in the place of the photographic image'. Importantly, the subsequent development of the photographs helps Austerlitz to reconstruct the events affected by his memory loss, a fact which echoes Freud's theory about the belated development of unconscious impressions. What remains ambiguous, however, is whether this subsequent engagement with the recorded photographs does indeed trigger a genuine process of recollection in Austerlitz, or whether the pictures merely provide a substitute which enables an 'external' reconstruction of the lost events.

In his book *Spectral Evidence: The Photography of Trauma*, Ulrich Baer develops a theory concerning the inherent structural similarity between trauma and photography, which bears some striking parallels to the discourse on trauma and photography in *Austerlitz*. In his study of photographs associated with hysteria and, more significantly, with the Holocaust, Baer argues that similar to the 'puzzlingly accurate imprinting on the mind of an overwhelming reality' in trauma, photography provides a 'mechanically recorded instant that was not necessarily registered by the subject's own consciousness' (2002: 8). Through this structural correspondence to the phenomenon of trauma, photographs can enable access to 'experiences that have remained unremembered yet cannot be forgotten' (2002: 7), functioning as testimonies of incidents which 'become . . . meaningful only in and as [their] representation' (2002: 12).

The role of photography in Austerlitz's search for his childhood follows a very similar pattern.[2] The images which Austerlitz recovers in his search for his past become substitutes for experiences that were either repressed as a result of traumatic experiences or were never adequately recorded in the child's consciousness in the first place. However, while the photographs in question play a central part in the protagonist's attempt at reconstructing his lost memories, they also illustrate the precarious character of this undertaking. Indeed, Austerlitz's engagement with photography in the context of the Holocaust poses the question of whether photography can indeed figure as a substitute for lost memory and experience or whether the pictures merely come to emphasise the aporetical nature of the process of remembrance.

Austerlitz's visit to Prague and the encounter with his former nanny Vera enable him to recover his Czech and to reconstruct many childhood memories. However, while the recollection of scenes of everyday life is relatively straightforward, the memory of his parents, especially of his mother, remains elusive. It is in this context that photography gains its full significance as a substitute for experiences that are inaccessible to conscious memory.

What underpins Austerlitz's search for his past and accounts for the inherently traumatic character of this undertaking is the (never explicitly thematised) discrepancy between his survival and his parents' murder in the Holocaust. As a consequence, then, the recuperation of the memory of his parents is inextricably linked with the task of confronting their murder by the Nazis, and the more general horrors of the Holocaust. The implications of this are illustrated in Austerlitz's engagement with photographs related to his childhood, a process which exceeds the reconstruction of the past as it is concerned with the task of coming to terms with the ultimately unrepresentable reality of his parents' death.

Central to this undertaking are two photographs which Austerlitz's former nanny Vera, another survivor haunted by the memories of the past, discovers in a volume of Balzac's *Comédie humaine*. Austerlitz's mother Agáta was an actress and opera singer. Correspondingly, both pictures are situated in a theatrical context, although she herself is depicted in neither of them. The first picture shows an unknown man and woman on a theatre stage in front of a painted mountain backdrop (Fig. 12.1).

> She had wondered, said Vera, what kind of play or opera had been staged in front of this alarming backdrop, and because of the high mountain range and the wild forest background she thought it might have been *Wilhelm Tell*, or *La Sonnambula*, or Ibsen's last play. The Swiss boy with the apple on his head appeared in my mind's eye, Vera continued; I sensed in me the moment of terror in which the narrow bridge gives way under the sleepwalker's foot, and imagined that, high in the rocks above, an avalanche was already breaking loose, about to sweep the poor folk who had lost their way (for what else would have brought them to these desolate

Fig. 12.1

surroundings) down into the depths next moment. Minutes went by, said Austerlitz, in which I too thought I saw the cloud of snow crashing into the valley. (A: 257–8/261–2)

The picture's impact on the viewers – Vera and Austerlitz – is diminished neither by the anonymity of the sitters nor by its openly artificial, staged setting. On the contrary, the viewers' imaginary, hallucinatory response is inextricably linked to the picture's theatricality: the painted backdrop and the two anonymous sitters who are imagined as an 'impresario, or a conjuror and his woman assistant' (A: 257/261). Because of their resemblance to Austerlitz's parents, they come to act as their substitutes in various catastrophic scenarios imagined by the viewers. The stage becomes a realm for the projection of various accidents, catastrophes and misfortunes, all of which are derived from the dramatic repertoire. The photograph's theatricality and the anonymity of the sitters are thus crucial in enabling the viewers, especially Austerlitz, to find an expression for the traumatic and inherently unrepresentable fates of his parents Agáta and Maximilian. Significantly, however, this confrontation is possible only with the help of auxiliary representational frameworks such as the photograph or the dramatic repertoire which, while enabling an imaginary, emotional engagement with the experience of trauma, also helps to displace this experience into a fictitious and anonymous photographic context. In this respect, we have to modify Baer's argument about the link between photography and trauma; photography becomes crucial for an engagement with repressed traumatic experiences not because it records what is normally excluded from consciousness but because it provides a substitute for these experiences and facilitates the viewer's retrospective, imaginary engagement with incidents which were never experienced, witnessed or photographed in the first place.[3]

Interestingly, the photographs and other forms of visual testimony with which Austerlitz engages in his search for the past are all in some respect linked to the theatrical sphere, a fact which underlines the importance of the fictional, theatrical realm for the engagement with trauma. However, while the photograph of the mountain scenery triggers the viewers' spontaneous and almost hallucinatory confrontation with catastrophe, the second photograph discovered by Vera poses more troubling questions about the implications of this notion of theatricality for the process of memory. This is a childhood portrait of Austerlitz himself, which shows him in the costume of the Rose Queen's pageboy in which he accompanied his mother to a masked ball (Fig. 12.2).

In contrast to the first image, the devices of costume and masquerade do not trigger an emotive, identificatory response in the viewer. The minute details such as the 'six large mother-of-pearl buttons' or the 'extravagant hat with the heron's feather in it' (A: 260/264) which are revealed when Austerlitz explores the photograph through a magnifying glass stand in marked contrast to the

Fig. 12.2

picture's inherent opacity, the 'blurred, dark area above the horizon' and the mysterious, almost supernatural appearance of the 'spectrally light' hair (A: 259/263). It is this conjunction of objectivity and opacity which resists any straightforward act of decoding. Despite prolonged scrutiny, then, Austerlitz has to admit that he 'could not recollect [himself] in the part' (A: 259/263), and, although he can identify details of his physical appearance, his photographic self ultimately remains alien to him.

Despite, or perhaps because of, this lack of recognition, however, the protagonist's account is reminiscent of his response to the picture of the mountain scenery. Austerlitz takes the bent arm concealed under the cape to be 'broken or in a splint', and this motif of physical wounding is extended into a sense of impending catastrophe.[4] Alongside his notion of a 'misfortune lying ahead' (A: 260/264), Austerlitz is also struck by an 'overwhelming sense of the long years that had passed' (A: 259/263). More clearly than in the previous accounts, then, the traumatic character of the photograph is associated with the conjunction of two temporal structures: first, the irredeemably past character of the photograph which radically separates it from the viewer and his present context; and secondly, the arrested moment preceding a catastrophe which will forever be preserved in its anticipation. Roland Barthes has accounted for the traumatic effect of this twofold temporal structure on the viewer:

> I read at the same time: *This will be* and *this has been*; I observe with horror an anterior future of which death is the stake. By giving me the absolute past of the pose (aorist), the photograph tells me death in the future . . . I shudder, like Winnicott's psychotic patient, *over a catastrophe which has already occurred*. Whether or not the subject is already dead, every photograph is this catastrophe. (1984: 96)

In the case of the childhood photograph, this traumatic structure of anticipation and repetition is intensified owing to the fact that the viewer of the photograph is also its sitter, and the protagonist therefore looks back onto his own ignorant but doomed self. More clearly than in the case of the previous photograph, the protagonist's feeling of radical alienation is tied in with this temporal structure of belatedness. As Baer argues, 'The photograph's deferral of an experience from the occasion of its registration may affect not only the viewer but also the photographed individual, who is preserved undergoing an event to which he or she can only later attach a meaning' (2002: 13).

As a consequence, the photograph's anticipation of catastrophe simultaneously contains a challenge for the viewer who discerns in the 'piercing, inquiring gaze of the page boy' the impossible challenge of averting the 'misfortune lying ahead' (A: 260/264). More clearly than in previous photographs, then, the photograph's traumatic, anticipatory character contains an imaginary ethical obligation, and although the task of averting the anticipated catastrophe is an impossible one, the photograph draws on another form of responsibility, namely, that of remembrance, in which Austerlitz is cast as the retrospective witness of an event which, because of its traumatic nature, is recorded in the technical media but excluded from individual memory or consciousness.

For my last example, I will now turn to another technical medium, namely, film, with which the protagonist also engages in a search for the memory and fate of his mother. Film differs from photography in that it lacks the latter's resonances of arrest and freezing, notions which make photography structurally comparable to the concept of trauma. As a result, film provides an alternative model of technical recording which, although it shares many of the characteristics associated with photography, also differs from photography in its temporal character, a fact which eventually enables an apparent moment of remembrance and recognition.

Having failed to reconstruct the image of his mother with the help of the photographs and Vera's accounts, Austerlitz tracks down a film of Theresienstadt, the ghetto where his mother was imprisoned, in the hope of discovering her in it. The film, entitled *Der Führer schenkt den Juden eine Stadt* [The Führer Gives a City to the Jews] (1944), was commissioned by the Nazis in order to document the '*Verschönerungsaktion* or general improvement campaign' (*A*: 339/343) of Theresienstadt undertaken to conceal the true state of the ghetto from a Red Cross commission.

Perhaps the ultimate paradox underlying Austerlitz's attempt to reconstruct the memory and fate of his parents with the help of the technical media is thus the fact that the film made by the Nazis uses the same strategies of staging, masquerade and theatricality that underpin the protagonist's attempts to reactivate his memory of the past through the two photographs recovered by Vera. The film implies that even the perpetrators have to resort to strategies of concealment and staging for the representation of their own crimes. A similar example of the Nazis' manipulation of visual testimonies is discerned by Max Ferber's uncle in *The Emigrants*, who mentions a photograph of the book-burning that took place in Würzburg on 10 May 1933. As the books were burnt in the evening, it was already too dark to take a photograph, and, as a result, the Nazi authorities 'simply took a picture of some other gathering outside the palace . . . and added a swathe of smoke and a dark night sky' (*E*: 183/274). From this, the uncle concludes that the entire Nazi regime 'has been a fake, from the very start' (*E*: 184/274). However, while this manipulation is clearly discernible in the photograph reprinted in the text, the deceptive character of the film is more intricate and less open to a deconstructive reading because the manipulations are performed on the reality recorded in it rather than on the resulting image. While this strategy of manipulation thus further complicates the testimonial function of the technical media, it also ties in with the previous photographic examples which anticipate, albeit indirectly, the impending catastrophe of the Holocaust. In the case of the film, then, Austerlitz's attempt to recuperate the image of his mother is inextricably linked to the more general task of confronting the film's illusory representational framework.

Prior to watching the film Austerlitz creates his own, imaginary version in which he pictures his mother in a number of idyllic scenes, for instance, as

> a saleswoman in the haberdashery shop, just taking a fine pair of gloves carefully out of one of the drawers, or singing the part of Olympia in the *Tales of Hoffmann* which . . . was staged in Theresienstadt in the course of the improvements campaign. (*A*: 343/346)

Austerlitz's imaginary version is marked by an uncanny complicity with the film's own dissimulating strategy, thus illustrating his investment in images which conceal, rather than reveal, the underlying traumatic reality behind the veil of reassuring normality. As in the case of Austerlitz's hysterical attack in Paris, then, the technical media do not merely provide access to experiences traumatically excluded from memory; they also act as a shield, a representational framework that distances from what it simultaneously reveals. Austerlitz's stance towards the film is underpinned by precisely this dichotomy between concealment and revelation, and in particular by the notion that the film contains hidden layers of meaning which can be extrapolated through a strategy of viewing which in itself bears manipulative characteristics.

The contrast between Austerlitz's imaginary version and the film could not be greater. Rather than providing, as Austerlitz imagined, a number of mini-narratives, the film is mainly concerned with the depiction of various tasks being carried out in the ghetto's workshops and factories. All Austerlitz can discern is 'an unbroken succession of strangers' faces emerg[ing] before [him] for a few seconds' (*A*: 344/347), and, instead of his being able to identify the face of his mother, the images 'merely flickered before [his] eyes as the source of continual irritation or vexation' (*A*: 345/348). The discontinuity and the fragmentary character of the images undermines the film's narrative continuity and invests it with a transient and fleeting character. In this respect, the film's images, which 'seemed to dissolve even as they appeared' (*A*: 345/348), echo Austerlitz's remarks about the latency of the photographic development process.

In order to counter this impression and to invest the film with some of the narrative continuity that characterises his own imaginary version, Austerlitz has a slow-motion copy made in which the original fourteen minutes are extended to an hour. This move is rather effective as it reveals 'previously hidden objects and people, creating . . . a different sort of film altogether' (*A*: 345/349). Whereas the shots of the workshops had previously been characterised by hectic movement, it now seems like the men and women 'were toiling in their sleep, so long did it take them to draw thread and needle through the air' (*A*: 345/349). Indeed, the slow-motion copy invests the depicted people with a ghostly, supernatural character:

> They seemed to be hovering rather than walking, as if their feet no longer quite touched the ground. The contours of their bodies were blurred and, particularly in the scenes shot out of doors in the broad daylight, had dissolved at the edges, resembling . . . the frayed outlines of the human hand shown in the fluidal pictures and electrographs taken by Louis Draget [*sic*] in Paris around the turn of the century. (*A*: 348/349)

What underpins this passage is the notion of a fundamental link between magic and technology, an association which had already been pointed out by Benjamin who states that film and photography 'make the difference between technology and magic visible as a thoroughly historical variable' (1999: 512). Austerlitz here refers to a specific episode in the history of photography, namely, its association with the realm of the supernatural. The example given in the text is the French photographer Louis Darget (and not, as in both the English and the German editions, 'Draget') who assumed that every living being emanates invisible rays which could be made visible on the photographic plate. His technique involved the physical contact between the referent's hand and the photographic plate and was later extended to so-called 'mental photography', which aimed at the photographic depiction of invisible fluids emitted by the sitter's thoughts and emotional states (cf. Krauss 1992: 48–51). The reference to Darget and his photographic experiments underlines the ghostly character of the retarded images and puts them into the context of a photographic practice that was founded on the notion of a privileged connection between photographic technique and the supernatural. In Austerlitz's case, too, the slow-motion copy makes visible what was previously invisible, and as such it undermines any clearcut distinction between the visible and the invisible, between manifest appearance and latent content, as well as between magic and technology.

One of the most uncanny effects of the slow-motion copy is that it draws attention to the damaged sections of the tape: flaws, which the viewer

> had hardly noticed before, now melted the image from its centre or from the edges, blotting it out and instead making patterns of bright white sprinkled with black which reminded me of aerial photographs taken in the far north, or a drop of water seen under the microscope. (*A*: 348/349–50)

The still reproduced in the text provides a striking example for this effect, as the blot which takes up more than half of the double-page illustration appears like a third, ghostly profile which is emerging next to the heads of two men and which fits in with the kinds of photographs of supernatural phenomena referred to by the protagonist (*A*: 346–7/350–1). The blots and stains resemble images seen through the microscope or from an aerial perspective, and as such they point to the more general extension of the range of human perception through the technical media.[5] More importantly, however, the physical flaws in the film disrupt and undermine the coherence of its staged, deceptive reality.

Ultimately, then, the extension and alteration of the realm of the visual yields the desired result for the viewer: in the shot of a musical performance, Austerlitz finally believes he has identified his mother amongst the audience:

> at the left-hand side, set a little way back and close to the upper edge of the frame, the face of a young woman appears, barely emerging from the black shadows around it, which is why I did not notice it at all at first. (*A*: 350/354) (Fig. 11.2)

As he had previously imagined, Austerlitz thus finally discovers his mother in the ghetto theatre which, as in the photograph of the painted mountain scenery, provides a privileged space of memory and recognition. Within the overall rationale of the film of Theresienstadt, however, the theatre gains an added significance as a self-reflexive reference to the theatrical, artificial reality staged for the visit of the Red Cross commission. And while Austerlitz imagined his mother in the lead role of Olympia in a performance of *The Tales of Hoffmann*, she is in fact merely a passive spectator of the dissimulating performance put on by the Nazis, a role in which she nearly merges with the surrounding darkness. At this point, Austerlitz's scrutiny of the slow-motion copy gains an urgent ethical, as well as personal, significance as it allows the depicted individual to emerge from darkness, invisibility and oblivion.

Despite his attempts to decelerate and even arrest the fleeting images, however, their transience is even inscribed into the still of his mother that Austerlitz copies from the Theresienstadt film:

> I run the tape back repeatedly, looking at the time indicator in the top left-hand corner of the screen, where the figures covering part of her forehead show the minutes and seconds, from 10:53 to 10:57, while the hundredths of a second flash by so fast that you cannot read and capture them. (*A*: 351/355)

While in other pictures it is the medium's materiality – its blots and stains – which invades and disrupts the representation, here it is its inherent temporality, its fleetingness, which is inscribed into the still and which partially obscures the image of the mother.

A comparison between the reprinted still and the protagonist's description reveals one minor incongruity, a detail that underlines the precarious nature of the image and the associated moment of recognition. While Austerlitz claims that his mother is 'wearing a three-stringed and delicately draped necklace which scarcely stands out from her dark, high-necked dress' (*A*: 351/354), the photograph inserted into the text shows only two strings clearly; guided by the text, the reader may momentarily discern the trace of a third string but this impression is called into question on closer scrutiny. The interrelation between text and image here invests the picture with an elusive, ghostly character, which blurs the boundaries between visibility and invisibility. There is, of course, the possibility that a comparison with the original film would bring to light the third string; ultimately, however, the very ambiguity surrounding its existence provides a potent symbol of the ambiguity and opacity which characterise the novel's discourse on the technical media and the process of remembering. While the protagonist attempts to arrest and preserve the memory of his mother through his narrative account, her image is already in the process of disappearing again, merging with the surrounding darkness and vanishing within a few seconds.

As I have attempted to demonstrate, Sebald's last novel illustrates the privileged but precarious role of the technical media in the representation and remembrance of the Holocaust and in processes of memory more generally. In this respect, photography in particular plays a central role in its capacity as both a theoretical model and a mode of visual testimony that accompanies the protagonist's quest for his repressed past. In both capacities, however, photography is inextricably linked to the failings of memory, to the latency of remembrance and the notions of forgetting and trauma, which repeatedly disrupt and undermine the process of recollection. Although photography in some cases enables a therapeutic, perhaps cathartic engagement with the past and the catastrophe of the Holocaust, in others it only emphasises the aporia inherent in the reconstruction of a traumatic incident. In this context, film plays a central role as it allows the viewer to alter and manipulate the supposedly objective representation of the past, thereby triggering a process of remembrance that apparently facilitates the redemption of its referents from invisibility and oblivion. Ultimately, however, both film and photography remain ambiguous as testimonies, not least because Sebald associates both media with strategies of concealment, staging and masquerade. As a consequence, these visual testimonies simultaneously figure as a protective shield that conceals underlying trauma. Throughout the novel, then, photographic and filmic images maintain an ambiguous role in relation to concepts of trauma and memory, enabling a moment of recollection while simultaneously illustrating the precarious if not impossible character of this undertaking.

NOTES

1. This notion of 'family resemblances' can be read on the level of a self-reflexive commentary; as J. J. Long has pointed out, the photographs inserted into Sebald's texts relate to each other by means of reflexive reference, that is, through similarity of motifs which mirror 'the overall thematics of the verbal narrative' but remain unacknowledged in the text (2003: 137). At the same time, however, the term 'family

resemblances' also has another, rather uncanny historical resonance, as it is reminiscent of the photographic experiments carried out by Francis Galton, Charles Darwin's cousin and the founder of the field of eugenics. Galton, whose writings provided the basis for the Nazis' racist politics, superimposed individual photographic portraits in order to generate the 'prototypical face' of, for instance, the Jew, the aristocrat or the criminal. Cf. Hamilton and Hargreaves 2001: 94–9.

2. Stefanie Harris in her article on photography in *The Emigrants* also comments on the similarity between photography and the 'discontinuous temporal structure' of trauma but does not explore in much detail the psychological implications of this connection (2001: 387).

3. Susan Sontag comments on this substitute function of photography, arguing that photographs provide 'not so much an instrument of memory as an invention of it or a replacement' (1979: 165).

4. 'Trauma', after all, means 'wound' in the original Greek.

5. Walter Benjamin coins the term of the 'optical unconscious' to describe the access to previously inaccessible visual spheres enabled by the technical media, a discovery whose significance he compares to that of the psychological unconscious (1999: 512).

PART V
HAUNTING, TRAUMA, MEMORY

13

TABOO AND REPRESSION IN W. G. SEBALD'S *ON THE NATURAL HISTORY OF DESTRUCTION*

Wilfried Wilms

'The truth of Auschwitz remains hidden in its ashes. Only those who lived it in their flesh and in their minds can possibly transform their experiences into knowledge. Others, despite their best intentions, can never do so' (Wiesel 1990: 166). For Elie Wiesel, there is an unbridgeable gap between the traumatic experiences of excessive, continued violence (what he calls the 'truth of Auschwitz') and the transformation, and ultimately transfer, of these experiences into readily communicable forms of expression. There is a specific quality about that kind of 'truth', Wiesel claims, something that separates it for all time from what we ordinarily label 'knowledge'. Because of its exclusive nature, it must exceed our normal understanding, perhaps even our imagination. The actual experience of this violence was buried with the victims who, according to Primo Levi, 'drowned' and never left the camps, as much so as it is still buried within those who were 'saved'. The others – the writer, the historian, the film-maker, the psychologist – remain outside that 'truth', hoping that perhaps the survivor will find a bridge to a past that will otherwise be lost for good. Knowledge of this kind – and perhaps we can call it unmediated knowledge for the sake of distinction – can come only from the victim; he or she alone is the ruler in the kingdom of memory. Thus only the camp survivor can provide an ultimate ruling over which transformation or representation at least comes close to being authentic, pure, appropriate or 'true,' and what is not. Others, as Wiesel maintains, no matter what their intentions or professions, are barred from such truth because they cannot occupy the authentic subject-position indispensable for the production of such pure knowledge. They remain outsiders to the 'truth of Auschwitz'.

There is, needless to say, an inherent danger in the assertion or construction of such exclusive agency, for – to raise just one obvious question – what happens to the reality of that traumatic chapter of lived history when its agents pass away? Will their heirs water down this pure knowledge and thus make it less authentic, real or true? Will it eventually be lost and even forgotten? The past decade has seen a tremendous rise in academic interest concerning the interplay of witnessing, memory, trauma and the role assigned to history within this web of entangled subject-positions – so much in fact that warnings of a surfeit of memory have been issued (Maier 1993). 'Witnessing – typically, witnessing based on memory,' LaCapra observed in *History and Memory after Auschwitz*, 'has emerged as a privileged mode of access to the past and its traumatic occurrences' (1998: 11). Yet LaCapra is critical of the equation of memory and history, finds it 'deceptive'. There is what he identifies as 'a tendency to go with memory's flow, mingle fact and fancy, provide ingratiating personal anecdotes or autobiographical sketches, and moot the question of the relation between history and fiction' (16). LaCapra certainly agrees with Wiesel that the unmediated knowledge of the 'truth of Auschwitz' (LaCapra prefers the term 'primary memory') belongs to the victim alone. Nonetheless, when investigating the role of the historian in whose hands the transfer of traumatic memory into history and knowledge rests, LaCapra reveals his clearly identifiable roots in the Enlightenment tradition. It is the historian, well aware of his own subject-position, who questions and tests memory against the demands of its empirical accuracy, because

> history also includes elements that are not exhausted by memory, such as demographic, ecological, and economic factors. More important, perhaps, it tests memory and ideally leads to the emergence of both more accurate memory and a clearer appraisal of what is or is not factual in remembrance. (20)

As, for instance, in the scandal surrounding Binjamin Wilkomirski's sham Holocaust-biography in the late 1990s. While a great number of studies of historical trauma focus, one way or another, on the Holocaust, I wish to depart from this landscape altogether while retaining the theoretical framework in order to show how its findings prove useful elsewhere. I will concentrate here on another experience of collective violence and trauma: the experience of the Allied bombing raids directed at civilian populations, particularly on civilians in German cities during the Second World War, and, more precisely, its place in post-war Germany's history and memory.

By the spring of 1945 most German cities were reduced to piles of rubble. Early encounters by war correspondents such as Janet Flanner and Martha

Gellhorn can hardly conceal the shocking magnitude of the desolation. Approximately 600,000 civilians had either been torn to pieces or were mangled by falling wreckage, had burnt to death in one of the many firestorms that raged through the cities, or suffocated slowly in their collapsed bunkers.[1] Graphic images of the time, for instance, those taken in Hamburg or Dresden, show corpses stacked like firewood in the city-centre streets where they were burned immediately to avoid epidemics. To gather the collected experiences of four years of air war, and ultimately evaluate them, demands first and foremost the description of a population that, by 1945, seemed to have returned to an existence resembling that of troglodytes. An assessment of these experiences should attempt to make these landscapes of destruction visible, and the stench of rotting corpses decaying underneath seemingly endless piles of rubble, sometimes decorated with a makeshift cross, tangible. The rats, maggots and flies – all that and much more had to be written down before it could possibly reach the memory banks of any generation, be it the generation that witnessed the violence or any born thereafter. And all that, once observed, had to be explained, justified or at least accounted for.

According to W. G. Sebald's controversial book *On the Natural History of Destruction*, however, the overwhelming reality of devastated German cities and their remaining inhabitants was never adequately addressed in language. Sebald triggered a debate on post-war literature when he claimed that Germany's writers, busy recovering a self-identity lost in inner emigration, failed in the face of such a task. The great novel of the bombing war was never written in Germany. Sebald is bothered by the absence of descriptions of the air raids; he fails to find what only the artist's 'synoptic and artificial view reveals' (*NHD*: 26/33). Sebald considers the artificial distance necessary if one is to supplement and comprehend the accounts of the eyewitnesses, who are themselves, he assumes, often products and victims of their overwhelmed and distorted senses. In his study of air war and literature, he observes that the unrestricted area bombing and its aftermath have left barely any trace in the German national consciousness, and that the public never engaged in a debate that focused on the question of whether the air raids could be justified on either strategic or moral grounds. What did surface, primarily in the late 1950s, was swiftly forgotten. The destruction of German cities, which at that time was historically unique, itself fell victim to what Sebald identifies as 'an almost perfectly functioning mechanism of repression' (*NHD*: 12/19). In Sebald's own words,

> People's ability to forget what they do not want to know, to overlook what is before their eyes, was seldom put to the test better than in Germany at that time. The population decided – out of sheer panic at first – to carry on as if nothing had happened. (*NHD*: 41/47)

His study plays out this central repression hypothesis in a variety of ways. The silence, he asserts, is a result of apathy, self-anaesthesia and suppression (*NHD*: 5/13, 11/19). We learn, moreover, that the devastation of the bombing war coincided with 'a desire to close down the senses', that it was protected or hidden by the 'tacit imposition of a taboo' in the years that followed (*NHD*: 24/30, 34/44). 'There was a tacit agreement, equally binding on everyone, that the true state of material and moral ruin in which the country found itself was not to be described' (*NHD*: 10/17). I will look very carefully at especially this last assertion. When Sebald thus describes the absence of memory as a defence mechanism, he also, of course, prescribes something we could label the moral task of writers: to come to terms with the bizarre campaign of destruction that surrounded them. This process might begin with nothing more than the mere description of the death and ruins. Yet this body of literature, Sebald declares, does not exist, give or take a handful of exceptions.[2] The terror of area bombing, whose ultimate aim was the dehousing of the German workforce (Kennett 1982: 129), allegedly caused suffering that was unspeakable. The language of that time, and even more so its speakers and writers, Sebald argues, reveal themselves as too feeble or unwilling to capture their dreadful experiences and thereby transform the 'primary memory' of what happened into knowledge for later generations.

1. THE PSYCHOLOGICAL ARGUMENT

Sebald's thesis presents us with a meld of two independent elements. It is an ambiguous fusion that is never addressed by Sebald himself, but must be unravelled in order to evaluate both the accuracy and thrust of his critique. When Sebald employs the now-common linguistic currency of trauma and memory, he attempts to describe the psychological reaction of individuals to an experience of collective and excessive violence. He is, like Wiesel, concerned about the transformation of this experience (the 'truth of area bombing', perhaps) into the collective 'secondary memory' of something like a national consciousness. For Sebald, as we have seen, the prime agent of such a transfer is not the historian but the artist – and especially the writer, whose alleged synoptic view is considered both capable of and responsible for producing accessible and authentic knowledge of the traumatic event. That Germany's post-war writers (as much as the general population), according to Sebald, did not simply suffer from a psychological pathology like amnesia, but rather actively chose not to carry out such a transformation is a different matter altogether. It is an issue that appears to point to a moral failure rather than an epistemological or psychological dilemma. For Sebald, they came to the decision to suppress their remembrances ('the population decided – out of sheer panic at first – to carry on as if nothing had happened'), that is, to detoxify the shocking reality by wilfully extinguishing its memory. I address this internal, psychological side of Sebald's repression hypothesis below.

The second element, the 'political' or 'external,' is something that Sebald's essay ignores. Any investigation, however, that expresses its astonishment about what was (or was not) written in the immediate aftermath of the war must include within its scope the administrative, organisational, social and economic circumstances in which literature or newspapers were produced.[3] What remains to be investigated, therefore, is how the notions of 'taboo' or 'repression' also allude to something other than the internal psychological taboo on remembering. Its external political dimension curiously falls by the wayside in Sebald's study. In Part 2, I will argue that repression also refers to the taboo on criticising the Allies because of the hideous crimes committed by or in the name of the Germans themselves. But let us focus on the implications of Sebald's psychological study first, since this dominates and guides his criticism.

As early as 1982, in an essay on Germany's post-war literature that contains the building blocks of his later book, Sebald expresses his bewilderment regarding the silence that surrounds the havoc caused by the Allied bombing campaign.[4] In the early 1980s, however, Sebald still operates mostly outside the theoretical and rhetorical framework of trauma, taboo and repression. His obvious discontent with literary reactions to and transformations of the bombing raids, especially those by Hermann Kasack and, to a degree, Hans Erich Nossack as well, were centred on the aesthetic notion of a new concept of literature appropriate to these unique experiences. Sebald is curious about the 'objective reality of the time, especially the devastation of Germany's cities' (1982: 347) and the consequence of witnessing such devastation on the individual's mental health or, on a far broader scale, the effects on social patterns of behaviour. Yet perusing the available literature he finds that he cannot gain access to the quiddity of the experience or its aftermath. According to Sebald, the literary representations of total destruction by and large reveal a habitual tendency to translate what must have been a most ugly reality of destroyed habitat into the narrative of a mythological no-man's-land, an aesthetic transformation that obscures what it is supposed to make visible. It is the 'rhetoric of fatalism that bars the view onto the technological undertaking of the destruction . . . Because of this constellation it was also not possible to reflect upon the agents of the destruction' (351). A discussion centring on notions of agency and responsibility, in keeping with this rationale, becomes unfeasible because of a language that prevents access to historical agents by removing them to a transcendent realm. It hides, along with the technological and organisational apparatus, the factual decision-making within the bombing campaign.[5] Sebald argues that even a text like Nossack's *Der Untergang*, which is for the most part merely descriptive, unfortunately camouflages the strategy of the Allied air forces as 'an example of God's justice' (350–1). The historically new experience that surpassed all imagination, Sebald concludes, required a culture of writing that it did not find at the time. Writers responded to the unknown by employing their old, familiar and, given the extraordinary circumstances, hopelessly unsuitable artistic tools. The language of fatalism and divine justice placed excessive strain on – or even replaced altogether – both the descriptive powers and the faculty of judgement. 'The interpretive pattern of the apocalypse' was, as Ursula Heukenkamp agreed, the 'language of a petrified experience' (2001: 475). It seems, then, given the traumatic nature of the experience and thus contrary to Wiesel's view, that not the insider but rather the outsider, both temporal and spatial, occupies a privileged position from which to describe the catastrophe. 'A description of the catastrophe,' Sebald asserts, 'is possible rather from its margins than from its very centre' (1982: 353). Only with a delay of more than three decades, and with the arrival of Alexander Kluge's *Der Luftangriff auf Halberstadt am 8. April 1945* in the 1970s, does the horror of this limit-event begin to be transformed into a knowledge that might survive the survivors. Sebald identifies Kluge as the first to unearth the 'traumatic and shock-like experiences, which – in complicated procedures of suppression – were consigned to amnesia by those affected'. Sebald's brief and somewhat unmediated excursion into trauma and memory argues that Kluge's text 'is based on the insight that experience in a true sense was simply not possible due to the overwhelming swiftness and entirety of the destruction' (357–8). The language of this passage points to the direction Sebald's later argument will take. When, in *On the Natural History of Destruction*, he harks back to the absence of literary reflections on the bombing raids, his focus has shifted somewhat from a discussion of literary models and artisanship to that of taboo and repression. The aesthetic verdict transmutes into a political commentary and the adoption of a moral position.

On the Natural History of Destruction maintains that the real condition of Germany's physical and moral annihilation was never supposed to be described – and that because of a universally binding and tacit agreement. Sebald claims that the Germans countered their apathy and lack of interest in what had just happened to them by expressing 'their intention of rebuilding their country' (*NHD*: 6/13).[6] Only very few authors 'ventured to break the taboo on any mention of the inward and outward destruction'. The gruesome experiences were relegated to 'an almost perfectly functioning mechanism of repression' (*NHD*: 11/18, 12/19). A 'desire to close down the senses' (*NHD*: 23/30) responded to the need to learn facts about the raids. 'The quasi-natural reflex, engendered by feelings of shame and a wish to defy the victors, was to keep quiet and look the other way,' Sebald asserts. The muteness of the Germans, their 'silence' and 'instinctive looking away' (*NHD*: 30–1/37–8), is the reason why we know so little about the experiences of the bombing raids. Ultimately, however, the scarcity of descriptions has its roots in the 'tacit imposition of a taboo' covering up the 'legacy of an existence among the ruins that was felt to be shameful' (*NHD*: 34/41, 36/43).

The experience of devastation and loss, Sebald tirelessly stresses, never left the realm of primary memory precisely because of this shame. The shame alone causes the ostensibly shocking inability to remember, thereby blocking the possibility of mourning, which will never take place in a society with such an amnesiac population.[7] The Germans collectively avoided the subject, acted as if nothing had happened, and decided to move on. It was a mutual agreement, publicly articulated in many so-called 'rubble films' of the time, which made Germans want to close their eyes before the apparent annihilation of the former master race. This aspect of Sebald's thesis employs 'taboo' as a willingly embraced, self-imposed censor of undesirable German memories. But can we reconcile this allegedly active forgetting ('handing over', 'shutting down') with Sebald's remark in his 1982 essay that 'experience in a true sense was simply not possible due to the overwhelming swiftness and entirety of the destruction'? Has his position changed with regard to the nature of the 'traumatic and shocklike experiences'? Did the Germans actively forget the bombing raids, or were these events, owing to their traumatic nature, inevitably going to be inaccessible, or eventually even lost? Sebald's rather straightforward attribution of agency must be scrutinised.

Trauma, as LaCapra observes, has an effect on primary memory as it 'creates a gap or hole in experience' (1998: 21). Cathy Caruth has investigated trauma's disruption of historical coherence, its effect beyond mere psychopathology. Caruth places trauma in a historical context and argues that it points to an interruption or incompletion in knowing. In trauma, witnessing unwillingly collapses.[8] The witness cannot fully register the truth or scope of an experience as it occurs owing to its overwhelming intensity. Traumatic history is thus history that is not owned in its entirety. It cannot be simply rejected, as Sebald seems to suggest throughout his argument. According to Caruth, in trauma '[t]he ability to recover the past is . . . closely and paradoxically tied up . . . with the inability to have access to it' (1995: 151–2). Several of the essays in the volume *Trauma: Explorations in Memory* conclude that trauma is not experienced as a mere repression or defence. Rather, the temporal delay allows the individual to function beyond the shock of the first moment.[9] Certainly, the event must register at some point, whether it is with the victims or later generations. But the question becomes more complex when it takes on a socio-political dimension. One must ask whether there is, on the one hand, a desire for that specific sort of testimony or witnessing, and, on the other hand, whether there exists political pressure that deems such testimony undesirable. A taboo on remembering is not only a private psychological affair, but also a political one. Moreover, the problems do not end with the issue of access. 'Recovery' of the distressing history necessitates, in addition, its transformation. 'Flesh' and 'minds' – to return to Wiesel's opening remark – do not talk, write, paint or tell on their own. They require a medium. Let us agree for a moment that the traumatic experience interrupts the familiar consistency of history. If this is the case, we can expect that any narrative of that very history will mirror the latter's ruptures and cracks.

In *On the Natural History of Destruction*, Sebald refers numerous times to the conceptual apparatus of trauma. The dreadful experiences of ruin and death 'obviously did not register on the sensory experience of the survivors' (*NHD*: 5/13). It is 'knowledge incompatible with any sense of normality' (*NHD*: 11/19); these experiences are 'beyond our ability to comprehend' (*NHD*: 25/32). During the last three years of the war, we could have observed throughout Germany what Sebald describes as 'distraught refugees vacillating between a hysterical will to survive and leaden apathy' (*NHD*: 29/36). What they were lucky enough to survive were 'experiences exceeding what is tolerable' (*NHD*: 79/85). And with regard to many mothers who, as several eye-witness accounts corroborate, carried their charred, shrivelled-up children in suitcases or as bundles out of the inferno, Sebald offers the following remark:

> We do not know what became of the mothers who fled carrying such burdens, whether and how they managed to readjust to normal life. Yet perhaps such fragmentary memories show that it is impossible to gauge the depths of trauma suffered by those who came away from the epicentres of the catastrophe. (*NHD*: 89–90/95)

Clearly, Sebald shares the observation that the traumatic event causes a rupture or block, that it dislocates the modes and boundaries of our understanding. However, the reaction of our sensory apparatus to an event of overwhelming power can also be one of numbness, or a refusal to register. While, on the one hand, Sebald seems willing to concede that the occurrences exceeded the capacity of comprehension, he suspects, on the other hand, that the resulting 'stereotypical phrases' or the 'apparently unimpaired ability . . . of everyday language to go on functioning' (*NHD*: 32/32) point to nothing but a suspicious lack of authenticity. The phrases and language – and this implied assertion is the guiding thrust of Sebald's angry analysis – display the moral failure of the very refusal to remember.

Trauma research indicates, however, that such a rejection is common, and certainly not a solid foundation for the criticism Sebald launches against an entire population that, allegedly, imposes a convenient taboo on its past arising from the shame it experienced. The complex transformation of trauma into narrative, and the inclusion of that narrative into a total (hi)story of the past, is simplified in *On the Natural History of Destruction* to a trouble-free elimination in order to move on. Sebald's argument neglects that such a process must suffer from its own incomprehensibility.[10]

2. The Political Argument

There is, ostensibly, ample evidence to support Sebald's claim of an internal paralysis and psychological taboo that left the experiences indescribable, or
labelled them as such. Yet looking at the second, more ambiguous political (or
external) aspect of the taboo – the suppression – will enable us to scrutinise his
thesis not only from within (for instance, via his treatment of trauma), but also
from outside the framework of his argument altogether. That silence was
'enjoined on' the past (*NHD*: 7/16) is only one of many assertions that could
potentially be taken quite literally, that is, linked with the political realm in
which obligations are made, and in particular with the (cultural) policies of the
Allied Military Government. What Sebald's psychological line of reasoning dis-
regards, especially with respect to book production in post-war Germany, are
the manifold dimensions that played key roles in the production process, elements such as the mission of re-education, the control of the media, and economic factors. How do censorship and licences, for example, or registration
and paper distribution in the zones of occupation inhibit or even prohibit what
an author writes or a publisher prints up to 1950, or even thereafter? How does
the desire for escapist literature or the economic successes of Adenauer's new
Republic affect the production of war literature? Can the surge of such literature in the late 1950s be seen in conjunction with the anti-American sentiment
prevailing (and worsening) in Germany at least until the Berlin crisis in 1961?[11]
Before 1961 it was primarily the bombing campaigns conducted by England
and America that characterised the image of Allied conquerors prone to excessive violence (Geyer 2001: 130). Sebald does not ponder such issues. It is legitimate, if not imperative, to raise these questions when investigating the complex
problem of whether the artistic denunciation of post-war Germany that Sebald
demands is truly (and only) the result of an internal suppression. Rather, the
collapse of witnessing goes hand in hand with a political course that reinforces
the taboo on remembering. The senior partners on the western side of the newly
emerging Iron Curtain were not particularly interested in reminding the bene-
ficiaries of the Economic Miracle of the havoc wreaked on Germany a few years
earlier. Once Germany became a necessary ally against communism, nobody
(neither the Germans nor the Americans and British) wished to recall the prob-
lematical raids that flattened Germany's cities and crushed its civilian population. 'Rubble literature' and 'rubble films' were unwelcome memory banks,
storing that part of Europe's history that both Germans and Allies attempted
to hide as much as possible behind the frail back of Heidi and the immaculate
beauty of the Alps.

We need not look far to discover that the cultural policies within the Allied
occupation zones aimed not only at the democratic re-education of the
Germans but also at suppressing awareness of a past bombing campaign that

could easily question the pedagogical qualifications of the teachers themselves. In post-war Europe's envisioned and imposed liberal and democratic order, an order of alleged superior humanity, the politics of active forgetting loomed large. In England and America, the activities of Bomber Command had become increasingly controversial both within segments of the public and within the government itself. And they became controversial despite the fact, as Stephen Garrett stresses, that the true character of the area offensive was 'systematically concealed from the British public' (Garrett 1996: 114). In the United Kingdom, Arthur Harris's veterans were soon confronted with their own, British version of an imposed taboo. In 1945, Garrett asserts, 'the general attitude of many . . . seemed to be that it would be best to forget [Bomber Command's] activities as quickly as possible' (84). Long before the end of the war, the Allies anticipated that the immense destruction caused by area bombing might collide with the intended and well-planned reorientation of the German population in the Western zones along liberal-democratic principles. Various issues were therefore identified that were '*not supposed to be* described', as Sebald phrased it.

The political dimension of this remark reveals its potential when we relate our investigation of Sebald's repression hypothesis to a project such as the 'Projection of Britain' in the British zone of occupation.[12] It brings us directly to the second mechanism of suppression that reinforces the assumed psychological reaction. As early as 1942–3, that is, at the same time as the intensification of Bomber Command attacks, the Americans and British intensified their efforts in the realm of 'Civil Affairs and Military Government', perhaps triggered by the collapse of Italy and the now apparent necessity (and shortcomings) of occupational government. The historian Gabriele Clemens claims that British cultural policies functioned within a much larger framework that exceeded the events of the Second World War. Cultural politics on the British side were what she terms 'Machtersatzpolitik' – politics in the realm of culture that were supposed to compensate for the apparent loss of direct political and military power of the British Empire in the aftermath of the Great War. The main task of the envisioned policies in all areas of cultural production and control in a post-war Germany was simple and straightforward: to promote Great Britain and British values. The projection of the 'British Way of Life' as an admirable example worthy of imitation contributed to and buttressed, at times even enforced, a continued silence about the bombings well into the semi-sovereign Federal Republic of Germany. Yet, we can imagine that in the years following 1945, this double task of forgetting Bomber Command's activities and of projecting the presumed superior British ideal proved to be a tremendous challenge. The positive projection of British (or, in general, humanist) values had to charm the audience into ignoring the devastation that literally framed their movie screen. All too present beyond the canvas was a permanent reminder of another, destructive England.

The prohibitive flip side of this policy, of course, was the necessary suppression of any negative self-image of the victorious Allies. They were not to surface in any cultural sphere, whether in books, films or on stage. The so-called *German Sub-Committee (GSC)*, a subsection of the *Joint Re-occupation Committee*, was central to these British efforts in the realm of culture. Within months of its founding in September 1943, the sub-committee produced several detailed drafts for the post-war control of the German media. Of greatest interest for the committee were the control and supervision of the publishing industry – a direct result of Britain's assumption that Germans had a high regard for books. Misinterpreting the tremendous influence of film and radio in Nazi Germany, the GSC believed that books had always influenced Germany's public opinion much more strongly than any other mass media. According to the GSC, special efforts were therefore required that focused on supplying Germany with adequate materials after an initial phase of cleansing public libraries. One of the most vocal opponents of these cultural policies implemented by the Military Government was the British publisher and socialist Victor Gollancz. The removal of books like Romain Rolland's *Mahatma Gandhi* so upset Gollancz that he accused the British military government of behaving like 'colonial masters' and 'Herrenvolk' (Gollancz 1947: 94).

Besides political re-education, the pacifying effect of entertainment was considered important, whether achieved through books or, more importantly, films. Clemens demonstrates persuasively that films in particular were intended to control the population (1997: 75–6). Ironically, because of the lack of adequate new films available for the image-hungry German audience, the British were soon forced to show cleansed versions of the very feature films the Nazis had used to steer a population tired of war through the darkest times. For the British effort, they were deemed even more desirable than the so-called rubble films that appeared between 1946 and 1949. Both the German audience and the British military government disliked the films. They neither re-educated the Germans nor did they help them to work through their immediate past. Most important in our context, however, is a third reason: the films, by their very nature, deal primarily with the landscapes of ruin, confronting the viewer with the surrounding reality. Homelessness, hunger, the black market and problems with returning soldiers, expellees, or refugees – themes that also dominate Heinrich Böll's rubble novel *The Silent Angel* – are paramount.[13] Rubble films are permanent visual reminders of the effect of terror bombing, and potentially trouble viewers instead of calming them. They are lasting visual testimonies of a campaign that was supposed to be suppressed and forgotten – a campaign that can stun the viewer in the twenty-first century just as much as in 1945. Since the projection of democratic values and Britain as an influential exemplary ideal was of prime importance, the Allies allowed nothing that would openly (or even potentially) criticise or defame the Allies. A curious example of British determination and thoroughness is the 1950 ban of the film depicting the sinking of the Titanic. Even one year after the immediate British control mechanism of censorship of films was replaced by the so-called *Freiwillige Selbstkontrolle* (Voluntary Self-Regulation) in what was now the semi-sovereign Federal Republic of Germany, the grim fate of the luxury liner was considered inappropriate for the German audience. Following enormous pressure from Britain (and against American inclination), its screening was forbidden in all German cinemas after a brief, unspectacular airing in the American zone. It contained, according to the British film officer under whose guidance voluntary self-regulation operated, strong anti-British propaganda since it allegedly presented the themes of materialism, greed and injustice as British vices (Peck 2000). Overall, books and films on war were considered extremely problematic. Great care was therefore exercised by the *BSC* to prevent the Germans from tackling their own immediate past via British literature. To appear as teachers or even prosecutors, the British feared, contained the possibility of provoking animosity towards England.

Clemens identifies two main reasons for this. First, war films of the victorious powers that repeatedly depicted the defeat of Germany would provoke negative reactions towards the British instead of identifying them as a desired ideal. Secondly, not the British but the United States and the Soviet Union were the true military superpowers after 1945 – a fact that the British did not want to see displayed in films or books. Clemens takes no notice, however, of the central moral issue of systematic area bombing that would inevitably be attached to any discussion concerning war. To engage with Germany's immediate past in the form of uninhibited British moralising will certainly feed into the discussion England's own chapter to the devaluation of all moral standards during the war – as, indeed, it did, after a delay of roughly four decades, in June 1992. The controversial debate surrounding the merits or ethical failure of Bomber Command flared up when the Queen Mother unveiled a statue honouring Sir Arthur Harris and the 55,000 men of Allied Bomber Command killed in action. Ten demonstrators were arrested when they shouted 'Harris was a mass murderer'. It would be of interest to know whether the demonstrators were referring to the perished civilians in German cities, or whether they were condemning 'Butcher' Harris because of the near-suicidal missions on which he sent his often inexperienced crews (Anon 1992; Tuohy 1991).

The great merit of Sebald's *On the Natural History of Destruction* is that it succeeds in lifting, to use Martin Broszat's famous phrase about the *Historikerstreit*, the 'general quarantine' (Broszat 1988: 3) under which the bombing raids were placed. It brings the horror of the area bombing into the public consciousness. Sebald correctly observes that the violent deaths of more than half-a-million civilians and the destruction of more than three million homes have not found an adequate voice in German literature. It would be an intellectual misdemeanour, however, to be satisfied with the suggestion that Germany's transition to a consumer society simply aided the welcomed collapse of witnessing by supporting an initial forgetfulness.[14] His overriding conviction that the ashamed German population was eager to return to their narrow-minded order of coffee and cake and thus themselves imposed a taboo on what they did not want to remember is, in its restrictedness, misleading.[15] Much in his book echoes this somewhat stereotypical assessment of the psychosocial deficiencies of the German petty bourgeois, stereotypes one would prefer to see dispensed with in favour of a more balanced analysis. In Sebald's study on air war and literature this hackneyed 'German' mentality returns in the form of an apathetic and wilfully amnesiac population that turns away from an ugly reality, a reality it hides with a pledge of secrecy. The story of the bombing war, for Sebald, is one of 'a persistent avoidance of the subject, or an aversion to it' (*NHD*: 93/99) on the part of its victims. One decides, whether in cold-blooded calculation or genuine shame, to carry on as if nothing had happened. Those who survived the bombing campaign in Germany seem to have experienced the taboo after 1945 quite differently. One woman, for instance, writes the following to Dieter Forte:

> The extent of the loneliness that came about because many questions could not be asked, because so many issues were taboo, because neither in history nor in literature were we allowed to draw parallels – this degree of loneliness was hard to endure. (Forte 1999)

Sebald's line of argument exhibits a rather selective historiography that, I would argue, has its roots in the complex difficulties of presenting Germans as victims at all (Bartov 2000: 29–40). Can any storyteller devote his or her energies to the feelings or sufferings of Germans trapped in their cellars or burning in the streets without injecting into the tale countless references to the crimes committed in their name? Is it not necessary to refer to Coventry before looking at Hamburg? Certainly, Sebald would answer. And in fact, he does. In particular, Sebald's angry response to the numerous letters and reactions his thesis triggered, a response that comprises the entire second half of *On the Natural History of Destruction* where he defends himself determinedly, signifies how profoundly the fear of revisionism parallels his laudable desire to raise the issues of taboo and repression in the post-1945 context. Although he expresses an interest in adding a new chapter, Sebald does not want to rewrite history. He urges that the 'majority of Germans today know, or so at least it is to be hoped, that we actually provoked the annihilation of the cities in which we once lived' (*NHD*: 103/109). If anyone wishes to discuss the bombing raids in a context of right and wrong, the sequence of action and reaction has to be clear. One last time, at the very end of *On the Natural History of Destruction*, he reminds his readers that Guernica, Warsaw, Belgrade and Rotterdam established the Germans as the pioneers of area bombing. What the Allies did, we are told, is what the Germans would have done. The difficulty and anxiety, perhaps especially for a member of the so-called second generation like Sebald himself, of describing the historical fact that German civilians, and among them many children, were killed in their hundreds of thousands, leads Sebald's argument astray insofar as it incorrectly limits the responsibility for this narrative void to German shame and self-pity. The intergenerational transmission of guilt seems here as visible as elsewhere. To put it more bluntly: Sebald's study itself bears the mark of a taboo typical of the 'bad conscience' of the Federal Republic of Germany. He himself is not a victim of the psychological taboo he observes on the side of his ancestors; rather, his interpretive wings are clipped from the start by the political taboo with which he himself grew up. The political taboo on criticising the Allies for the attacks on civilians is the blind spot of his own observations. Sebald's study is sustained by a gesture that seeks and finds blame or failure on the side of the now ashamed and speechless German perpetrator who makes a taboo of the massive destruction of his home and life. Both his fierce rejection of anything that only remotely smells of revisionism, and the pressure to generate politically correct assertions, leads him to produce an inaccurate historical assessment.

One can hardly object to the contention that the bombing campaign was swept underneath the carpet by the Allies. 'There was', as Garrett asserts for England, 'a seeming effort to discourage . . . detailed examination of Bomber Command's activities' (Garrett 1996: 34). Any confrontation with the immediate past, any question relating to the issue of agency and responsibility, could not avoid approaching the piles of rubble that were, for many years, part of the new Germany. What was not supposed to be described was therefore war as such. To steer clear of the recent technological mass-murder in the process of cultural reorganisation was, for obvious reasons, very much in the interest of victors who were decidedly unwilling to look back. And the cultural officers responsible for the educational manifestations that were permitted to reach the light of day, made that perfectly clear to any publisher or film producer at the time. Sebald's unspoken internal taboo, exclusively at work among the ashamed and disillusioned former 'master race', this inner and self-inflicted mechanism of suppression reserved for the defeated Germans, fails to acknowledge or recognise the powerful hand of Allied cultural politics in occupied Germany. Their claim to be the cradles of democracy and humanity is at stake amidst the ruins of cities like Cologne, Hamburg or Dresden. For many, especially the younger generations who are still kept by and large ignorant of this chapter of European history, the 'truth of area bombing' is not so much hidden by the new buildings that replaced the rubble. Rather, it is still anxiously hidden under a cloak of excessive moral tact.

NOTES

1. Based on the *Strategic Bombing Surveys* and Germany's *Federal Office for Statistics*, 600,000 is the number Sebald operates with.

2. The most prominent texts are Kasack (1949), Ledig (1999), Nossack (1976).
3. Gwienow-Hecht (1999) offers an illuminating analysis of the editorial policies that characterised ten years of the American-sponsored *Die Neue Zeitung* in occupied Germany.
4. In 1982, Sebald sets out to 'answer the more than overdue question why the air attacks on German cities . . . and the societal life forms radically changed by the catastrophic destruction, were rarely ever discussed in German literature' (Sebald 1982: 345).
5. For a concise overview of the administrative development of the campaign in England, see Garrett 1996; for the United States, see Schaffer 1985; for a general history, see Kennett 1982.
6. Huyssen focuses on 'the desire for repeated new beginnings', a desire he interprets as 'a peculiar German repetition compulsion of the post-fascist decades' (Huyssen 2001).
7. Moeller's *War Stories* (2001) deviates from the pattern of analyses claiming a general collapse of memory in post-war Germany. Instead, he argues that Germans remembered 'selectively', turning the stories of German POWs and expellees into a narrative of German victimisation.
8. The 'collapse of witnessing' is an expression used by Dori Laub. See Felman and Laub 1991: 57–92.
9. Historical examples discussed by Schäfer (1985) confirm this position. German anthropologist Baelz was the first to speak of an 'emotional paralysis' in the context of the Tokyo earthquake in 1894. He describes a catatonia that triggered a defence mechanism so strong that the people calmly attempted to save their lives without any feeling of panic. Baelz quoted in Panse 1952: 8–9 and 90–6.
10. '[T]he transformation of the trauma into a narrative memory that allows the story to be verbalized and communicated, to be integrated into one's own, and others', knowledge of the past, may lose both the precision and the force that characterizes traumatic recall' (Caruth 1995: 153).
11. For a concise, if self-congratulatory analysis of German-American encounters in post-1945 Germany, see Geyer 2001.
12. For a comparative study that investigates the activities of all four victors by focusing on Berlin, see Schivelbusch 1998.
13. Böll's example of rubble literature offers little or no consolation while it describes life in the immense ruins of Cologne. The story depicts a devastated, poverty-stricken hopelessness and is precisely the sort of text Sebald deems suitable to bear witness to the destruction and misery from a distance. However, Böll's *Silent Angel*, submitted to his publisher Middelhauve in August of 1950 and even announced in the publisher's catalogue, was not actually published until 1992.
14. For Sebald, however, the causality is that clear, even in the realm of politics. The 'reconstruction of the country . . . prohibited any look backward. It did so through the sheer amount of labour required . . . pointing the population exclusively towards the future and enjoining on it silence about the past' (*NHD*: 7/16).
15. Some of those affected display a 'lack of moral sensitivity bordering on inhumanity' as they seem, scandalously, determined 'to drink coffee in the normal way on Hamburg balconies' in July 1943 (*NHD*: 42/48).

14

SEEING THINGS: SPECTRES AND ANGELS IN W. G. SEBALD'S PROSE FICTION

Jan Ceuppens

Does the work of W. G. Sebald hold a promise? Can the dead he evokes, to quote Marx, bury the dead and make way for future redemption? Do Sebald's (hi)stories of loss and destruction point to an end of history in a reconciliatory moment, even to some kind of transcendence? Or would such a promise be an obscenity in view of the horrors that loom behind the biographies on which his stories are based? These are the most general and most ambitious questions the present chapter attempts to tackle.

The following remarks constitute an attempt to analyse a number of motifs that point to such a model of history in Sebald's work by connecting them to the notions of the spectre, the uncanny and repetition, as a preliminary step towards clarifying a certain turn in literary theory which uses these notions. My approach is limited to selected passages from Sebald's *The Emigrants*, briefly making reference to his earlier *Vertigo*. The two works are tied together by a number of structural similarities, motifs and themes that set them apart from Sebald's other novels. *The Emigrants*, one could even claim, is a variation on *Vertigo*, and the readability of both books is greatly enhanced when they are juxtaposed.

LEVELS OF REPETITION

The most striking structural feature of Sebald's narratives is repetition. We are presented with a first-person narrator acting as a witness to events happening to or inflicted on others, or rather: a narrator telling the life stories of third

parties as they were told to him by the third parties themselves or by eyewitnesses. In many cases, especially in key passages, the narrator's sources are
written records of some kind – diaries, letters, archival documents. In other
words, what the narrator does with striking regularity is *read*.

In *The Emigrants*, the most intricate example of this procedure can be found
in 'Ambros Adelwarth', where the narrator (re)constructs his great-uncle's
biography from accounts given by his American relatives, Aunt Fini and Uncle
Kasimir, by former psychiatrist Dr Abramsky, and by Ambros himself through
his travel journal for 1913. These accounts partly overlap, creating a perspectivist view on the subject and presenting Adelwarth's biography in an achron-
ological manner. For example, the re-narration of the journal ends with a
somewhat enigmatic entry, which the reader is able to interpret in the light of
earlier revelations about Adelwarth's later life:

> Memory, he added in a postscript, often struck me as a kind of dumbness.
> It makes one's head heavy and giddy, as if one were not looking back
> down the receding perspectives of time but down on the earth from a great
> height, from one of those towers whose tops are lost to view in the clouds.
> (*E*: 145/215)

The image of the tower, which might otherwise serve as a metaphor of omnis-
cience, here stands for a distance that blurs vision. It causes the kind of
Schwindelgefühle or vertigo that formed the title of Sebald's first prose work,
the German containing a deliberate ambiguity between 'dizziness' and 'swindle'.

A striking characteristic of both the first-order narrator and his second-order
'oral' sources is that they seem to have an infallible memory at their disposal.
The narrator's impossibly complete memory is one of the many strategies
employed by Sebald to indicate that, in spite of their apparent realism, his narratives are fictional, not factual. But as we shall see below, the capacity of the
characters to remember does not provide them with a clearer view of things, or
help them to understand their fate. Indeed, memory seems only to lead to an
'unhappy consciousness', as Adelwarth states explicitly in the journal entry
quoted above.

This is a synecdochic way of demonstrating that witnessing, or bearing
witness, is always in some way a repetition without a final word: the narrator
is no more able to turn the stories into a final statement than are the other characters. And this form would then conform to Sebald's central subject, namely,
the irretrievability of a memory which is forever lost, since no repetition can
ever hope to render it in an 'authentic' way. If, however, this is the 'truth' behind
The Emigrants, it is merely yet another instance of postmodern relativism,
refuting itself since it *does* tell a truth about its subject after all. One possible
solution to this interpretative dilemma is to see repetition or representation in
itself, even if it is a 'hopeless' endeavour, as a way of remaining faithful to an

irrecuperable past and of opening a space for a promise. Sebald's *The Emigrants* thematises this logic of repetition by foregrounding questions of spectrality.

THE RETURN OF THE SPECTRE

In discussing the motif of the spectre in Sebald, the obvious starting point is a character that appears only implicitly in *The Emigrants*, but explicitly in *Vertigo*: the intra- and intertextual leitmotif of the undead hunter Gracchus from Franz Kafka's eponymous story. More than just a leitmotif, however, this ghost also becomes a thematic connection through which Kafka and Vladimir Nabokov – the latter the more visible of the two in *The Emigrants* – can be read together.

Gracchus is a classic example of a ghost or spectre: a person who never made it to the beyond but instead got stuck in an eternal limbo, not completely taken up into a non-corporeal other world, nor yet fully corporeal.[1] The clearest connection between *Vertigo* and *The Emigrants* is in the last sentence of Kafka's story. In a fragment of the story deleted by Kafka from the final manuscript, the dialogue between the hunter and the mayor of Riva ends:

> 'I am forever,' replied the Hunter, 'on the great stair that leads up to it. On that infinitely wide and spacious stair I clamber about, sometimes up, sometimes down, sometimes on the right, sometimes on the left, always in motion. The Hunter has been turned into a butterfly.' (Kafka 1993: 272)

We can only speculate about why Kafka decided to omit the butterfly, but a plausible reason would be that he interpreted it as too positive, as a sign of a possible transfiguration or redemption. It is generally accepted that the name Gracchus is really a word-play on Kafka's own name, the Italian 'gracchio' meaning the same as the Czech 'kavka': jackdaw. Kafka was always quite lucid about his own fate as an outcast, and so the positive transfiguration of the hunter into a butterfly seems incongruous. But even the butterfly cannot escape from the 'earthly waters' and is stuck on the stairs that would lead to the world beyond.

In *The Emigrants*, there are a number of references to and quotations from 'The Hunter Gracchus'.[2] A striking instance is the story of the 'stag's leap'. The narrator recalls how his primary school teacher would show his pupils 'how an image could be broken down into numerous tiny pieces – small crosses, squares or dots – or else assembled from these' (*E*: 31/47). The 'crosses, squares or dots' are mechanical tools that enable the pupils to produce the recognisable image of a stag. This image is itself applied by Bereyter as a didactic tool: the 'Legend of the Stag's Leap' to which he refers tells the story of a white stag that made its escape from a group of hunters by taking an enormous leap across a deep valley. One of the versions of this legend is set in the hamlet of Falkensteig in the Black Forest. It is hard not to think of the hunter Gracchus, who came from the Black Forest and died while hunting down an animal (albeit a chamois rather than a stag). The stag's leap may then well be a symbol for an unattainable goal – another reference to the unfinished mission of the hunter.

But the hunter and the butterfly motifs are also connected, in *The Emigrants*, in a way that renders the butterfly image even more ambiguous than it already was in Kafka (or in *Vertigo*). The link lies in the strange character of 'the man with the butterfly net' who appears in a number of different guises (cf. Sill 1997). The butterfly hunter is the guise in which Nabokov repeatedly appears in his own autobiography, *Speak, Memory* (1967), and both author and book are explicitly mentioned by Sebald's narrator: in the Henry Selwyn story, a slide of Henry Selwyn reminds the narrator of a picture of Nabokov (*E*: 15–16/26), and Paul Bereyter meets his companion Lucy Landau while she was reading Nabokov's autobiography (*E*: 43/65). The recurrence of the butterfly man could, of course, be seen as a *leitmotif*, a means of ensuring the text's coherence. But within Sebald's poetics, in which coincidence plays such an important role, it would seem to have a wider scope.

Before turning to this more general point, however, let us first take a closer look at the contextual embedding of the motif. The first two occurrences of the butterfly man still seem realistically motivated, but he acquires uncanny qualities as soon as we look at some of his other appearances.[3] Nabokov appears for the first time in person as the 'butterfly man' in Ithaca, where Ambros spends his last years in a mental institution; indeed, he mentions the man with the net just before going into what will be his last shock treatment. Nabokov appears twice in 'Max Ferber': as the little boy whom Ferber's mother mentions in her diary, and as the grown-up butterfly hunter who crosses Ferber's path on the Grammont mountain near Lake Geneva. This last and most elaborate Nabokov episode is highly overdetermined. First of all, it is set in the same landscape that has already served as a place of remembrance in 'Dr. Henry Selwyn', and is the site of the Hotel Eden, Ambros Adelwarth's first place of work after his definitive departure from his German homeland. For Ferber, too, it is tied to a recollection – he visited the lake region with his father in 1936 – and he now finds it ostensibly unchanged, and so alluring that he considers throwing himself into it. But then the man with the butterfly net 'suddenly appeared before him – like someone who's popped up out of the bloody ground' (*E*: 174/259). This sudden appearance plunges Ferber into a spate of amnesia, a 'lagoon of oblivion' (*E*: 174/259), from which he cannot even free himself by trying to render the butterfly hunter's face in a drawing.

The suggestion is that both 'hunters' – Gracchus and Nabokov – play a similar role in both texts. The image of the butterfly is combined with that of the hunter. Read from this perspective, the sentence omitted by Kafka can no longer be ascribed any redemptive meaning. The butterfly becomes something to be caught and displayed as a museum piece, a metaphor of death rather than of transfiguration or life. But this still does not account for the insistence with which these two characters recur in Sebald's narratives. In his discussion of the motif, Oliver Sill (1997: 621) refers to a similar character from a German folk song, mentioned by Walter Benjamin: the little hunchback ('bucklicht Männlein'). It is no coincidence that Sill should refer to Benjamin, since Benjamin's *Berlin Childhood*, in which the hunchback appears, is an important intertext for *The Emigrants*. The uncanny hunchback is always there, popping up wherever the subject goes. Sill reads the hunchback as a metaphor of forgetfulness (621) in stark contrast to the Nabokov motif, whose meaning would, in his view, be (compulsive) recollection. This opposition may seem too clearcut, but even so, we are confronted with two modes of remembering that keep coming back in *The Emigrants*, two modes that exist in a paradoxical relationship: a constant repetition that resists appropriation or integration into some sort of symbolic order, and a liberating, 'usable', 'communicative' or 'functional' memory. This is where the logic of the spectre could provide us with a helpful conceptual tool.

While it has been of interest to scholars of fantastic literature for some time, the spectre has recently become fashionable as a philosophical notion, especially since the publication of Jacques Derrida's *specters of marx* (1994). As always, Derrida draws his operative term from existing texts rather than importing notions from an extraneous system. In this case, the *Communist Manifesto* and *The German Ideology* provide him with the 'quasi-transcendental' term that facilitates his deconstructive reading.[4] The spectre is a revenant, a 'thing' that keeps coming back, especially when you least expect it. It is a past one would like to shake off but never quite can, a metaphor for the kind of inheritance one can never really assume, since it is not simply given but imposes itself.

Marx's *The Eighteenth Brumaire of Louis Bonaparte* (1852), which is interesting for its literary as well as its philosophical, political and historiographical merits, is concerned with such a comeback, and is central to Derrida's reflections. Marx's text hinges on something that has long fascinated Derrida: the (im)possibility of repetition. Marx quotes Hegel in saying that historical events always occur twice, but adds that while the first occurrence is a tragedy, the second is a farce. Yet things are complicated by the very example that prompted Marx's comment in the first place: the French Revolution of 1789 sought its own language in that of ancient Rome, and abandoned this historical garb as soon as it outgrew it, whereas the 1848 'revolution', which eventually cleared the way for Louis Bonaparte, seemed like a mere parody of that of 1789/1794 and, indirectly, also of those Roman costumes and customs. Marx's contention is that a real proletarian revolution would not need the kind of historical orientation that shaped the events of 1848, or even 1789: a *real* revolution would obtain its 'poetics' – Marx's word – from the future rather than the past, and would no longer need any models. To put it differently, history is a burden, to be forgotten in order to reach new ground. But Marx does not address the question of how this is to be achieved. He would seem to imply that the action required is a leap into the unknown – hoping that the necessary 'poetics' will arrive in time. For Derrida, the advent of such a poetics and of a pure revolution not tainted by history and the logic of repetition is an impossibility; it will have to remain a promise. What we have is the existing situation of alienation. This, it would seem, is where Sebald's characters are caught: in a melancholy inability to appropriate and bury their past – and to turn to the future. The question is whether this melancholy position is also Sebald's.

A commentary Peter Fenves wrote on Derrida's Marx book may prove useful in exploring this issue further. Inspired by Benjamin's concept of history, Fenves introduces the distinction between spectres and angels. The spectre, as we have seen, is that which, in its endless return or repetition, defies the very notion of singularity. The one thing one wants to reach and 'incorporate', the singularity of a person or event, is forever lost under a pile of representations of 'the same'. Conversely, the angelic or messianic would be that which is absolutely singular, unique, different, but it would, as such, be a promise that could never be attained in its 'pure' form.[5] This idea of 'purity' is precisely what Derrida reproaches Marx with: a pure revolution, the arrival of the angels, can never be attained. Perhaps the choice between the endless repetition of available patterns – the recycling of old clothing, so to speak – and an attempt to reach the singular who (or which) would then no longer have to be remembered is still too neat; the real question would be: how can one be faithful to the promise of the singular event by using the clothes of the past?

Returning to *The Emigrants*, the questions raised by Fenves seem to find an expression in the Nabokov/Gracchus figure. It would seem difficult to interpret it as an angel, of course, since it certainly does not bring memories to a standstill, referring rather to a past that will not rest. At the same time, however, its call for representation may just be the thing that makes a promise possible – if not redeemable. The spectral past is simultaneously that which sets in motion a desire for redemption and that which prevents us from ever reaching it.

GHOSTLY DWELLINGS

The question of the singular appearing or at least remaining visible as a promise can be reformulated in terms of the uncanny, which, according to Freud's definition, is the appearance of the unfamiliar within the familiar. Yet this equation is not unproblematic, since the uncanny is also tied to a return: the return of the repressed or, to use Schelling's phrase, which Freud quotes, of things that 'should have remained secret, hidden, latent, but which have come to light' (Freud 1919). If we seek to analyse the links between the return of the repressed, the uncanny and the promise of a singularity, the presence of the architectural in Sebald's work would seem to provide a good point of access.

The very word 'unheimlich', as analysed by Freud, derives from notions such as home or dwelling (*Heim, Heimat*), so that this affiliation seems rather obvious, especially in view of the long-standing literary tradition of the haunted house (Vidler 1992: 26–8). Architecture is of immense importance to Sebald, and although it becomes a general theme only in *Austerlitz*, it is also present in *The Emigrants*. It is introduced in a somewhat enigmatic reference at the beginning of 'Dr. Henry Selwyn', where a whole series of resemblances and comparisons is set in motion:

> The sash windows, each divided into twelve panes, glinted blindly, seeming to be made of dark mirror glass. The house gave the impression that no one lived there. And I recalled the château in the Charente that I had once visited from Angoulême. In front of it, two crazy brothers – one a parliamentarian, the other an architect – had built a replica of the façade of the palace of Versailles, an utterly pointless counterfeit, though one which made a powerful impression from a distance. The windows of that house had been just as gleaming and blind as those of the house we now stood before. (*E*: 4/9)

The impression the house gives is not deceptive, since its inhabitants are indeed mostly absent: while his wife Elli is abroad on business most of the time, Selwyn himself prefers to live in the small tower-like garden house he calls a 'folly'. The narrator and his wife decide to rent an apartment in a side wing which reminds Elli of a dovecote (*E*: 9/15); the only other person who lives there is the maid, Elaine, whose behaviour the tenants find unsettling – with her shorn hair, she reminds the narrator of an asylum inmate. The only time the house is actually used for a social occasion is a visit from Selwyn's friend Edwin Elliott, during which a slide show takes place that resembles a séance, conjuring up ghosts who do not age:

> The low whirr of the projector began, and the dust in the room, normally invisible, glittered and danced in the beam of light by way of a prelude to the pictures themselves . . . *Strangely enough*, both Edwin and Dr Selwyn made a *distinctly youthful impression* on the pictures they showed us, though at the time they made the trip, *exactly ten years earlier*, they were already in their late sixties. (*E*: 16–17/27–8; my emphasis)

The word that prompted Derrida's study of Marx, 'Gespenst', appears only once in *The Emigrants*, and it is precisely in a passage which describes the Selwyns's house.[6] It is used as an adjective, 'gespenstisch' ('ghostly'), in the narrator's reflection on the strange architecture of the house: there is a whole network of hidden corridors and entrances allowing the servants to go about their work without meeting with their 'betters', as it is ironically phrased. This is a second, invisible household underneath the visible life of the family: another scene possessing a different reality, perhaps even the 'real' substructure of the affluent life on the surface. If we take this description allegorically, other connotations come to mind. In a book both recounting memories and thematising memory, it seems almost too obvious to interpret this as a metaphor for the mind's workings: unknown to the house's proprietors, things go on behind their backs – they are, so to speak, not in complete control. The narrator's comment certainly points in such a direction:

> Often I tried to imagine what went on inside the heads of people who led their lives knowing that, behind the walls of the rooms they were in, the shadows of the servants were perpetually flitting past. I fancied they ought to have been afraid of those ghostly creatures. (*E*: 9–10/17)

Memories that cannot be shaken off are here represented in spatial terms. Something within a system of meanings and categories turns out to resist categorisation, it leads a life of its own within that system, or again: it is the uncanny, an appearance of the unfamiliar within the familiar. It would seem that this uncanny only appears when the reader adopts a different perspective on the image presented, when he looks at it obliquely. This, arguably, is the narrator's approach.

The temporal structure of this haunting becomes clear in the description of another haunted house that appears in the 'Max Ferber' episode. It is the house owned by the Lanzbergs at Bad Kissingen. Luisa Lanzberg, Max Ferber's mother, recalls it in her memoirs:

> To me the house, which the people of Kissingen soon took to calling the Lanzberg Villa, always remained essentially a strange place. The vast, echoing stairwell; the linoleum flooring in the hall; the corridor at the back where the telephone hung over the laundry basket and you had to hold the heavy receivers to your ears with both hands; the pale, hissing gaslight; the sombre Flemish furniture with its carved columns – there was something distinctly creepy [*unheimlich*] about all of it, and at times I feel quite definitely that it did steady and irreparable harm to me. (*E*: 208–10/314)

For all its grandeur, then, the Lanzberg Villa could surely pass for a haunted house. The archaic telephone, too, intrudes into the lives of the house's inhabitants with an 'uncanny violence'. Luisa's unease arguably reflects the general sense of alienation that accompanied the Jews' ascent to 'a position in middle-class life' (*E*: 208/312), something on which Sebald himself has written extensively (*UH*: 40–64). It is nevertheless surprising to find that the very place identified by the outside world with the name of the family is a strange place to Luisa Lanzberg; furthermore, it does her harm, or at least, that is how she perceives it many years later. The only place she thinks of as home, and which is also associated with all kinds of family occasions and Jewish feasts, is the small village of Steinach, the lost, idyllic origin. Could this be a model of how things ought to be – a paradise lost, to which one can only ever hope to return?

JERUSALEM

If there is one powerful image for the redemption of history, the coming of the Messiah and the fulfilment of the divine promise to mankind (or the chosen people), it is the celestial Jerusalem – another topic of Sebald's own essayistic reflections on Jewish culture (*UH*: 44–5). Formerly a city of wonders in the midst of a promised land, Jerusalem has fallen prey, as outlined in *The Emigrants*, to decay as a consequence of wars and scorched-earth politics (a phrase that sounds eerily familiar).

Jerusalem is the last station in Ambros Adelwarth's 1913 travel diary. Ambros, Cosmo Solomon's travelling companion and putative lover, first gives a detailed description of the Jerusalem of 1913, which turns out to be one more instance of a ghostly dwelling. The room in which the two travellers are accommodated foreshadows the lugubrious experience that is to come: 'One cannot say what period or part of the world one is in' (*E*: 136/203). The first walk through the city gives 'a frightful impression': '*Une malédiction semble planer sur la ville.* Decay, nothing but decay, marasmus and emptiness' (*E*: 137/204). The whole passage echoes earlier descriptions of Deauville. Aunt Fini recalls, again in astonishing detail, the image offered to her by Ambros himself of the fashionable resort and meeting place of the rich and famous, where the most outrageous things are possible. The present-day Deauville in which the narrator finds himself, however, is a deserted provincial town, where most large buildings are closed, the former first-class hotel Rochers Noirs is on the verge of ruin, and the Hotel Normandy gives the narrator the impression of a fake pavilion at a world fair. None of these buildings seems to be quite of this world any more, and neither does the Jerusalem Ambros and Cosmo visited in 1913.

Jerusalem returns, in 'Max Ferber', in the form of the scale model of Solomon's temple, which is made by one 'Frohmann, of Drohobycz' and appears to Ferber in a dream (*A*: 176/262). The dream scene comprises another intertextual reference – this time to Joseph Roth's *The Wandering Jews* (1927) – and also refers intertextually to Sebald's own work, *The Rings of Saturn*, in which one Thomas Abrams is engaged in a similar project (*RS*: 241–9).[7] In Roth's version, however, the description is given a distinctly ironic tone:

> Frohmann claims to have spent seven years building this minitemple, and I believe him. To build a model temple in accordance with the description in the Bible must cost as much labour as love . . . Very few visitors come and look. The old folks are already familiar with it, and the young people want to go to Palestine and build roads, not temples. (Roth 2001: 73–4)

In Ferber's dream, the irony is gone, and the model acquires a different value:

> Just look, said Frohmann: you can see every crenellation on the towers, every curtain, every threshold, every sacred vessel. And I, said Ferber, bent down over the diminutive temple and realized, for the first time in my life, what a true work of art looks like. (E: 176/262–3)

Perhaps we could, like Ferber himself, interpret the model temple as a metaphor for the artist's work: a loving, detailed reconstruction of what was and might come back, and an act of homage to the builders of its original. That, at least, is implied in Roth's further account, where his initial irony is abandoned for the tone of praise that characterises most of his text: 'Frohmann is the guardian of tradition and of the only great architectonic work the Jews have ever produced, and for that reason will never forget' (Roth 2001: 74). One may infer that this is also the reason for Ferber's admiration, albeit in a dream. The dream of authenticity and the passing on of tradition seems to be something of which Ferber himself, constantly reworking his paintings and drawings, is incapable.

GERMANY

Of course, the homeland that is really lost to most of these emigrants – and also the narrator – is not Jerusalem but Germany. 'Germany' is at once a figment or illusion (or a promise), on the one hand, and a haunted, deserted place on the other. What interests Sebald is not so much Jewish culture or emigration, but the place – or rather, non-place – it acquired in German culture after the Second World War. It may therefore be rewarding to take a closer look at the descriptions of contemporary Germany in *The Emigrants*.

Max Ferber does not know present-day Germany, and cannot bring himself to go there. He does, however, hold a vivid imaginary view of it: 'To me, you see, Germany is a country frozen in the past, destroyed, a curiously extraterritorial place, inhabited by people whose faces are both lovely and dreadful' (E: 181/270). This matches Paul Bereyter's response to his 'hometown' S, as reported by his friend Lucy Landau, which is described as 'a miserable place . . ., which in fact he loathed and, deep within himself . . . would have been pleased to see destroyed and obliterated, together with the townspeople, whom he found so utterly repugnant' (E: 57/84). In spite of his feelings, however, and in contrast to Ferber, Bereyter does feel the need to return to S often, since he is, in Lucy Landau's words, 'German to the marrow' (E: 57/84), but these trips end only in depression.

In contrast, there is the sentimental nostalgia evoked by Luisa Lanzberg's journal. Here, we are confronted with an almost idyllic representation of a Germany in which Jewish families blend in unproblematically. Yet this is hardly the state Sebald conceived as his utopia, since the depiction itself already shows signs of doubt. In retrospect, Luisa Lanzberg sees her family's moving to Bad Kissingen as 'the first step on a path that grew narrower day by day and led inevitably to the point I have now arrived at' (*E*: 208/312). Written in 1939, the implications of this entry are obvious. But even the earlier memories of a happy childhood in the village of Steinach are discredited by the narrator's initial remark that 'it almost goes without saying that there are no Jews in Steinach now' (*E*: 193/290).

The narrator himself then decides to make enquiries at Bad Kissingen to find out what became of the city's Jewish community. The Germany he finds seems to be inhabited by hostile or freakish characters; there is the monstrous fellow-passenger on the train to Kissingen, of whom the narrator cannot say 'whether the physical and mental deformity . . . was the result of long psychiatric confinement, some innate debility, or simply beer-drinking and eating between meals' (*E*: 219/328). Then there is the hotel. In contrast to the other hotels he stays in, it is newly renovated, but the welcome is rather frightening:

> The woman at reception, who had something of the mother superior about her, sized me up as if she were expecting me to disturb the peace, and when I got into the lift I found myself facing a weird old couple who stared at me with undisguised hostility, if not horror. (*E*: 219/329)

His investigations lead him to the one place that still bears witness to the former Jewish presence at Kissingen – the cemetery. (Here, the book seems to have come full circle, since a picture of a cemetery is also what it started with.) Of course, it can only have this testimonial function for the narrator, since apparently no one else ever goes there, as can be gathered from the state it is in: 'a wilderness of graves, neglected for years, crumbling and gradually sinking into the ground amidst tall grass and wild flowers under the shade of trees' (*E*: 223/334). It would seem that this is the promised land of the (German) Jews, the one place where they can feel at home and – as the narrator stresses – bear their own names: the cemetery. At least, the narrator's comment on seeing the graveyard that it 'had little to do with cemeteries as one thinks of them' (*E*: 223/334) may point in this direction. In fact, the description comes close to the ones discussed by Sebald in his essay on German-Jewish literature (*UH*: 54–5). The cemetery, the only Jewish place where flowers bloom, is the true community to return to, the home where no one will be denied a resting place or a name. But does this imply that deliverance is only possible in a world beyond death? If this were so, we would be dealing with a messianism that fits into the dogmatic Christian view of history. But it hardly does justice to Sebald's text, since it never looks beyond this world – the cemetery itself *is* the homeland, the place where memory is kept, the only tradition that can be passed on. Again, there is a tension between this 'tradition' – in this context, calling it spectral is only too obvious – and the possibility of escaping its logic of repetition (illustrated, for instance, in the seemingly endless list of Jewish names), of leaving the cemetery behind and finding a life of one's own.

THE PILGRIM'S PROMISE

The Emigrants, a perspectivist, multi-layered view of the biographies of a number of émigrés, seems to lay claim to biographical truth. It thereby purports to understand the lives that it narrates. This tendency would seem to be reinforced by Sebald's archaic tone, reminiscent of the nineteenth-century tradition about which Sebald has also written several essays. At the same time, his text provides us with numerous indications to the contrary: that this is all too contrived to be an authentic report. This was already apparent in the original title of Sebald's first prose book, which, as I have argued, can be seen as a blueprint for *The Emigrants*: *Schwindel. Gefühle*. The title of the English translation, *Vertigo*, renders only one of the two possible meanings, the other being 'swindle'. The entire text could thus be considered a hoax, a most inappropriate response to the horrors it thematises, were it not for the insistence with which the narrator keeps coming back to the same point, keeps looking into things more and more deeply.

So the promise in Sebald's text may lie in its openness, not only in its constant appeal to other texts but also in its constant tension between presenting the reader with a pretty, picture-postcard image on the one hand and 'leaving the story untold' or preserving the possibility of yet another twist on the other. *The Emigrants* is perhaps best summed up by the promise made by Hebel's shrewd pilgrim in a story Paul Bereyter liked to recite to his class. Although it is a hoax, the fascination it exerts remains, not least by virtue of the names that it evokes: 'When I return, then shall I bring unto you a sacred seashell from the shores of Askalon, or a Rose of Jericho' (Hebel 1961: 114).

The author wishes to thank Tom Toremans and Daniel Jaspers for taking the time to revise an earlier version of this text.

NOTES

1. See Martin Klebes's chapter in this volume for a more detailed summary of the story.
2. An almost verbatim quotation from 'The Hunter Gracchus' story can be found in Ambros Adelwarth's diary, where he describes how Cosmo and he sail into a small harbour on the Asian side of the Golden Horn: 'two men were squatting on the quay playing dice' (*E*: 133), and some lines further down 'a grey pigeon about the size of a full-grown cockerel' (*E*: 134). This is surely not just a playful reference, as the reader has already learned that Cosmo and Ambros are destined to sink slowly into insanity shortly after their Middle Eastern journey.
3. This is a strong sign of fictionality in Sebald's texts: the improbable coincidence of Nabokov's appearing in all four biographies should make it clear that the author is not simply recounting a number of emigrants' biographies. Fictionalisations of this

type should also warn the reader against identifying the narrator with the actual author.

4. The term quasi-transcendental, coined by Rodolphe Gasché, was later taken up by Geoffrey Bennington in his introduction to Derrida's work (Bennington 1993). Derrida takes such quasi-transcendentals (such as 'écriture', 'différance', 'pharmakon' and so on) from the text he is reading and then 'reinscribes' them: they become the pivotal points for the whole reading, without, however, escaping the general – finite – horizon of that text. Put differently, they are an attempt to take a 'marginal' point of view that facilitates a new view of the meaning construed in a text, without, however, offering some form of external, objective perspective. Or, again: you may not be able to get out of the system, but you can look at it obliquely. The term 'spectre' became prominent in Derrida's work only after Bennington's introduction was published, but it is an obvious candidate for the list given above, a ghost being precisely something that tries but fails to escape finitude.

5. See Fenves 1997. In *specters of marx*, the 'messianic' becomes operative mainly in the last chapter, which is aptly called 'apparition of the inapparent'. It is, however, a motif Derrida has repeatedly worked on, mostly with reference to Walter Benjamin. Interestingly, the messianic and the angelic are also connected by Sebald himself in an essay on Kafka's *Castle* (UH: 87–103).

6. The 'Max Ferber' episode contains an interesting parallel to this description, when the narrator recalls how the otherwise deserted hotel Arosa is filled with life in the evenings, when 'travelling gentlemen' come and go, making 'stairs creak'. The commotion they cause is referred to as 'toings and froings' in the English translation (E: 155/228–9), while the German original actually has 'Spuk' (spectre, haunting, but also bustle), a word also discussed by Derrida in relation to Marx's *German Ideology*.

7. In the German original, the character is called Alec Garrard, which is the real-life modelmaker's name. A number of characters have been renamed in the English translations; it seems this was done in the first place to emphasise the fictionality of the stories: Aurach was changed to Ferber to avoid identification with real-life painter Frank Auerbach (two images by Auerbach were omitted in the English version, probably for the same reason), Garrard was changed to Abrams. It is unclear whether this is true of all such cases; when, for example, Henry Selwyn's wife is no longer called 'Hedi' but 'Elli', while his friend Edward Ellis becomes 'Edwin Elliott', this may have other reasons. But apart from the biographical side of the question, a more general reflection on the role of proper names in Sebald is required; Denneler (2001) makes a number of interesting points on the subject.

15

FACING THE PAST AND THE FEMALE SPECTRE IN W. G. SEBALD'S *THE EMIGRANTS*

Maya Barzilai

W. G. Sebald's *The Emigrants* consists of four separate narratives, varying in length, named after the four main protagonists: Dr Henry Selwyn, Paul Bereyter, Ambros Adelwarth and Max Ferber (Aurach in the German edition). The anonymous narrator, a male witness-character, records his ongoing attempts to uncover the life stories of these characters, one a distant relative, the other his schoolteacher, and the other two mere acquaintances. Thus the fascination with the past in *The Emigrants* centres mainly around four men, figures who once lingered on the margins of the narrator's life and have slowly become the focal point of his thoughts and journeys. It may be further maintained that the investigation of these life stories becomes a form of male bonding between the narrator and his subjects as he discovers not only their tales of emigration and/or persecution but also, at times, the stories of their intimate relationships and sexual preferences. Moreover, male bonding appears as a theme within these life stories: two of the male protagonists are reported to have formed close friendships or erotic relationships with other men.

Yet whereas descriptions of lasting intimate connections with women are scarce in *The Emigrants*, female figures are not completely absent. First, characters such as Lucy Landau and Aunt Fini support the structure of male homosocial desire by mediating the process of memory retrieval. Second, some female figures are depicted as spectres of a disruptive past that challenge characters and narrator alike to face up to traumatic historical events that have not been sufficiently confronted or worked through. Sebald introduces these spectral (m)other figures mainly in the last narrative, 'Max Ferber', where he addresses – more directly than in any of the other stories – the history of Jewish persecution during the Second World War. The feminisation of the Jewish past in Sebald's writing also recalls the issue of the effeminate and uncanny construction of the Jew prior to the Second World War. By portraying uncanny and implicitly queer male (Jewish) protagonists as well as by aligning female figures with a horrific Jewish-German past that cannot be faced directly, Sebald exposes, reinterprets and perhaps even reinstates certain racial and sexual stereotypes. Accordingly, it is not surprising that those male characters who avoid confrontation with their traumatic pasts are often also incapable of forming long-lasting relationships with women. In what follows I shall explore the different gender configurations that appear in *The Emigrants* and the connections between them through a historical-cultural reading of Sebald's use of female spectres.

'THE OTHER PERSUASION': HOMOSOCIAL DESIRE IN *THE EMIGRANTS*

Three out of the four protagonists featured in *The Emigrants* were never married, and none bore offspring. Paul Bereyter whose early love, Helen Hollaender, was deported during the war, did have an intimate late-life relationship with Lucy Landau. However, the only married man out of the four, Dr Henry Selwyn is estranged from his wife, Elli (Hedi in the German edition), and lives as 'a kind of ornamental hermit' in a remote corner of his garden (*E*: 5/11). In addition, the narrator's own partner, Clara, who is mentioned in the first narrative, does not reappear in the subsequent three stories and no other female partner is mentioned, thereby accentuating the narrator's intense preoccupation with the stories of these men.

Selwyn's exposition of his troubled marriage seems to occur almost incidentally, in the context of the story of his stay in Berne before the First World War, where, instead of furthering his medical training, he '[took] more and more to mountain climbing' (*E*: 13/23). In this setting he meets Johannes Naegeli, a 65-year-old alpine guide 'of whom, from the beginning, he was very fond' (*E*: 13–14/23). Summing up his travels with Naegeli, Selwyn claims that 'never in his life, neither before nor later, did he feel as good as he did then, in the company of that man' (*E*: 14/24). Yet this blissful male bonding is short lived; after the outbreak of the war, Selwyn returns to England and is drafted, whereas Naegeli disappears, to resurface only after seven decades. He was assumed to have fallen into a crevasse in the Aare glacier, and so the bond between the two men is broken off without any possibility of parting (*E*: 15/24). Upon hearing of Naegeli's disappearance Selwyn is plunged into a deep depression, as though he himself had been buried in the ice instead of his beloved friend (*E*: 15/25). In the process of telling his story to the narrator and Clara, Henry Selwyn explicitly compares the painful parting from Naegeli at the outbreak of war to his relationship with Elli whom he had married after the war: 'Even the separation from Elli . . . did not cause me remotely as much pain as the separation from Naegeli' (*E*: 14/24). Moreover, the growing estrangement from Elli contrasts with Selwyn's continued imaginary bond with Naegeli who seems closer whenever he comes to the character's mind, despite the fact that they never again met after their farewell in Meiringen (*E*: 15/24). The tale of the alpine guide indeed frames the whole episode, in accordance with Selwyn's sense of closeness to his lost friend, whereas the narrative of marriage and separation becomes a relatively minor event within the larger story of male bonding.

The narrative devoted to Ambros Adelwarth, the narrator's long-dead great uncle, takes up the theme of male bonding that appeared in its nascent form in the story of Naegeli and Selwyn. Adelwarth, another emigrant of German origins, is best characterised by his vocation as butler or manservant, as one who takes care of the affairs of others but whose own identity and history remain enigmatic. Adelwarth ultimately becomes the valet and travelling companion of Cosmo Solomon, son of one of the wealthiest Jewish families in New York. In relating this episode in Adelwarth's life, the narrator's uncle, Kasimir, reveals the 'tragic' homosexual aspect of the relationship between Adelwarth and Solomon. More explicitly, Kasimir states that Ambros Adelwarth was 'of the other persuasion, as anyone could see, even if the family always ignored or glossed over the fact. Perhaps some of them never realized' (*E*: 88/128–9). The family's inability or unwillingness to see what was lying just beneath the surface, to acknowledge Adelwarth's 'other persuasion', matches the valet's own difficulties in accessing his memories as well as the defensive emphasis he put on external appearances, conveying the impression of a 'hollowed-out' man (*E*: 88/129).

In *Between Men: English Literature and Male Homosocial Desire*, Eve Kosofsky Sedgwick demonstrates how gendered power relations in specific social and historical settings tend to form a triangular asymmetry – that is, two men bond through the mediation of a woman. This asymmetry manifests itself by 'the radically disrupted continuum . . . between sexual and nonsexual male bonds, as against the relatively smooth and palpable continuum of female homosocial desire' (1985: 23). Functioning as the locus of patriarchal power, male relationships are subject to more careful scrutiny and control, resulting in what Sedgwick describes as 'ideological homophobia, ideological homosexuality, or some highly conflicted but intensively structured combination of the two' (1985: 25). Following Sedgwick's analysis of gendered relationships in Western society, the portrayals of homosocial bonding in *The Emigrants* may be said to exemplify the 'radically disrupted continuum' between sexual and nonsexual male relationships. Although homosexual undertones appear in the story of Selwyn and the alpine guide, they remain unvoiced and thus repressed rather than 'palpable'. In the case of Cosmo and Ambros, despite the fact that 'anyone could see' that

Adelwarth was queer, his homosexuality retains the status of 'a terrible family secret' long after his death (*E*: 123/181). Indeed, in the narrator's dream that is set in 1913 at the French resort where Cosmo and Ambros had once vacationed together, their representation reveals the force of familial and societal homophobia as well as of homosexual fixation. Even though at this stage the narrator is clearly aware of his relative's 'other persuasion', the intriguing possibility that the two men, master and servant, were lovers is not made explicit in his telling of the dream. It is perhaps the indefiniteness of the Solomon–Adelwarth relationship that triggers the intense scrutiny exhibited in the dream by the gossiping vacationers and the narrator himself (*E*: 122–5/180–4).

In contrast to the heavily freighted bonds between men, relationships with women are represented either as stories of estrangement (Elli) or as late-life companionships (Lucy) that lack erotic intensity. When female characters appear in the book, they often act as conduits of memory between men. Both Lucy Landau in the second narrative and Aunt Fini in the third transmit to the narrator the life stories of Bereyter and Adelwarth respectively, so that a triangulated form of storytelling takes place. Although the stories of these women are also briefly recounted, they invariably serve as minor characters whose role it is to provide the narrator with access to the past. In other words, they contribute to the construction of the narrator's 'postmemory', a term used by Marianne Hirsch to describe the memory of the second generation whose connection to the events preceding their birth, to memory's 'object or source is mediated not through [their own] recollection but through an imaginative investment and creation'.[1] The story of Luisa Lanzberg's memoirs constitutes an exception as her son, Max Ferber, hands over the package containing almost a hundred pages of her handwritten memoirs to the narrator (*E*: 192/289). Although this package is a commodity that strengthens the bond between the two men, it should be stressed that Ferber becomes the channel through which the narrator gains access to the mother's memoirs.

Finally, in the process of retracing Selwyn's and Ferber's life stories, the feminine role of mediation apparently becomes superfluous since the narrator himself converses with these protagonists and ultimately forms close connections with them. Not surprisingly, although Selwyn pays his respects to Clara, the narrator's partner, by bringing produce from his garden, it is only when Clara is conveniently 'away in town' that Selwyn uses the opportunity to confide in the narrator (*E*: 18/30). As a result, the two narratives that frame *The Emigrants* question the necessity and importance of the role of women as oral transmitters of familial memory between men, a role reserved in the book only for those cases in which the men are already long dead. From another perspective, in first and last narratives the function of female mediation becomes incorporated into the male-male relationship, strengthening the male bond and charging it with further erotic undertones.

FEMALE SPECTRES: THE GENDERED REPRESENTATION OF THE
JEWISH-GERMAN PAST

As Sedgwick claims, 'the status of women, and the whole question of arrangements between genders, is deeply and inescapably inscribed in the structure even of relationships that seem to exclude women' (1985: 25). However, whereas Sedgwick appears to view the position of the excluded woman primarily in functional terms as that commodity trafficked between men or used to cement male bonds, one might also consider this position in symbolic terms. Whether inscribed within male relationships or excluded from them, Sebald also depicts women as the *haunting* other, the one who 'can only appear by disappearing' (Derrida 1988: 275). Furthermore, inhabiting a 'space of intervention', a cultural 'beyond', these spectres of past loss or future death at times possess in Sebald's writing the power to destabilise certain male-dominated structures such as the triangulated structure of remembrance (Bhabha 1994: 4, 9–10). Accordingly, the story of Max Ferber, in which the theme of the haunting woman is fully developed, counterbalances the previous narratives in which women appeared, if at all, in subsidiary roles. Yet although the woman as haunting other undermines normative homosocial triangulation, she may further be read as fulfilling a different set of male fantasies. The (m)other is not only the object of erotic desires in the Oedipal scheme, but also a source of death wishes and fears stemming from the view of female sexuality as marked by lack (of male genitals).[2] Such male fantasies notwithstanding, the female spectres in *The Emigrants* display significant erotic and symbolic power and thus cannot be easily dismissed as mere conduits of male desire or memory.

The representation of female spectres is closely linked in the final narrative to Ferber's and the narrator's confrontation with a Jewish-German past that incessantly haunts the present. In general, the infiltration of the past into the present through descriptions of haunted, disintegrating places and of ghostly people in *The Emigrants* stands in contradistinction to what Sebald terms 'the lack of memory that marked the Germans, and the efficiency with which they had cleaned everything up' after the Second World War (*E*: 225/338). Concurrently, Sebald's characters and narrator confront the 'dumbness' of memory – that is, the limits of their understanding of the past and the possibility of its reconstruction (*E*: 145/215). Indeed, for Ambros Adelwarth and other characters, the return of memories late in life is represented as an emotionally precarious event, awakening destructive forces that literally drive them toward death (see *E*: 173–4/258–9). At the limits of memory's reach, or at the point where the act of remembering no longer heals but, rather, may lead one to despair, madness and even death, Sebald frequently evokes a haunting female figure. These figures are conjured up in relation to recollections of Germany and, in particular, to the persecution of the Jews. Consequently, the representation of the past by means of female figures is most prevalent in the last narrative: through the story of the painter Max Ferber whose parents were murdered by the Nazis, Sebald confronts, more directly than elsewhere in *The Emigrants*, the memory of the Holocaust. Sebald's overdetermined marking of the recent traumatic past as feminine in Ferber's narrative retrospectively affects our perception of the gender relations portrayed in the previous narratives.

A haunting female figure presides over Ferber's account of his relationship to Germany from where he only just escaped in 1939. It is only during the narrator's 'late reunion' with Ferber, approximately twenty-five years after their first acquaintance, that Ferber discloses his memories of the period before the war and his current attitude toward Germany: 'a country frozen in the past, destroyed, a curiously extraterritorial place' (*E*: 181/270). As Ferber relates, he never revisited Germany, fearing that 'the insanity lodged in [his] head' whenever he thinks of it might 'really exist' out there (*E*: 181/270). Yet, while Ferber does not visit Germany himself, he is visited by a gendered hallucination that comes from this 'extraterritorial' land. She is depicted as 'a beautiful woman wearing a ball gown made of grey parachute silk and a broad-brimmed hat trimmed with grey roses' (*E*: 181/271). In the meeting between Ferber and his female apparition, both erotic and deathly fantasies find their expression. The grey lady hastens toward him 'like a doctor afraid that she may be too late to save a sinking patient'; simultaneously, she causes him to fall into 'a swoon', losing any sense of how the scenario continues after that point. In the midst of this uncertainty as to whether 'the grey lady' intends to save Ferber or to cause him distress and loss of his senses, she removes her hat and peels off her fencing gloves, charging the scene with eroticism. In this sense, the woman represents the compelling forces of attraction toward Germany, the site of Ferber's familial trauma, as well as the destructive and annihilating (not to mention castrating) potential of facing the 'fragmentary scenes that haunt [his] memory' (*E*: 181–2/271).[3]

In a posthumously published interview, Sebald employs the term 'horror' to designate the experience of facing the Holocaust: 'the horror of persecution in its ultimate forms' (Jaggi 2001a). In another interview, Sebald tellingly makes use of the image of Medusa's head to explain the difficulty of writing about the events of the Holocaust: 'I don't think you can focus on the horror of the Holocaust. It's like the head of the Medusa: you carry it with you in a sack, but if you looked at it you'd be petrified' (Jaggi 2001b). It is instructive to read these expressions in the context of Freud's short essay 'Medusa's Head', since, as Sarah Kofman has noted, Freud himself uses the term 'Grauen' (horror) in this essay to designate the anxious male reaction 'when confronted by a woman's ... genitals (represented symbolically by the Medusa's head)' (1985: 29).[4] The complex symbol of the Medusa's head, according to Freud's interpretation, serves to isolate the horrifying effects of the female genitals and the terror of castration they may evoke from their pleasure-giving effects; however, the stiffening into stone, or defensive 'erection', in face of this 'sight' may indicate that the two dichotomous effects are inextricably linked in the male psyche (Freud 1922: 212–13). Accordingly, the repetition of the adjective 'grey' ('grauer' and 'grauen')[5] in the portrayal of Ferber's spectre possibly evokes the 'horror', 'Grauen' of facing this spectre of the German past who is, obviously, also extremely desirable and 'beautiful'.

Moreover, Ferber describes the recurring scenes as 'silent' ones, since the 'grey lady understands only her mother tongue, German', a language he has not spoken since parting from his parents at Munich airport in 1939. Yet ironically, Ferber's disclosure is narrated in German, the 'muted' language he claims not to have spoken since then (*E*: 182/271). The silence that accompanies the female other may symbolise Ferber's dislocation and deep disconnection from the place and language in which he was brought up. When he finally reveals segments of his life in Germany to the narrator, his memory appears to be 'shot full of holes', retaining very few details of his early childhood and, above all, of severing himself from his parents (Hirsch 1997: 22–3; *E*: 182, 187/271–2, 279). It is not surprising, then, that faced with the 'grauen' spectre of the German lady, Ferber closes his eyes in a swoon, avoiding the lethal gaze of this lovely Medusa who represents those literally unspeakable realms of his life, the 'lagoon[s] of oblivion' (*E*: 174/259).

In contrast to the grey lady who symbolises Ferber's petrified memory of his lost mother country and mother tongue, the diaries of Ferber's deceased mother represent the possibility of writing and creating even under Nazi rule. Moreover, in this case the haunting woman cannot be regarded as a male invention or vision, but stands as a force of creativity in her own right. Upon concluding his narrative, Ferber entrusts the narrator with a 'paper package . . . containing a number of photographs and almost a hundred pages of handwritten memoirs penned by his mother . . . between 1939 and 1941' (*E*: 192/288). Rather than describing the events of the moment, Luisa Ferber (née Lanzberg) prefers to write, 'with a passion that was beyond [Ferber's] understanding' of her childhood experiences (*E*: 193/288). The 'truly wonderful' quality of Luisa's writing, especially considering those bleak times, contributes to Ferber's professed ambivalent response to this manuscript. On second reading, the memoirs seemed to him 'like one of those evil German fairytales' in the sense that they magically propel Ferber to carry on to the very end, 'till [his] heart breaks', with the work of 'remembering, writing, and reading' (*E*: 193/289). Hence, like the compulsive visions that haunt Ferber's memories, the reading of his deceased mother's memoirs clearly does not relieve him or enable some form of working through. Rather, recalling the Medusa's head, this maternal text casts a spell over him, binding him to the destructive force of the past that continues to reshape his present.

The narrator upon whom Ferber finally bestows the burdensome package of memoirs is moved to travel to Bad Kissingen where Ferber's mother's family used to reside. There he attempts to enter the old Jewish cemetery. However, the narrator soon discovers that the keys to the cemetery gate, given to him by a 'panic-stricken bureaucrat in a particularly remote office' of the town hall, do not fit the lock and so decides to climb the wall (*E*: 221–2/331–4). The act of climbing the cemetery wall reinforces the difficulties that the German visitor, supplied with an inadequate set of distinctively German keys, must face when endeavouring to enter this site of Jewish memorial. Surmounting the obstructions, the narrator finally reaches the graves where, among other sights, he is touched 'by the symbol of the writer's quill on the stone of Friederike Halbleib, who departed this life on the 28th of March 1912' (*E*: 224/336). Imagining the deceased woman with pen in hand, reminiscent of Luisa Ferber's reconstruction of her childhood memories, the narrator, whom we may also picture jotting down the lines we read, is overcome by sudden feelings of identification with this unknown figure and with unmediated grief over her loss. 'It feels as if *I* had lost her', he writes, 'and as if *I* could not get over the loss despite the many years that have passed since her departure' (*E*: 224–5/336–7). Known to the narrator only by her gravestone, Friederike Halbleib epitomises the inexorable process of 'remembering, writing, and reading' that takes place in the narrative of 'Max Ferber' over and through the lost body of the dead Jewish mother. Thus by means of her haunting and creative presence, the spectral woman may induce a rearrangement of gender power relations, disrupting the male-female-male asymmetry that Sebald installs in some of the earlier stories. The relations linking the narrator, Luisa Lanzberg, and Friederike Halbeib may be read as such a new constellation.

According to Diane Jonte-Pace in *Speaking the Unspeakable*, the 'counterthesis' of the mother as the uncanny, disrupting emblem of death rather than the beloved, eroticised object, emerges with uncharacteristic directness in Freud's 'The Theme of the Three Caskets'. In this essay, Jonte-Pace argues, the mother is transformed into an emblem of death itself, into the 'Goddess of Death', and is not merely re-figured as a 'dead mother' (2001: 57–8). Consequently, Freud exposes 'a mythic account of love and choice . . . as a complex and highly ambiguous attempt both to escape from death and to embrace death as one embraces the mother' (2001: 60, 58–9). A similar development from the image of the 'dead mother' to 'Mother Death' takes place at the end of *The Emigrants* in a scene that alludes to the myth of the three Fates, and so perhaps also to Freud's essay. The narrator recalls a photograph of three young Jewish women working at a loom in the Lodz ghetto in Poland during the early 1940s. This photograph is the last in a series exhibiting the ghetto streets and various production sites that the narrator screens, as it were, on 'an infinitely deep stage' in his mind (*E*: 235–6/350–2). Despite the obvious fabrication of these photographs, because of the directing gaze of Walter Genewein, accountant of the Lodz ghetto and amateur photographer, they nevertheless allow some form of access to ghetto life and to the Jewish slave-workers. (It is important to note, too, that the story of Walter Genewein and his colour photographs is historically accurate and that the collection is preserved today in the Jewish Museum of Frankfurt.)

Yet it is at this point of most direct contact with the horror of Jewish persecution that Sebald prefers not to reproduce the photographs but, rather, to describe them in words, withholding this image from the reader.[6] This choice also endows the photographs with a mythic, unimaginable quality. Furthermore, in describing the image of the weavers, the narrator recasts these unknown women as the mythological Fates: 'Nona, Decuma and Morta, the daughters of night' who determine the destiny and length of human life with their spindle, scissors and thread. Simultaneously symbolising the end of Sebald's narrative thread, these 'daughters of the night' ironically seem to possess the power to escape the boundaries of their own death-in-photograph, causing the narrator to 'sense that all three of them are looking across at [him]' (*E*: 237/355). Undermining the boundaries of the photographic still(ness) through their uncanny gaze, the weavers/Fates also awaken the ambivalent emotional forces, discussed above in relation to the 'grey lady', of seduction and destruction. On the one hand, they are clearly ordinary young women, the middle one even appears as a 'blonde [who] has the air of a bride about her'; on the other hand, they represent the 'Goddesses of Death', the fearsome Fates, who also threaten to return from the dead (*E*: 237/355).

In thus laying bare, rather than disguising, the deadly nature of the silent photographic subjects as both young brides and 'daughters of the night', the closing scene of *The Emigrants* diverges from the 'wishful reversal' in Shakespeare's plays and in folktales, a reversal that transforms the mythological Fates into desirable brides among whom a choice must be made. In 'The Theme of the Three Caskets', Freud interprets this reversal as expressing the human struggle against the verdict of mortality. Yet, as he also shows, traces of the original myth involving the Goddess of Death may still be found in the 'free' choice that always falls on the third woman, supposedly the Goddess of Love, who is characteristically 'dumb', 'concealed' or otherwise serves as a reminder of the third scissor-wielding Fate (1913: 294–5, 299–300). By contrast, in the closing scene of *The Emigrants*, the original myth is accentuated since the narrator explicitly compares the three women to the Fates and cannot withstand for long the 'steady and relentless' gaze of the third woman, possibly the Goddess of Death herself. Just as Ferber 'closes [his] eyes in a swoon' when visited by his grey lady, so the narrator must look away from the photographed weaver. Her gaze appears to bridge the distance between past and present and forces the narrator to face and, eventually, turn away from the fate of this spectre in which his own fate is enfolded.

It is also crucial to note that in this last scene Sebald's narrator, a man of the same nationality as the author, confronts the spectre of the Jewish past in the guise of the suffering women condemned to premature, unnatural death. Nevertheless, by positioning himself in the position occupied by Genewein and his camera, the narrator partially identifies with the perpetrator, with the man who captured the ghetto inhabitants on film possibly against their will and for purposes beyond their control. At the same time, he casts the three weavers in the role of the Fates who determine the course and length of human life, thus placing both his own fate and the fate of his text in their formidable hands. Thus, unlike the previous graveyard scene in which the narrator takes in his arms, so to speak, the figure of the long-deceased female writer 'as if *he* had lost her', at the close of the book his reaction towards the ghetto image, a more recent memorial, is far more restrained. In addition to the all-too-human denial of death identified by Freud, Sebald's post-Holocaust German narrator specifically exhibits, through his averted gaze, a threefold convergence: an intense guilt, a sense of unalterable complicity and a recognition of the impact of recent German history on his life. I would further argue that while the weavers are the objects of both the narrator's and the photographer's gaze, the stronger and more significant interaction in this passage occurs between the narrator and the third daughter of the night.

WHAT LIES BEYOND: A BRIEF JEWISH HISTORY OF SEBALD'S SPECTRAL IMAGERY

Sebald's conflation between 'Roza, Luisa and Lea' and 'Nona, Decuma and Morta' – between the Jewish weavers in the ghetto and the mythological Fates with their deadly gaze – raises several questions concerning the implications of this final passage. As I have demonstrated, the history of European Jewry in the twentieth century is often marked as feminine in Sebald's writing. The relationship to the past sometimes takes the form of a relationship between a living male character and a female spectre that haunts his days and nights. But why does Sebald resort to the image of an absent, dead or ghostly woman in order to convey the inaccessibility of a traumatic past as well as the difficulty of integrating past and present? Furthermore, what is the connection, if any, between the feminisation of the Jewish-German past and the privileging of relationships between men throughout the book?

I would like to gesture toward one possible response to these questions by noting that Sebald's writing draws on a rich variety of culturally and historically bound themes and images. Among these sources are not only Freud's interpretation of the myths of the three Fates and the Medusa's head but also his understanding of the uncanny. Indeed, Sebald's study of nineteenth- and twentieth-century Austrian literature, mainly by Jewish authors, entitled *Unheimliche Heimat*, indicates his interest in the concept of the uncanny.[7] Contemporary criticism has reintroduced this concept, among others, into the fin-de-siècle context that informed Freud's writing. Such analyses vividly demonstrate how Freud's psychoanalytic world-view was affected by his difficult position as an assimilated Jew threatened by the rise of racial anti-Semitism during his lifetime. A short review of some of the socio-historical perspectives on Freud may thus provide a basis for re-examining the appearance of uncanny female spectres in Sebald's writing in the context of Jewish remembrance.

In 'The Uncanny Jew: A Brief History of an Image', Susan Shapiro explains that the European Jew was often portrayed by both non-Jewish and Jewish modern thinkers as a ghostly, wandering figure, devoid of home and nation, thereby 'disrupting and haunting [other peoples' homes], making them "Unheimliche" [uncanny]' (1997: 65). In 'The Uncanny', Shapiro argues, Freud, too, grapples with the collective cultural image of the Jew as a 'living corpse'; however, in a move that may be interpreted as either defensive or analytical and interpretive, Freud attempts to both 'displace' and 're-envision' this trope 'by reading the uncanniness of the Jew into the very structures of the unconsciousness within everyman' (1997: 70). Moreover, 'the primary anxiety' that generates such a sense of 'Unheimlichkeit' is thus understood 'not in racial terms, but explicitly in terms of sexual difference' (1997: 71). In *Unheroic Conduct* Daniel Boyarin claims, more broadly, that Freud's 'relative abandonment' of his study of hysteria in favour of the heterosexual Oedipus narrative signifies a growing fear of exhibiting certain traits that would mark him as queer – namely, hysteria, melancholia and passivity (1997: 214–15).[8] Yet, if the Oedipal master-thesis may be interpreted as a defensive barrier against the association of Jews with homosexuality, it is also important to examine the function of the 'counterthesis' (which figures the mother as an emblem of death and loss rather than as an object of desire) in relation to the historical-cultural forces that shaped Freud's thought. As Jonte-Pace demonstrates, at times Freud links Jewishness with the uncanny mother, and 'is not simply engaging in a hyper-masculinization of Judaism' (2001: 80, 96). The 'counterthesis' of mother-death rather than mother love may therefore be understood as Freud's partial analysis of the 'inevitable ambivalence' of assimilated Jews at that period concerning both their Jewishness and their participation in Gentile society (Jonte-Pace 2001: 80).

In Sebald's writing, an analogous 'counterthesis' plays an important role in both constructing the Jewish man as uncanny and possibly homosexual and associating Jewishness, or Jewish history in general, with the spectral woman. Indeed, a dead Jewish bride/mother symbolising the Holocaust haunts the narrative of 'Max Ferber', recalling the 'ghostlike function' of the pre-oedipal mother in Freud's texts. Moreover, Sebald's characters and narrator exhibit a mixture of fear, repugnance and attraction toward the female spectres they encounter, just as the mother figure is 'the object of [Freud's] fascinated and horrified gaze' (Sprengnether 1990: 5). In reading *The Emigrants*, the image of the wandering, homeless Jew cannot but also come to mind, along with the stereotypical gendering of Jewish men as feminine and/or queer. Although the Jewish identity of the four male protagonists is often partial or unmarked, they do exhibit those characteristics of melancholia, passivity and homoeroticism said to have constructed the homosexual and the Jew alike in fin-de-siècle central Europe and perhaps also in other periods (Boyarin 1997: 215).

Furthermore, the close correlation in *The Emigrants* between the remembrance of Jewish persecution, the fear of death and the female body or sexuality may well explain the tendency of the emigrant-survivors to turn away from women as viable erotic objects. Clearly, the weight of a traumatic past (be it consciously remembered or not) contributes to the protagonists' inability to form new relationships, to create new families and homes for themselves. This is especially true when, as in the case of Max Ferber, visions connected to the German past are represented in highly gendered terms. In order to avoid the unbearable 'sight' of the past, it seems that one must also turn away from the supposedly uncanny female body. Thus Sebald's protagonists, who live under the 'poisonous canopy' of past suffering and loss, find themselves unable to fully 'escape from Jewish queerdom into gentile, phallic heterosexuality', as Freud possibly endeavoured to do in his later theories of sexuality (*E*: 191/286; Boyarin 1997: 215).

The theme of mother death in Sebald's writing discloses not only the victims' complex relation toward their past and sexual identity but also the German narrator's relation toward the Jewish-German history he uncovers. Consequently, female spectres repeatedly emerge in *The Emigrants* at specific inter-cultural and inter-racial junctures: when a Jewish survivor is haunted by his German mother tongue and mother country; when a narrator of German origins trespasses in order to visit a Jewish cemetery preserved on German land; or when that narrator recalls a photograph of Jewish slave-workers taken at a Polish ghetto by an Austrian accountant. The desired and feared female apparitions are positioned, then, not only at the edge of memory but also on the border between German and Jewish memory, at the possible meeting-point of the two cultures in the aftermath of the Holocaust. In this respect, Sebald consciously uses spectral women to create a highly ambivalent and vexed picture of postwar German-Jewish relations. However, at the same time, he also succeeds in suggesting the difficulties, *shared* in different ways by Jews and Germans, in attempting to uncover the traumatic history of Jewish extermination.

In summary, female spectres provide in *The Emigrants* an effective means of representing complex issues of remembrance and inter-cultural relations under the shadow of a traumatic past. However, in view of the Jewish-Freudian significance of this uncanny imagery, Sebald's conflation of the emotive reaction toward the history of Jewish persecution with that toward the woman and her body is problematic. As a German author (born in 1944) who constantly questions his right to engage creatively with the Jewish past, Sebald is clearly aware of the moral and aesthetic dangers of 'writing about the subject [of the systematic extermination of whole peoples and groups], particularly for people of German origins' (Jaggi 2001b). Nevertheless, the question of how one should assess the moral achievement of this work arises from the unacknowledged cultural and historical background of certain terms and tropes that Sebald employs to characterise his male protagonists and to portray their relations to the past. To what extent, one may ask, is Sebald's recourse to images that carry with them misogynistic and anti-Semitic historical traces intended to foreground the continuing dangerous resonance of these images, thereby heightening our awareness of contemporary misogyny and racism? And does his writing, however inadvertently, repeat and reinforce this disturbingly persistent heritage?

Sebald does not provide, in *The Emigrants*, any clear-cut stance concerning such queries but, rather, ends the book with the ambivalent response of his narrator toward the ghetto image. On the one hand, whereas Freud, according to Shapiro and Boyarin, attempted to universalise so-called Jewish features and displace them into purely sexual terms, Sebald consciously evokes the trope of the uncanny or 'bent' Jew in connection with the partial retrieval of tales of Jewish emigration and persecution. Moreover, the concluding scene of his book juxtaposes Jewish history and Greco-Roman myth so that the universalised, gendered distinction between the male spectator and the female spectres does not obliterate or mask the Jewish identity of the weavers, resulting in a complex and troublesome interplay of sexual and ethnic tensions. Hence although the female figures of the past may be silent – like the grey German lady who haunts Ferber's studio, or the three photographic subjects frozen in time – the unspeakable is spoken in *The Emigrants* in the sense that the gendered experience of the uncanny finally takes place in a historical context that recalls, albeit indirectly, 'the horror of [Jewish] persecution in its ultimate form'.

On the other hand, if Freud's ambivalent and partial introduction of the haunting 'counterthesis' may be explained as an attempt to analyse, from the perspective of a threatened Jew, 'the ways in which anti-Semitism, homophobia, and misogyny are intimately interconnected in the unconscious', Sebald's analogous use of female spectral imagery, from his post-Holocaust German position, seems more difficult to account for (Jonte-Pace 2001: 81). That the main protagonists of Sebald's works are consistently male, whereas women appear either as conduits of male memory or as dead mothers/lovers, may suggest that in the German imagination Jewish difference continues to be configured as both feminine and homosexual. Ultimately, by portraying his narrator's ambivalent reaction toward the Jewish-German past in highly gendered and culturally bound terms, Sebald privileges a viewpoint that filters all incomprehensible or horrific events through male anxiety.

NOTES

1. Hirsch 1997: 22. In *Family Frames*, Hirsch further explains that 'postmemory characterises the experience of those who grow up dominated by narratives that preceded their birth, whose own belated stories are evacuated by the stories of the previous generation shaped by traumatic events that can be neither understood nor recreated' (22).
2. See for example Kofman 1985: 20, 83–4; Sprengnether 1990: 5–6; Jonte-Pace 2001.
3. In 'The Uncanny', published close to the time of the writing of 'Medusa's Head', Freud cites the female genital organs as an example of 'what arouses' in certain 'neurotic men' this specific form of uncanny 'dread and horror' since they stand as a reminder of the mother's body, of 'the entrance to the former *Heim* [home] of all human beings' (1919: 219, 245).
4. Freud describes the Medusa as 'das abgeschnittene Grauen erweckende Haupt der Medusa (the horrifying decapitated head of Medusa)' (1922 [1940]: 273).
5. Likewise, in the previous narrative, 'Ambros Adelwarth', the narrator himself is haunted in his dreams by a similar woman, a *'femme au passé obscur'* also dressed in 'grey' silk, who perhaps symbolises the mystery of Adelwarth's identity in general and his sexual identity in particular (*E*: 125–6/185).
6. The abundance of 'documentary' evidence interwoven throughout *The Emigrants*, including both old, historical photographs of various characters and images taken from the narrator's travels, makes this choice not to reproduce the ghetto photographs even more conspicuous for the reader accustomed to Sebald's employment of actual images.
7. Sebald's title refers mainly to the Jewish sense of exile from the collective and, at times, false *Heimat* that Germany became for authors such as Jean Améry, the very paradigm of unreality (*UH*: 141). Sebald's self-imposed exile from Germany following his emigration to England in 1966 may also partially illuminate his investment in the issue of emotional and physical exile from one's land and home.
8. The cultural developments that induced Freud's fear of being marked as queer include 'the racialisation/gendering of anti-Semitism, the fin-de-siècle production of sexualities, including the "homosexual", and the sharp increase in contemporary Christian homophobic discourse' (Boyarin 1997: 208).

NOTES ON CONTRIBUTORS

Maya Barzilai is currently pursuing a Ph.D. in Comparative Literature at the Hebrew University of Jerusalem. She specialises in post-Second World War German and Hebrew literature, and photography theory.

John Beck teaches American and English Literature at the University of Newcastle upon Tyne. He is author of *Writing the Radical Centre: William Carlos Williams, John Dewey, and American Cultural Politics* (2001).

Greg Bond is Head of Languages at the University of Applied Sciences, Wildau, Berlin. He has published widely on German and English literature of the twentieth century.

Jan Ceuppens teaches courses in literature and translation in the Applied Linguistics Department at Vlekho/Hogeschool voor Wetenschap en Kunst in Brussels. He is completing a doctoral thesis on W. G. Sebald's *The Emigrants*.

Carolin Duttlinger is Fellow and Tutor in German at Wadham College, Oxford. Her doctoral thesis was on Kafka and photography, and she has published articles on Kafka, Benjamin, Freud and Adorno.

Russell J. A. Kilbourn teaches Cultural Studies and Critical Theory in the English Department at McMaster University in Hamilton, Ontario. He has published on comparative literature, cinema and cultural studies, and is currently working on W. G. Sebald and modernity.

Martin Klebes is currently Visiting Assistant Professor of German at Kenyon College, and the translator of Ernst-Wilhelm Händler's debut novel *City with Houses* (2002).

Massimo Leone lectures in Semiotics at the University of Siena, Italy, and is Fulbright scholar at the University of Berkeley, USA. He is the author of *Religious Conversion and Identity* (2003).

J. J. Long is Senior Lecturer in German at the University of Durham. He is the author of *The Novels of Thomas Bernhard* (2001), and has published widely on twentieth-century fiction.

Colin Riordan is Professor of German at the University of Newcastle upon Tyne. He has published widely on post-war German literature, and is the editor of *Green Thought in German Culture: Historical and Contemporary Perspectives* (1997). Since 1997 he has been working on environmental discourse in German literature.

Martin Swales is Professor of German at University College, London, and has published extensively on German literature of the nineteenth and twentieth centuries, including studies of Realism, the *Bildungsroman*, the *Novelle* and Thomas Mann.

George Szirtes is a poet, critic and translator. He has published some dozen books of poetry, most recently *Selected Poems* (1996), *The Budapest File* (2000) and *An English Apocalypse* (2001). His poetry and translations from the Hungarian have won several major prizes.

Simon Ward is Lecturer in German at the University of Aberdeen and the author of *Negotiating Positions* (2001), a study of Wolfgang Koeppen.

Anne Whitehead is Lecturer in Contemporary Literature and Theory at the University of Newcastle upon Tyne. She has published numerous articles on trauma theory and modern fiction. She has a monograph, *Trauma Fiction*, forthcoming with Edinburgh University Press in 2004.

Wilfried Wilms is Assistant Professor of German Studies at Union College, Schenectady. He has published on eighteenth-century political configurations, and is currently researching a book on the Allied bombing campaign in World War II and the politics of memory.

John Zilcosky is an Assistant Professor of German and Associate Member of the Centre for Comparative Literature at the University of Toronto. He is the author of *Kafka's Travels: Exoticism, Colonialism, and the Traffic of Writing* (2003), and has published widely on German and American literature, travel writing and literary theory.

BIBLIOGRAPHY

Texts by W. G. Sebald

Works in German

Note: The following lists Sebald's major literary works and a selection of his criticism. A comprehensive list of Sebald's literary and critical writings is provided by Markus R. Weber, 'Bibliographie', in Heinz Ludwig Arnold (ed.) (2003), *W. G. Sebald*, Munich: Text + Kritik, pp. 112–17.

(1980), *Der Mythus der Zerstörung im Werk Döblins*, Stuttgart: Klett.

(1982), 'Zwischen Geschichte und Naturgeschichte: Versuch über die literarische Beschreibung totaler Zerstörung mit Anmerkungen zu Kasack, Nossack und Kluge', *Orbis Litterarum*, 37, 345–66.

(1985), *Die Beschreibung des Unglücks: Zur österreichischen Literatur von Stifter bis Handke*, Salzburg: Residenz.

(1986), 'Die Zerknirschung des Herzens: Über Erinnerung und Grausamkeit im Werk von Peter Weiss', *Orbis Litterarum*, 41, 265–78.

(1988), *Nach der Natur: Ein Elementargedicht*, Nördlingen: Greno.

(1990), *Schwindel. Gefühle*, Frankfurt am Main: Eichborn.

(1992), *Die Ausgewanderten: Vier lange Erzählungen*, Frankfurt am Main: Eichborn.

(1995a), *Die Ringe des Saturn: Eine Englische Wallfahrt*, Frankfurt am Main: Eichborn (edition quoted: paperback reprint, Frankfurt am Main: Fischer, 1997).

(1995b), *Unheimliche Heimat: Essays zur österreichischen Literatur*, Frankfurt am Main: Fischer.

(1998), *Logis in einem Landhaus: Über Gottfried Keller, Johann Peter Hebel, Robert Walser und andere*, Munich: Hanser.

(1999), *Luftkrieg und Literatur: Mit einem Essay über Alfred Andersch*, Munich: Hanser.

(2001), *Austerlitz*, Munich: Hanser.

(2003), *Campo Santo*, Munich: Hanser.

and Jan Peter Tripp (2003), *'Unerzählt': 33 Texte und 33 Radierungen*, Munich: Hanser.

(no date), *Verleihung des Heine-Preises 2000 der Landeshauptstadt Düsseldorf an W. G. Sebald*, Düsseldorf: Kulturamt der Landeshauptstadt Düsseldorf.

Works in English

(1996), *The Emigrants*, trans. Michael Hulse, London: Harvill.

(1998), *The Rings of Saturn*, trans. Michael Hulse, London: Harvill.

(1999), *Vertigo*, trans. Michael Hulse, London: Harvill.

(2001a), *Austerlitz*, trans. Anthea Bell, London: Hamish Hamilton.

(2001b), *For Years Now*, London: Short Books.

(2002), *After Nature*, trans. Michael Hamburger, London: Hamish Hamilton.

(2003), *On the Natural History of Destruction*, trans. Anthea Bell, New York: Random House.

Interviews

Angier, Carole (1996), 'Who is W. G. Sebald?', *The Jewish Quarterly*, 164 (Winter 1997/97), 10–14.

Balzer, Burkhard (1993), 'Bei den armen Seelen: Ein Gespräch mit W. G. Sebald', *Saarbrücker Zeitung*, 16 March, 10.

Bovenschen, Sven (1993), 'Menschen auf der anderen Seite: Gespräch mit W. G. Sebald', *Rheinische Post*, 9 October.

Bigsby, Christopher (2001), 'In Conversation with W. G. Sebald', *Writers in Conversation*, Norwich: Arthur Miller Centre.

Cuomo, Joe (2001), 'Interview with Joe Cuomo', *New Yorker*, 3 September.

Jaggi, Maya (2001a), 'The Last Word', *The Guardian*, 21 December.

Jaggi, Maya (2001b), 'Recovered Memories', *The Guardian*, 22 September.

Pfohlmann, Oliver (1999), 'Ist Bücherschreiben eine Verhaltensstörung?', *Saarbrücker Zeitung*, 6 January.

Siedenberg, Sven (1996), 'Anatomie der Schwemut: Gespräch über sein Schreiben und die Schrecken der Geschichte', *Rheinische Merkur*, 19 April.

Wittmann, Jochen (1997), 'Alles schrumpft: Ein Besuch bei W. G. Sebald, dem deutschen Autor in England', *Stuttgarter Zeitung*, 27 November.

Wood, James (1998), 'An Interview with W. G. Sebald', *Brick*, 59, 23–9.

SECONDARY WORKS ON W. G. SEBALD

Aciman, A. (1998), 'Out of Novemberland', *New York Times Review of Books*, 3 December [http://www.nybooks.com/articles/641].

Albes, Claudia (2002), 'Die Erkundung der Leere: Anmerkungen zu W. G. Sebalds "englisher Wallfahrt" *Die Ringe des Saturn*', *Jahrbuch der deutschen Schillergesellschaft*, 46, 279–305.

Annan, Gabriele (2001) 'Ghost Story', *New York Review of Books*, 1 November [www.nybooks.com/articles/14722].

Arnold, Heinz Ludwig (ed.) (2003), *W. G. Sebald*, Munich: Text + Kritik.

Atlas, J. (1999), 'W. G. Sebald: A Profile', *Paris Review*, 41:151, 278–95.

Ayren, Armin (1998), 'Sebald über Canetti', in Gerhard Köpf (ed.), *Mitteilungen über Max*, pp. 9–20.

Bauer, Karin (forthcoming), 'The Good European: W. G. Sebald's *Austerlitz* as Nomadic Narrative', in Scott Denham and Mark McCulloh (eds), *Reading W. G. Sebald: Essays from the Third Occasional Davidson Symposium on German Studies*.

Bere, Carol (2002), 'The Book of Memory: W. G. Sebald's *The Emigrants* and *Austerlitz*', *Literary Review*, 46.1, 184–92.

Boehncke, Heiner (2003), 'Clair obscur: W. G. Sebalds Bilder', in Heinz Ludwig Arnold (ed.), *W. G. Sebald*, pp. 43–62.

Braun, Michael, and Hermann Wallmann (1995), 'Bilder einer sich zermahlenden Erde: Briefwechsel über Bücher II: *Die Ringe des Saturn* von W. G. Sebald', *Basler Zeitung*, 11 October, 7–8.

Ceuppens, Jan (2002), 'Im zerschundenen Papier herumgeisternde Gesichter: Fragen der Repräsentation in W. G. Sebalds *Die Ausgewanderten*', *Germanistische Mitteilungen*, 55, 79–98.

Craven, Peter (1999), 'W. G. Sebald: Anatomy of Faction', *Heat*, 13, 212–24.

Denneler, Iris (2001), *Von Namen und Dingen: Erkundungen zur Rolle des Ich in der Literatur am Beispiel von Ingeborg Bachmann, Peter Bichsel, Max Frisch, Gottfried Keller, Heinrich von Kleist, Arthur Schnitzler, Frank Wedekind, Vladimir Nabokov, und W. G. Sebald*, Würzburg: Königshausen und Neumann.

Dyer, Geoff, et al. (2002), 'A Symposium on W. G. Sebald', *Threepenny Review*, 89, 18–21.

Franklin, Ruth (2002), 'Rings of Smoke', *The New Republic*, 23 September.

Fuchs, Anne (2003), 'Phantomspuren: Zu W. G. Sebalds Poetik der Erinnerung in *Austerlitz*', *German Life and Letters*, 56, 281–98.

Hall, Katharina (2000), 'Jewish Memory in Exile: The Relation of W. G. Sebald's *Die Ausgewanderten* to the Tradition of the *Yizkor* Books', in Pól O'Dochartaigh (ed.), *Jews in German Literature since 1945: German-Jewish Literature?*, Amsterdam: Rodopi, pp. 153–64.

Harris, Stephanie (2001), 'The Return of the Dead: Memory and Photography in W. G. Sebald's *Die Ausgewanderten*', *German Quarterly*, 74, 379–91.

Heidelberger-Leonard, Irene (2001), 'Melancholie als Widerstand', *Akzente*, 48:2, 122–30.

Hellweg, Patricia (1998), 'Lokaltermin Wertach', in Gerhard Köpf (ed.), *Mitteilungen über Max*, pp. 21–31.

Huyssen, Andreas (2001), 'On Rewritings and New Beginnings: W. G. Sebald and the Literature about the *Luftkrieg*', *Zeitschrift für Literaturwissenschaft und Linguistik*, 124, 72–90.

Juhl, Eva (1995), 'Die Wahrheit uber das Ungluck: Zu W. G. Sebald *Die Ausgewanderten*', in Anne Fuchs and Theo Harden (eds), *Reisen im Diskurs: Modelle literarischer Fremderfahrung von den Pilgerberichten bis zur Postmoderne*, Heidelberg: Winter, pp. 640–59.

Kastura, Thomas (1996), 'Geheimnisvolle Fahigkeit zur Transmigration: W. G. Sebalds interkulturelle Wallfahrten in die Leere', *Arcadia*, 31, 197–216.

Kochhar-Lindgren, Gray (2002), 'Charcoal: The Phantom Traces of W. G. Sebald's Novel-Memoirs', *Monatshefte*, 94, 368–80.

Köhler, A. (2002), 'Die Durchdringung des Dunkels: W. G. Sebald und Jan Peter Tripp – ein letzter Blickwechsel', *Neue Zürcher Zeitung*, 14 December, 73.

Köpf, Gerhard (ed.) (1998), *Mitteilungen über Max: Marginalien zu W. G. Sebald*, Oberhausen: Laufen.

Korff, Sigrid (1998), 'Die Treue zum Detail: W. G. Sebalds *Die Ausgewanderten*', in Stephan Braese (ed.), *In der Sprache der Täter: Neue Lektüren deutschsprachiger Nachkriegs- und Gegenwartsliteratur*, Opladen: Westdeutscher Verlag, pp. 167–97.

Long, J. J. (2003), 'History, Narrative, and Photography in W. G. Sebald's *Die Ausgewanderten*', *Modern Language Review*, 98, 118–139.

Loquai, Franz (ed.) (1995), *Far from Home: W. G. Sebald*, Bamberg: Fußnoten zur Literatur.

Loquai, Franz (ed.) (1997), *W. G. Sebald*, Eggingen: Isele.

McCulloh, Mark (2003), *Understanding W. G. Sebald*, Columbia, SC: University of South Carolina Press.

Parry, Anne (1997), 'Idioms for the Unrepresentable: Post-War Fiction and the Shoah', *Journal of European Studies*, 108, 417–32.

Romer, Stephen (2002), 'Beyond Strangeways', *The Guardian*, 6 July.

Schuhmacher, Heinz (1998), 'Aufklärung, Auschwitz, Auslöschung: Eine Erinnerung an Paul Bereyter', in Gerhard Köpf (ed.), *Mitteilungen über Max*, pp. 58–84.

Scott, Joanna (2002), 'Sebald Crawling', *Salmagundi*, 243–54.

Sill, Oliver (1992), 'Migration als Gegenstand der Literatur: W. G. Sebalds *Die Ausgewanderten*', in Armin Nassehi and Georg Weber (eds), *Nation*,

Ethnie, Minderheit: Beiträge zur Aktualität ethnischer Konflikte, Vienna: Böhlau, pp. 309–30.

Sill, Oliver (1997), '"Aus dem Jäger ist ein Schmetterling geworden": Textbeziehungen zwischen Werken von W. G. Sebald, Franz Kafka und Vladimir Nabokov', *Poetica*, 29, 596–623.

Sontag, Susan (2002), 'A Mind in Mourning', *Where the Stress Falls*, London: Jonathan Cape.

Weber, Markus (2003), 'Die fantastische befragt die pedantische Genauigkeit: Zu den Abbildungen in W. G. Sebalds Werken', in Heinz Ludwig Arnold (ed.), *W. G. Sebald*, pp. 63–74.

Williams, Arthur (1998), 'The Elusive First Person Plural: Real Absences in Reiner Kunze, Bernd-Dieter Huge, and W. G. Sebald', in Arthur Williams, Stuart Parkes and Julian Preece (eds), *'Whose Story?': Continuities in Contemporary German-Language Literature*, Bern: Lang, pp. 85–113.

Williams, Arthur (2000), 'W. G. Sebald: A Holistic Approach to Borders, Texts and Perspectives', in A. Williams, S. Parkes and J. Preece (eds), *German-Language Literature Today: International and Popular?*, Oxford: Lang, pp. 99–118.

Williams, Arthur (2001), '"Das korsakowsche Syndrom": Remembrance and Responsibility in W. G. Sebald', in Helmut Schmitz (ed.), *German Culture and the Uncomfortable Past: Representations of National Socialism in Contemporary Germanic Literature*, Aldershot: Ashgate, pp. 65–86.

OTHER WORKS

Adler, H. G. (1955), *Theresienstadt 1941–45: Das Antlitz einer Zwangsgemeinschaft. Geschichte, Soziologie, Psychologie*, Tübingen: Mohr.

Adorno, Theodor W., and Max Horkheimer (1997 [1944]), *Dialectic of Enlightenment*, trans. John Cumming, London: Verso.

Anon (1992), 'Ten Arrests at Unveiling of "Bomber" Harris Statue', *Financial Times*, 1 June.

Augé, Marc (1995 [1992]), *Non-Places: Introduction to an Anthropology of Supermodernity*, trans. John Howe, London: Verso.

Augustine (1988), *Confessions*, trans. R. S. Pine-Coffin, Harmondsworth: Penguin.

Bachelard, Gaston (1983 [1942]), *Water and Dreams: An Essay on the Imagination of Matter*, trans. E. R. Farrell, London: Pegasus.

Baer, Ulrich (2002), *Spectral Evidence: The Photography of Trauma*, Cambridge, MA: MIT Press.

Bakhtin, Mikhail (Valentin Nikolaevič Vološinov) (1930), 'Konstrukcija vyskazyvanija', *Literaturnaja učeba*, 3, 65–87.

Barthes, Roland (1982 [1970]), *Empire of Signs*, trans. Richard Howard, New York: Hill and Wang.

Barthes, Roland (1984 [1980]), *Camera Lucida*, trans. Richard Howard, London: Flamingo.

Bartov, Omer (2000), 'Germany as Victim', *New German Critique*, 80, 29–40.

Baudrillard, Jean (1995), *The Gulf War Did Not Take Place*, trans. Paul Patton, Bloomington: Indiana University Press.

Benjamin, Walter (1977 [1928]), *The Origin of German Tragic Drama*, trans. John Osborne, London: New Left Books.

Benjamin, Walter (1982), *Das Passagen-Werk*, in Benjamin Walter, *Gesammelte Schriften*, ed. Rolf Tiedemann and Hermann Schweppenhäuser, vol. 5, Frankfurt am Main: Suhrkamp.

Benjamin, Walter (1999 [1930]), 'Little History of Photography', in Benjamin Walter, *Selected Writings*, trans. Rodney Livingstone et al., ed. Michael W. Jennings, Howard Eiland and Gary Smith, Cambridge, MA: Harvard University Press, vol. 2, 1927–34, pp. 507–30.

Benjamin, Walter (2002a [1936]), 'The Work of Art in the Age of Its Technological Reproducibility', in Benjamin Walter, *Selected Writings*, vol. 3, pp. 101–33.

Benjamin, Walter (2002b [1950]), 'Berlin Childhood around 1900', in Benjamin Walter, *Selected Writings*, trans. Edmund Jephcott at al., ed. by Michael W. Jennings, Howard Eiland and Gary Smith, Cambridge, MA: Harvard University Press, vol. 3, 1935–8, pp. 344–413.

Bennett, Alan (2003), '2002 Diary', *London Review of Books*, 2 January, 5.

Bennington, Geoffrey (1993), 'Derridabase', in Geoffrey Bennington and Jacques Derrida, *Jacques Derrida*, Chicago: University of Chicago Press, pp. 3–316.

Bernheimer, Charles (1993), 'Fetishism and Decadence: Salome's Severed Heads', in Emily Apted and William Pietz (eds), *Fetishism as Cultural Discourse* (Ithaca: Cornell University Press), pp. 62–83.

Bhabha, Homi K. (1994), *The Location of Culture*, London: Routledge.

Boa, Elizabeth, and Rachel Palfreyman (2000), *Heimat, a German Dream: Regional Loyalties and National Identity in German Culture 1890–1990*, Oxford: Oxford University Press.

Böhme, Gernot (1992), *Natürlich Natur: Über Natur im Zeitalter ihrer technischen Reproduzierbarkeit*, Frankfurt am Main: Suhrkamp.

Böll, Heinrich (1995 [1992]), *The Silent Angel*, trans. Breon Mitchell, New York: Picador.

Borges, Jorge Luis (1972 [1964]), 'Tlön, Uqbar, Orbis Tertium', trans. James E. Irby, in Donald A. Yates and James E. Irby (eds), *Labyrinths*, Harmondsworth: Penguin, pp. 27–43.

Boyarin, D. (1997), *Unheroic Conduct: The Rise of Heterosexuality and the Invention of the Jewish Man*, Berkeley: University of California Press.

Broszat, Martin (1988), 'Was heißt Historisierung des Nationalsozialismus?', *Historische Zeitschrift*, 247:1, 1–14.

Browne, Sir Thomas (1958 [1658]), *Urn Buriall and The Garden of Cyrus*, ed. John Carter, Cambridge: Cambridge University Press.

Budick, Sanford, and Wolfgang Iser (eds) (1989), *Languages of the Unsayable: The Play of Negativity in Literature and Literary Theory*, New York: Columbia University Press.

Burckhardt, Jacob (1956 [1905]), *Weltgeschichtliche Betrachtungen: Über geschichtliches Studium*, in Jacob Burckhardt, *Gesammelte Werke*, vol. 4, Basel: Schwabe.

Buzard, James (1993), *The Beaten Track: European Tourism, Literature, and the Ways to Culture, 1800–1918*, Oxford: Oxford University Press.

Caillois, Roger (1961 [1958]), *Man, Play and Games*, trans. M. Barash, New York: Free Press of Glencoe.

Calvino, Italo (1992 [1993]), *Six Memos for the Next Millennium*, trans. P. Creagh, London: Cape.

Caruth, Cathy (ed.) (1995), *Trauma: Explorations in Memory*, Baltimore: Johns Hopkins University Press.

Chamisso, Adalbert von (1900), *Werke*, vol. 2, ed. Heinrich Kurz, Leipzig and Vienna: Bibliographisches Institut.

Cixous, Hélène (1986), 'The Laugh of the Medusa', in H. Adams and L. Searle (eds), *Critical Theory since 1965*, Tallahassee: Florida State University Press, pp. 309–20.

Claasen, H. (1947), *Gesang im Feuerofen*, Düsseldorf: Schwann.

Clemens, G. (1997), *Britische Kulturpolitik in Deutschland 1945–1949: Literatur, Film, Musik und Theater*, Stuttgart: Steiner.

Coates, Peter (1998), *Nature: Western Attitudes since Ancient Times*, Cambridge: Polity.

Conte, Joseph M. (2002), *Design and Debris: A Chaotics of Postmodern American Fiction*, Tuscaloosa: University of Alabama Press.

Davidson, Arnold (1987), 'How to Do the History of Psychoanalysis: A Reading of Freud's *Three Essays on the Theory of Sexuality*', *Critical Inquiry*, 13:2, 252–77.

Deleuze, Gilles (1990 [1969]), *The Logic of Sense*, trans. Mark Lester with Charles Stivale, ed. Constantin V. Boundas, New York: Columbia University Press.

Derrida, Jacques (1978), 'The *Retrait* of Metaphor', *Enclitic*, 2:2, 5–34.

Derrida, Jacques (1988 [1981]), 'The Deaths of Roland Barthes', trans. Pascale-Anne Brault and Michael Naas, in Hugh J. Silverman (ed.), *Philosophy and Non-Philosophy since Merleau-Ponty*, New York: Routledge, pp. 259–96.

Derrida, Jacques (1992 [1989]), 'How to Avoid Speaking Denials', in Harold

Coward and Toby Foshay (eds), *Derrida and Negative Theology*, Albany: SUNY Press, pp. 73–142.

Derrida, Jacques (1994 [1993]), *specters of marx, the state of the debt, the work of mourning and the new international*, trans. Peggy Kamuf, New York: Routledge.

Eco, Umberto (1976), *A Theory of Semiotics*, Bloomington: Indiana University Press.

Eco, Umberto (1979), *The Role of the Reader: Explorations in the Semiotics of Texts*, Bloomington: Indiana University Press.

Eksteins, Modris (2000 [1989]), *Rites of Spring: The Great War and the Birth of the Modern Age*, Boston: Houghton Mifflin.

Eliade, Mircea (1964), *Shamanism: Archaic Techniques of Ecstasy*, New York: Bollingen Foundation.

Enzensberger, Hans Magnus (ed.) (1990), *Europa in Ruinen: Augenzeugenberichte aus den Jahren 1944 bis 1948*, Frankfurt am Main: Eichborn.

Felman, Shoshana (2003), *Writing and Madness: Literature/Philosophy/Psychoanalysis*, Stanford: Stanford University Press.

Felman, Shoshana, and Dori Laub (1991), *Testimony: Crises of Witnessing in Literature, Psychoanalysis, and History*, New York: Routledge.

Fenves, Peter (1997), 'Marx, Mourning, Messianity', in Hent De Vries and Samuel Weber ed., *Violence, Identity, and Self-Determination*, Stanford: Stanford University Press, pp. 253–70.

Forte, Dieter (1999), 'Menschen werden zu Herdentieren', *Der Spiegel*, 7 April.

Frank, Manfred (1989), 'Aufbruch ins Ziellose', *Kaltes Herz, Unendliche Fahrt, Neue Mythologie: Motiv-Untersuchungen zur Pathogenese der Moderne*, Frankfurt am Main: Suhrkamp.

Frank, Manfred (1995), *Die unendliche Fahrt: Die Geschichte des Fliegenden Holländers und verwandter Motive*, Leipzig: Reclam.

Freud, Sigmund (1953–74), *The Standard Edition of the Complete Psychological Works of Sigmund Freud*, ed. and trans. James Strachey, London: Hogarth Press.

Freud, Sigmund (1900), *The Interpretation of Dreams*, in Sigmund Freud, *Standard Edition of the Complete Psychological Works*, vols 4 and 5.

Freud, Sigmund (1905), *Three Essays on the Theory of Sexuality*, in Sigmund Freud, *Standard Edition of the Complete Psychological Works*, vol 7.

Freud, Sigmund (1913), 'The Theme of the Three Caskets', in Sigmund Freud, *Standard Edition of the Complete Psychological Works*, vol. 12, pp. 289–301.

Freud, Sigmund (1917), *Introductory Lectures on Psycho-Analysis Part III*, in Sigmund Freud, *Standard Edition of the Complete Psychological Works*, vol. 16.

Freud, Sigmund (1919), 'The Uncanny', in Sigmund Freud, *Standard Edition of the Complete Psychological Works*, vol. 17, pp. 217–56.

Freud, Sigmund (1920), *Beyond the Pleasure Principle*, in Sigmund Freud, *Standard Edition of the Complete Psychological Works*, vol. 18, pp. 1–64.

Freud, Sigmund (1922 [1940]), 'Medusa's Head', in Sigmund Freud, *Standard Edition of the Complete Psychological Works*, vol. 18, pp. 273–4.

Freud, Sigmund (1939), *Moses and Monotheism*, in Sigmund Freud, *Standard Edition of the Complete Psychological Works*, vol. 23, pp. 1–137.

Freud, Sigmund (1989a), 'Das Unheimliche', in Sigmund Freud, *Studienausgabe*, ed. Alexander Mitscherlich, Angela Richards and James Strachey, vol. 4, Frankfurt am Main: Fischer, pp. 241–74.

Freud, Sigmund (1989b), *Jenseits des Lustprinzips*, in Sigmund Freud, *Studienausgabe*, vol. 3, pp. 213–72.

Friedländer, Saul (1993), *Memory, History, and the Extermination of the Jews of Europe*, Bloomington: Bloomington University Press.

Frisch, Max (1979), *Der Mensch erscheint im Holozän*, Frankfurt am Main: Suhrkamp.

Garrett, Stephen A. (1996), *Ethics and Airpower in World War II: The British Bombing of German Cities*, 2nd edn, New York: St. Martin's Press.

Gasché, Rudolphe (1994), *Inventions of Difference: On Jacques Derrida*, Cambridge, MA: Harvard University Press.

Geimer, Peter (2002), *Die Vergangenheit der Kunst: Strategien der Nachträglichkeit im 18. Jahrhundert*, Weimar: Verlag und Datenbank für Geisteswissenschaften.

Geyer, Michael (2001) 'America in Germany: Power and the Pursuit of Americanization', in Frank Trommler and E. Shore (eds), *The German-American Encounter: Conflict and Cooperation between Two Cultures, 1800–2000*, New York: Berghahn, pp. 121–44.

Gilman Sander (1993), *Freud, Race and Gender*, Princeton: Princeton University Press.

Gleick, James (1998 [1988]), *Chaos: The Amazing Science of the Unpredictable*, London: Vintage.

Goethe, Johann Wolfgang von (1994 [1816–17]), *Italian Journey*, trans. Robert R. Heitner, Princeton: Princeton University Press.

Gollancz, Victor (1947), *In Darkest Germany*, Hinsdale: Regnery.

Goodbody, Axel (1997), 'Catastrophism in Post-War German Literature', in Colin Riordan (ed.), *Green Thought in German Culture: Historical and Contemporary Perspectives*, Cardiff: University of Wales Press, pp. 159–80.

Goodin, Robert (1992), *Green Political Theory*, Oxford: Polity.

Guerrier, Yves, and François Bassères (1984), *Le vertige et le vertigineux*, Paris: Roger Dacosta.

Gwienow-Hecht, Jessica C. E. (1999), *Transmission Impossible: American*

Journalism as Cultural Diplomacy in Postwar Germany 1945–1955, Baton Rouge: Lousiana State University Press.

Hamilton, Peter, and Roger Hargreaves (2001), *The Beautiful and the Damned: The Creation of Identity in Nineteenth Century Photography*, Aldershot and Burlington: Lund Humphries.

Harbison, Robert (1991), *The Built, the Unbuilt and the Unbuildable: In Pursuit of Architectural Meaning*, London: Thames and Hudson.

Hayles, N. Katherine (1990), *Chaos Bound: Orderly Disorder in Contemporary Literature and Science*, Ithaca: Cornell University Press.

Hebel, Johann Peter (1961), *Poetische Werke: Nach den Ausgaben letzter Hand und der Gesamtausgabe von 1834 unter Hinzuziehung der früheren Fassungen*, Munich: Winkler.

Hegel, Georg Friedrich Wilhelm (1975), *Aesthetics: Lectures on Fine Art*, trans. T. M. Knox, Oxford: Oxford University Press.

Heidegger, Martin (1992 [1924]), *The Concept of Time*, trans. William McNeil, Oxford: Blackwell.

Heukenkamp, Ursula (2001), 'Gestörte Erinnerung: Erzählungen vom Luftkrieg', *Amsterdamer Beiträge zur neueren Germanistik*, 50:2, 469–92.

Hirsch, Marianne (1997), *Family Frames: Photography, Narrative and Postmemory*, Cambridge, MA: Harvard University Press.

Homer (1997), *The Odyssey*, trans. Robert Fagles, New York: Penguin.

Hutcheon, Linda (1988), *A Poetics of Postmodernism: History, Theory, Fiction*, London: Routledge.

Jonte-Pace, Diane (2001), *Speaking the Unspeakable: Religion, Misogyny and the Uncanny Mother in Freud's Cultural Texts*, California: University of California Press.

Kafka, Franz (1983a), 'Fragment zum "Jäger Gracchus"', in Franz Kafka, *Beschreibung eines Kampfes*, pp. 248–51.

Kafka, Franz (1983b), *Hochzeitsvorbereitungen auf dem Lande und andere Prosa aus dem Nachlaß*, ed. Max Brod, Frankfurt am Main: Fischer.

Kafka, Franz (1983c) 'Der Jäger Gracchus', in Franz Kafka, *Beschreibung eines Kampfes: Novellen, Skizzen, Aphorismen aus dem Nachlaß*, ed. Max Brod, Frankfurt am Main: Fischer, pp. 75–9.

Kafka, Franz (1983d), 'Josefine, die Sängerin oder das Volk der Mäuse', in Franz Kafka, *Erzählungen*, Frankfurt am Main: Fischer, pp. 200–16.

Kafka, Franz (1983e), *Tagebücher 1910–1923*, Frankfurt am Main: Fischer.

Kafka, Franz (1991), *The Great Wall of China and Other Works*, trans. Malcolm Pasley, Harmondsworth: Penguin.

Kafka, Franz (1993), *Nachgelassene Schriften und Fragmente*, vol. 1, ed. Malcolm Pasley, Frankfurt am Main: Fischer.

Kafka, Franz (2000), *Metamorphosis and Other Stories*, trans. Malcolm Pasley, Harmondsworth: Penguin.

Kasack, Hermann (1949), *Die Stadt hinter dem Strom*, Frankfurt am Main: Suhrkamp.

Kennett, L. (1982), *A History of Strategic Bombing: From the First Hot-Air Balloons to Hiroshima and Nagasaki*, New York: Scribner's Sons.

Kluge, Alexander (1977), 'Der Luftangriff auf Halberstadt am 18. April 1945', in Alexander Kluge, *Neue Geschichten: Hefte 1–18*, Frankfurt am Main: Suhrkamp, pp. 33–106.

Kofman, Sarah (1985 [1980]), *The Enigma of Woman: Woman in Freud's Writings*, trans. Catherine Porter, Ithaca: Cornell University Press.

Krauss, Rolf H. (1992), *Jenseits von Licht und Schatten: Die Rolle der Photographie bei bestimmten paranormalen Phänomenen – ein historischer Abriß*, Marburg: Jonas.

LaCapra, Dominick (1998), *History and Memory after Auschwitz*, Ithaca: Cornell University Press.

LaCapra, Dominick (2001), *Writing History, Writing Trauma*, Baltimore and London: Johns Hopkins University Press.

Ledig, Gert (1999 [1956]), *Vergeltung*, Frankfurt am Main: Suhrkamp.

Leone, Massimo (2004a), *Religious Conversion and Identity: The Semiotic Analysis of Texts*, London and New York: Routledge.

Leone, Massimo (2004b), 'Literature, Travel and Vertigo', forthcoming in *Proceedings of the Royal Irish Academy Conference on Modern Language Studies*.

Leys, Ruth (2000), *Trauma: A Genealogy*, Chicago and London: University of Chicago Press.

Lukács, Georg (1971 [1916]), *The Theory of the Novel: A Historico-Philosophical Essay on the Forms of Great Epic Literature*, trans. Anna Bostock, Cambridge, MA: MIT Press.

MacCannell, Dean (1976), *The Tourist: A New Theory of the Leisure Class*, New York: Schocken.

McCole, John (1993), *Walter Benjamin and the Antinomies of Tradition*, Ithaca: Cornell University Press.

Maier, Charles S. (1993), 'A Surfeit of Memory? Reflections on History, Melancholy and Denial', *History and Memory*, 5, 136–51.

Mandelbrot, Benoit B. (1991), 'How Long Is the Coast of Britain?', in Timothy Ferris (ed.), *The World Treasury of Physics, Astronomy, and Mathematics*, Boston: Little, Brown, pp. 447–55.

Manetti, Giovanni (1998), *La teoria dell'enunciazione: Le origini del concetto e alcuni più recenti sviluppi*, Siena: Protagon.

Marx, Karl (1979 [1852]), 'The Eighteenth Brumaire of Louis Bonaparte', in Karl Marx and Frederick Engels, *Collected Works*, vol. 11, London: Lawrence & Wishart, pp. 99–197.

Melchior-Bonnet, Sabine (2001), *The Mirror: A History*, trans. Katherine H. Jewett, New York: Routledge.

Merchant, Carolyn (1992), *Radical Ecology: The Search for a Livable World*, New York and London: Routledge.

Moeller, Robert G. (2001), *War Stories: The Search for a Usable Past in the Federal Republic of Germany*, Berkeley: University of California Press.

Mortley, Raoul (1986), *From Word to Silence II: The Way of Negation, Christian and Greek*, Bonn: Hanstein.

Nabokov, Vladimir (1967), *Speak, Memory: An Autobiography Revisited*, London: Weidenfeld and Nicolson.

Niederland, William G. (1980), *Die Folgen der Verfolgung*, Frankfurt am Main: Suhrkamp.

Nietzsche, Friedrich (1966), *Werke*, ed. Karl Schlechta, Munich: Hanser.

Nossack, Hans Erich (1976 [1948]), *Der Untergang*, Frankfurt am Main: Suhrkamp.

Noyes, John K. (2004), 'Nomadism, Nomadology, and Postcolonialism: Empire, Writing, Theory', forthcoming in *Interventions: The International Journal of Postcolonial Studies*.

O'Brien, Susie, and Imre Szeman (2003), *Popular Culture: A User's Guide*, Scarborough, Ontario: Nelson.

O'Riordan, Timothy (1976), *Environmentalism*, London: Plon.

Panse, Friedrich (1952), *Angst und Schreck in klinisch-psychologischer und sozialmedizinischer Sicht*, Stuttgart: Thieme.

Peck, Robert E. (2000), 'The Banning of Titanic: A Study of British Postwar Film Censorship in Germany', *Historical Journal of Film, Radio and Television*, 8, 1–17.

Percy, Walker (1975), *The Message in the Bottle*, New York: Farrar, Strauss.

Robben, Antonius C. G. M., and Marcelo M. Suarez-Orozco (eds) (2000), *Cultures under Siege: Collective Violence and Trauma*, Cambridge: Cambridge University Press.

Roth, Joseph (2001 [1976]), *The Wandering Jews*, trans. Michael Hofmann, London: Granta.

Schäfer, Hans Dieter (1985), *Berlin im Zweiten Weltkrieg: Der Untergang der Reichshauptstadt in Augenzeugenberichten*, Munich: Piper.

Schaffer, Ronald (1985), *Wings of Judgment: American Bombing in World War II*, New York: Oxford University Press.

Schama, Simon (1995), *Landscape and Memory*, London: HarperCollins.

Schivelbusch, Wolfgang (1998), *In a Cold Crater: Cultural and Intellectual Life in Berlin 1945–1948*, trans. Kelly Barry, Berkeley: University of California Press.

Sedgwick, Eve Kosofsky (1985), *Between Men: English Literature and Male Homosocial Desire*, New York: Columbia University Press.

Shapiro, Susan (1997), 'The Uncanny Jew: A Brief History of an Image', *Judaism*, 46, 63–78.

Simmel, Georg (1959 [1919]), 'The Ruin', in Georg Simmel, *Georg Simmel, 1858–1918: A Collection of Essays with Translations and a Bibliography*, ed. K. H. Wolff, tr. D. Kettler, Columbus: Ohio State University Press, pp. 125–33.

Simmel, Georg (1996 [1903]), 'The Metropolis and Mental Life', in Georg Simmel, *Modernism: An Anthology of Sources and Documents*, eds V. Kolocontroni, Jane Goldman and Olga Taxidou, Chicago: University of Chicago Press, pp. 51–60.

Solnit, Rebecca (2000), *Wanderlust: A History of Walking*, London: Viking.

Sontag, Susan (1979), *On Photography*, Harmondsworth: Penguin.

Soper, Kate (1995), *What Is Nature? Culture, Politics, and the Non-Human*, Oxford: Blackwell.

Sprengnether, Madelon (1990), *The Spectral Mother: Freud, Feminism, and Psychoanalysis*, Ithaca: Cornell University Press.

Steller, Georg Wilhelm (1988), *Journal of a Voyage with Bering 1741–1742*, ed. with an introduction by O. W. Frost, trans. Margritt A. Engel and O. W. Frost, Stanford: Stanford University Press.

Stock, Brian (1996), *Augustine the Reader: Meditation, Self-Knowledge, and the Ethics of Interpretation*, Cambridge, MA: Harvard University Press.

Swales, Martin (1997), *Epochenbuch Realismus*, Berlin: Erich Schmidt.

Thoreau, Henry David (1994 [1862]), 'Walking', in Paul Lauter (ed.), *The Heath Anthology of American Literature*, vol. 1, 2nd edn, Lexington: Heath, pp. 2079–2100.

Tuohy, William (1991), 'New Statue to Bomber Chief Raises German Ire', *Los Angeles Times*, 25 October.

Vidler, Anthony (1992), *The Architectural Uncanny: Essays in the Modern Unhomely*, Cambridge, MA: MIT Press.

Vogel, Steven (1996), *Against Nature: The Concept of Nature in Critical Theory*, Albany: SUNY Press.

Wiesel, Elie (1990), *From the Kingdom of Memory: Reminiscences*, New York: Summit Books.

Williams, Raymond (1988), *Keywords: A Vocabulary of Culture and Society*, London: Fontana.

Williamson, George (1935), 'Mutability, Decay, and Seventeenth Century Melancholy', *English Literary History*, 2:2, 121–150.

Yates, Francis (1966), *The Art of Memory*, Chicago: University of Chicago Press.

Zilcosky, John (2003), *Kafka's Travels: Exoticism, Colonialism, and the Traffic of Writing*, New York: Palgrave.

Zilcosky, John (2004), 'The Writer as Nomad?: The Art of Getting Lost', forthcoming in *Interventions: The International Journal of Postcolonial Studies*.

INDEX

Aciman, Andre, 84
acting out (Freud), 13
Adler, H. G., 13, 149, 150
Adorno, Theodor W., 43n, 47
aerial bombing *see* air war
aesthetics, 7, 10, 11, 28, 46, 59, 64, 66, 67,
    69, 71n, 90, 92, 98, 156, 179, 180,
    214
agency, 14, 61, 179, 181, 188
air war, 5, 11, 14–15, 39, 55, 60, 65, 66,
    116, 176–88
Albes, Dawn, 118n, 119n
Altdorfer, Albrecht, 34, 39, 69
Améry, Jean, 118n, 153n, 216n
amnesia, 78, 81, 180, 181, 187, 193
anamnesis, 144, 145
angel, 195
    of history (Benjamin), 67
anti-Semitism, 15, 80, 213, 215, 216n
apocalypse, 31, 49–50, 51, 55, 65, 82,
    180
apomnesis, 145
architecture, 13, 61, 140, 141, 143, 144,
    146–7, 152, 157, 159, 195–6, 199
area bombing *see* air war
Augustine, Saint, 143
    Confessions, 13, 144–5, 153
Auschwitz, 133, 175, 176
authenticity, 50, 62, 175, 191, 199, 201

Baer, Ulrich, 14, 155, 160, 163, 165
Balzac, Honoré de, 24, 161
Barthes, Roland, 105, 106
    Camera Lucida, 131, 155, 165
    Empire of Signs, 104, 119n
Bassères, François, 92
Baudrillard, Jean, 148
Beckett, Samuel, 119n
beginnings, 95–6, 97, 101n
belatedness, 8–9, 24, 159, 160, 165, 216n
Benjamin, Walter, 28, 67–8, 91, 97, 98,
    155, 157, 168, 171n, 194, 195, 201n
Bennett, Alan, 40
Bering, Vitus Jonassen, 33, 53
Bernhard, Thomas, 5, 38, 39, 43n
Boa, Elizabeth, 6, 7
Böll, Heinrich, *The Silent Angel*, 185,
    189n
Bomber Command, 184, 186, 188
bombing *see* air war
Borges, Jorge Luis, 11, 68, 82
    'Tlön, Uqbar, Orbis Tertius', 80–1, 83,
    87, 88
Boyarin, Daniel, 213, 215
Broszat, Martin, 186
Browne, Thomas, 39, 43n, 82, 83, 84, 88,
    111
butterfly man, 10, 42, 64, 135–6, 195; *see
    also* Nabokov, Vladimir